D0316788

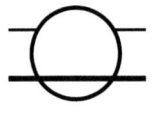

DISABILITY, HUMAN RIGHTS AND EDUCATION

Disability, Human Rights and Society

Series Editor: Professor Len Barton, University of Sheffield

The *Disability, Human Rights and Society* series reflects a commitment to a particular view of 'disability' and a desire to make this view accessible to a wider audience. The series approach defines 'disability' as a form of oppression and identifies the ways in which disabled people are marginalized, restricted and experience discrimination. The fundamental issue is not one of an individual's inabilities or limitations, but rather a hostile and unadaptive society.

Authors in this series are united in the belief that the question of disability must be set within an equal opportunities framework. The series gives priority to the examination and critique of those factors that are unacceptable, offensive and in need of change. It also recognizes that any attempt to redirect resources in order to provide opportunities for discriminated people cannot pretend to be apolitical. Finally, it raises the urgent task of establishing links with other marginalized groups in an attempt to engage in a common struggle. The issue of disability needs to be given equal significance to those of race, gender and age in equal opportunities policies. This series provides support for such a task.

Anyone interested in contributing to the series is invited to approach the Series Editor at the Department of Educational Studies, University of Sheffield.

Current and forthcoming titles

F. Armstrong and L. Barton (eds): *Disability, Human Rights and Education*
M. Corker: *Deaf and Disabled, or Deafness Disabled? Towards a Human Rights Perspective*
M. Corker and S. French (eds): *Disability Discourse*
M. Moore, S. Beazley and J. Maelzer: *Researching Disability Issues*
J. Read: *Disability, the Family and Society: Listening to Mothers*
A. Roulstone: *Enabling Technology: Disabled People, Work and New Technology*
C. Thomas: *Female Forms: Experiencing and Understanding Disability*
A. Vlachou: *Struggles for Inclusive Education: An Ethnographic Study*

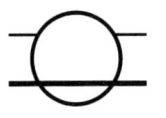

DISABILITY, HUMAN RIGHTS AND EDUCATION
Cross-cultural perspectives

Edited by
Felicity Armstrong and Len Barton

Open University Press
Buckingham · Philadelphia

Open University Press
Celtic Court
22 Ballmoor
Buckingham
MK18 1XW

e-mail: enquiries@openup.co.uk
world wide web: http://www.openup.co.uk

and
325 Chestnut Street
Philadelphia, PA 19106, USA

First Published 1999

A catalogue record of this book is available from the British Library

ISBN   0 335 20457 0 (pb)   0 335 20458 9 (hb)

Library of Congress Cataloging-in-Publication Data
Disability, human rights and education: cross cultural perspectives/
   Felicity Armstrong and Len Barton (eds).
      p.   cm. – (Disability, human rights and society)
      ISBN 0-335-20458-9. – ISBN 0-335-20457-0 (pbk.)
      1. Handicapped – Social conditions.   2. Handicapped – Education.
   3. Human rights.   I. Armstrong, Felicity.   II. Barton, Len. III. Series.
   HV1568.D568   1999
   305.9'0816–dc21   99-13640
                                                                            CIP

Typeset by Type Study, Scarborough
Printed in Great Britain by St Edmundsbury Press Ltd, Bury St Edmunds, Suffolk

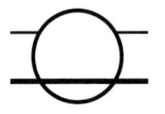

Contents

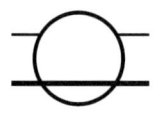

Notes on contributors

Derrick Armstrong is a lecturer in education in the Department of Educational Studies, University of Sheffield, UK, and Programme Director for the university's work in Trinidad and Tobago.

Felicity Armstrong is a lecturer in the Department of Educational Studies at the University of Sheffield, UK, and a member of the Inclusive Education Research Centre.

Len Barton is the Director of the Inclusive Education Research Centre in the Department of Educational Studies at the University of Sheffield, UK. He is the founder and editor of the international journal, *Disability and Society*.

Nathalie Bélanger is Assistant Professor in the Departments of Curriculum, Teaching and Learning and Sociology and Equity Studies in Education at the Ontario Institute for Studies in Education of the University of Toronto. In addition, she conducts research through the Centre de recherches en éducation franco-ontarienne. She has a particular interest in the sociology and history of special education.

Robert Chimedza is a lecturer in Special Education in the Department of Teacher Education at the University of Zimbabwe. He is also the Coordinator of Special Education in the University College of Distance Education at the same institution. He is a graduate of Michigan State University (PhD).

Karen Dunn is Principal Lecturer in Psychology at Sheffield Hallam University, UK. Her teaching and research interests are in social understandings of childhood and atypical development. She has published widely in the area of education and developmental psychology.

Nicolas Garant has a doctorate in political science from the Université Paris I – La Sorbonne. His main research interests include political thought and comparative studies. His doctoral thesis was on the work of Weber, Shumpeter and

Ortega y Gasset. He has played leadership roles in a wide range of organizations, each concerned with providing opportunity and equity. He has authored and edited many books concerning social policy, humanpower programmes, self-help mutual aid, education and disability.

Alan Gartner is Dean for Research at The Graduate School and University Centre, The City University of New York, USA. His research interests include social policy, education and disability.

Anders Gustavsson is Acting Professor at the Department of Education, Stockholm University. He has published a number of articles and books in the field of disability studies. In collaboration with researchers in other countries, he has edited *Intellectual Disability in the Nordic Welfare States* and *Social Definitions of Disability*.

Farhad Hossain is a research fellow at the Department of Administrative Science, University of Tampere, Finland, teaching intercultural communication and development studies. In the 1980s he was an NGO activist in Bangladesh. His current research includes issues relating to the sustainability of NGO-led development in Asian countries. He co-edited *NGOs under Challenge. Dynamics and Drawbacks in Development*, 1998, Ministry of Foreign Affairs of Finland, Helsinki.

Dorothy Kerzner Lipsky is Director of the National Center on Educational Restructuring and Inclusion at the City University of New York. Her research has been funded by federal and state agencies, local school districts, and private foundations. Projects include those in general and special education, transition, family support issues and international reviews of services for students with special needs.

John Lewis is a senior lecturer in the Department of Special Education at the Hong Kong Institute of Education, and has lectured previously on disability issues at Australian and British universities. John has held numerous teaching, policy and administrative posts in a variety of special education and government settings, and taught secondary students for six years in Papua New Guinea.

M. Miles has worked since 1978 in the development of disability resources in South Asian and Southern African countries. In recent years he has been researching the histories of responses to disabilities in Asia, Africa and the Middle East.

Michele Moore works in the Inclusive Education Research Centre at the University of Sheffield, UK, as a lecturer carrying out research and writing on a variety of disability matters. She is particularly interested in issues affecting the lives of disabled children and their families.

Ann Cheryl Namsoo was until recently Director of the Trinidad and Tobago Unified Teachers' Association/University of Sheffield Masters Courses. She is currently a full-time doctoral student at the University of Sheffield.

Susan Peters is an associate professor in Teacher Education and Special Education at Michigan State University. She was awarded a Fulbright Scholarship for study in Zimbabwe (1993), and is a member of the core faculty in African studies. She has held many leadership positions in disability rights organizations in the United States over the past 20 years.

Helen Phtiaka has been an assistant professor at the University of Cyprus since 1992. She obtained a PhD at Cambridge University. Her research interests cover many areas, such as special needs, deviant behaviour, teaching and learning styles, home–school relations and qualitative research methodology. She has published widely in international journals and is the author of two books, published by the British Library Research and Development Department, and Falmer Press.

Patricia Potts is a member of the Inclusive Education Group at the UK Open University, where her particular interests include the development of inclusive education in urban settings, both in the UK and in China, the history and geography of education for students who experience difficulties in communication, mobility or social relationships, teacher education for women and critiques of stage theories of child development.

Marcia Rioux, who holds a PhD in Jurisprudence and Social Policy from the University of California, Berkeley School of Law, is President of the Roeher Institute, Canada's national institute for education, information and the study of public policy related to disability. She has published numerous articles, papers and books on disability and human rights issues and has worked in the Caribbean, Latin America and Europe. Her research interests lie in the area of human rights, equality of outcome and social well-being.

Roger Slee is Dean of the Faculty of Education at the University of Western Australia. He holds the Chair in Teaching and Learning and is the Founding Editor of the *International Journal of Inclusive Education*. His books include: *Is There a Desk with My Name on It?* (Falmer Press, 1993), *Changing Theories and Practices of Discipline* (Falmer Press, 1995), *School Effectiveness for Whom?* (with Gaby Weiner and Sally Tomlinson, Falmer Press, 1998) and *The Inclusive School* (Falmer Press).

Anastasia Vlachou-Balafouti currently teaches in the Department of Pre-School Education, University of Athens, and in the Department of Social Work, Technological and Educational Institute of Patra. She has worked in both comprehensive and special secondary schools and has been involved in national and cross-national teaching and research projects in the areas of special/inclusive education. She has worked and studied in the educational systems of Greece, Canada and England and is the author of the book *Struggles for Inclusive Education* (Open University Press 1997).

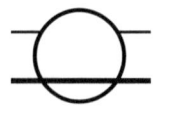

Foreword

Mike Oliver

In recent years the increasing pace of globalization and the virtual disappearance of colonialism have had an important impact on the academy. As academics we can no longer pursue our own interests secure in the knowledge that our intellectual activities are bounded by our nation state or merely ponder on how we can export our ideas to the rest of the world. We have been forced to recognize that we have as much, if not more, to learn from others as they have from us.

In the newly emerging area of disability studies this is as true as it is in other more established parts of the academic curriculum. This book makes an outstanding contribution both to our understanding of disability and to developing a global approach to disability studies. It takes as its focus the concept of human rights and seeks to apply it both to the issues of disability and education but it recognizes that the very idea of human rights is itself problematic.

Each of the chapters develops its own understanding of human rights located within the society and culture it discusses and what quickly emerges from these individual discussions is that these different conceptions both shape particular meanings and definitions of disability which in turn produce different educational responses to disability.

What is refreshing about the individual contributions is that they adopt a critical and reflective approach based upon insider perspectives. This is unlike much comparative work which merely reproduces dominant, and usually, government's own descriptive perspectives on what is happening. As such the book will not be a comfortable read either for those of us who think we are doing quite well in establishing the human rights of disabled people nor those who would like to do better when circumstances allow.

This book, therefore, provides an important example of the way we need to approach our attempts to understand the worlds to which we are moving, not just in respect of our understanding of disability but of understanding every aspect of ourselves and our lives.

Mike Oliver
Professor of Disability Studies
University of Greenwich

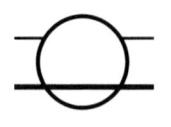

Acknowledgements

We would like to thank Jacinta Evans for her constructive and encouraging support in the development of this book, and also to express our thanks to Helen Oliver for her typing, patience and good humour throughout the production of the manuscript.

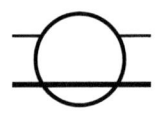

Introduction

Len Barton and Felicity Armstrong

The production of this book has been a difficult, disturbing and exciting task. It has involved struggles over how to describe, understand and make tentative connections between different political and economic systems, historical influences, cultural values, conceptual meanings, policies and practices. The realities of such dilemmas are, for example, expressed in the different theoretical and writing styles that the contributors have used in order to analyse the societies they are discussing.

In each society struggles are taking place within and between different interest groups contesting the rights to speak, to challenge particular perspectives and to offer alternative ideas and interpretations concerning these complex and fundamental issues of disability, human rights and education. In this context, the extent to which the voices of disabled people are part of this conflictual engagement for representation and change is of crucial importance.

All the contributors, including ourselves, are unsure, confused and exercised over a series of personal dilemmas in relation to several aspects of the agendas and questions raised in this book. None of us is complacent and we recognize the immensity of the work which still needs to be done. This includes the importance of a critical engagement with the material presented in this book.

One of the immense difficulties which each author has had to engage with is that of attempting to make connections between the wider structuring influences of economic conditions and political systems, globalization and the illuminating detail of micro, situational aspects of social experience. We greatly sympathize with Whitty *et al.* (1998) and their perceptive analysis of some of the key factors involved. They maintain:

Seeking to integrate the one with the other inevitably means that the theoretical clarity will sometimes be politically obscured by empirical messiness, while what appear to be significant details in particular institutional and national contexts may get lost in the attempt to make broader generalisations.

(Whitty *et al.* 1998: 6)

Given the underexamined nature of the topics addressed in this book and their contestable and complex nature, it is inevitable that it contains ambiguities and contradictions that illustrate the messiness of this process.

The focus of this book is concerned with the rights, position and experience of disabled children and adults in different societies. It raises contentious issues for reflection and debate, and this is highlighted in the variety of perspectives and insights offered by the authors. From our perspective, this book should not be viewed as another attempt to impose Western standards and values on other cultures. Western attitudes, values and practices are far from exemplary in the area of human rights and disability, and there is no room for assuming any society has a preordained prerogative to speak for, about and at other societies defined as 'developing' or 'Third World'. Racism, imperialism and dogmatism should not be allowed to pass unchallenged and unnoticed under the guise of discourse and intervention legitimated in terms of 'aid', 'support' and 'advice'. All societies have much to learn and develop in this matter, not least in terms of generating an open curiosity about different cultures that allows us to listen better, to take notice and to dismantle preconceived ideas about values and practices in different social contexts, including within our own societies.

We have attempted to bring together a group of contributions that will be informative, thoughtful and thought provoking. The centrality of debate and dialogue at a cross-cultural level is one of the most urgent tasks and, sadly, one of the most neglected and underdeveloped in this area. Learning to listen to one another, to develop critical discourses and, at the same time, to strengthen our respect for each other is absolutely essential in this developing learning encounter. As part of this, we have attempted not to interfere with the language or terminology used by authors in their chapters, and this means there is a certain lack of uniformity in this area which we hope you will find understandable.

Within and across societies, individuals and groups have different understandings, values, interpretations and discourses with regard to issues of human rights and disability. The chapters in this book reflect this in both the content and emphasis that they give to important concepts and ideas.

During the process of reading these chapters and discussing them together and with their authors, we have come across, and are beginning to recognize, concepts and ways of understanding issues that are new to us. This has been a stimulating experience. It has also provoked some questioning and re-evaluation of some of our own firmly lodged images and principles, and we have found this process both uncomfortable and creative.

A number of contrasting perspectives on human rights and disability issues emerge in this book, which presents important questions with regard to human rights issues, discourses and practices. The writers are all concerned, in different ways, about how disability is defined and how disabled people interpret and deal with the ignorance, superstition, fear and prejudice that are features of their daily experience. Disabling barriers of an institutional, attitudinal, material and ideological nature are viewed through critical perspectives. The distinctive cultural influences on how disabling images and concepts are established are also an important feature in the analyses offered.

These 'analyses' should not be seen as complete or fixed, but rather as beginnings, openings, towards further debates and struggle. They may be used to test out dominant images of how human rights are understood and interpreted in different contexts. They could lead to questions about *why* discourses of human rights are positioned as being concerned with 'others', rather than with 'our own' communities. And, most importantly, they can be used to make connections between wider issues and questions concerning human rights and education in 'our own' and 'other' societies. This is important because, without these connections, it is only possible to 'fix' *some* equality issues for *some* groups in a provisional and make-shift sort of way. After all, if schools become open and accessible to disabled students, but once admitted they are then at risk of exclusion and discriminatory treatment on the grounds of race, gender, class, poverty or their status as refugees, what questions does this raise about human rights? If we see the question of human rights as concerning *all* members of *all* societies, including, of course, all children and young people – whether they go to school or not – then the arguments, challenges and efforts undertaken by those involved will be more powerful and more unified in terms of understanding and changing the structures and processes that exclude and oppress groups within and across different communities.

This book is based on a cross-cultural approach which acknowledges and examines connections and differences between and within societies, and tries to avoid an approach based on a homogenizing search for 'sameness' and similarities, opposites and differences. Societies are themselves highly diverse, both in terms of cultures and social practices and in terms of policy making and interpretation. In England, for example, there are enormous differences based on class and culture between different communities and in terms of local policy making and interpretation regarding the rights of disabled people. These reflect important differences in histories, values and relationships between different groups in society. 'Culture' is itself a contested concept. Stuart Hall reconceptualizes 'culture' as follows:

- Culture is not settled, enclosed or internally coherent. In the modern world, culture, like place, is a meeting point where different influences, traditions and forces intersect.
- A culture is formed by the juxtaposition and co-presence of different cultural forces and discourses and their effects. It does not consist of fixed elements but of the process of changing cultural practices and meanings.

- The identities which culture helps to construct are not guaranteed in their 'sameness' by some simple origin or fixed in their eternal belongingness to shared values and meanings.

(Hall 1995: 187)

As editors, we might want somehow to marshal and organize in advance the material for this book by imposing some key questions or frameworks on contributors. (To some extent we have done this simply by using the language of 'disability', 'rights' and 'education' in our title and editors' statement for authors, and hence suggesting that such concepts are universally shared and understood in the same way.) As editors, we might have decided to identify a number of possible characteristics that could be taken to indicate an awareness of disability as a human rights issue in different societies. We could then draw themes and questions together in order to 'make comparisons', thus imposing some kind of coherence on the material in the book. These 'characteristics' might include:

- The extent to which an organization of disabled people is present in a society and is attempting to provide alternative conceptions through literature, songs, poetry, education, drama and public demonstration.
- The extent to which there is appropriate legislation in place which is informed by a human rights perspective and is centrally concerned with anti-discrimination and equity.
- The extent to which disability studies is an established feature of higher education institution courses.
- The extent to which schools are open and inclusive in terms of their access, organization, pedagogy, curriculum and ethos.

But any attempt to draw up a list of criteria for measuring the recognition of rights needs to be treated with suspicion for three reasons. First, the ways in which 'rights' are conceptualized and understood in different cultures are diverse and not easily recognized by people living outside those cultures. Second, such a list represents a number of assumptions about the particular structures and practices present in any society. Third, the act of creating such a list of criteria assumes some right to define the framework and language within which issues are to be discussed.

One of the worrying features of a great deal of our thinking in relation to these issues is ethnocentricity. This includes the way in which we think in narrow, stereotypical forms as if our conceptions, experiences and interpretations are the *only* ones of significance. What these chapters demand of us is to engage actively with the issues they raise in order that we can reflect back on our own values and ideas in ways which are both critical and imaginative.

This is not to imply that this will be a comfortable experience, or that the accounts provided do not express some of the messiness and contradictory nature of social life. In the struggle for understanding there will be moments when we are unsure, and uncertain about what to do. Self-tolerance and tolerance of others must be an essential feature of this process.

The rationale for the book

This book is not in any sense a survey of a number of countries or an attempt to draw comparisons between countries. While authors have written about aspects of particular societies, in general they have not attempted to give an overview of disability issues or educational structures in a particular country. Such an attempt would inevitably involve all kinds of homogenizing generalizations and distortions. More often, authors have focused on a particular aspect – sometimes in a very personal account – of their work, the work of others and their developing perceptions about it, to draw out a number of reflections, propositions and questions.

In a sense it would be wrong to say that any countries are 'represented' in this book. Indeed, there is no attempt to represent countries or areas. The selections made concern our choice of contributors, rather than a search for material on particular countries deemed 'to represent' the 'different parts of the world'. Such a project would be contradictory to our aim of trying to avoid crude generalizations and flattened out descriptions, distortions and artificial representations of, and imposed relationships between, countries. There are some important connections and relationships readers will want to try out and make, perhaps, during the reading of this book. An essential means of challenging and removing ignorance, prejudice and misunderstandings is open debate. This involves listening to new voices, establishing trust and earning mutual respect. It is a demanding and difficult task. Authors have included a number of questions that have emerged for them during their thinking and writing. These questions are sometimes difficult and provocative. For example, they may require readers to dismantle some of the conceptual furniture that has been an important part of their thinking, or they may ask readers to try and make some connections between ideas and practices which seem – at first – so disparate as to be totally unconnected. There are no 'answers' to these questions, but their purpose is to encourage imaginative and critical reflection on the part of the reader. Each reading of the book will be individual and unique.

One example of a way of making sense of this book would be to highlight how the major themes of the book relate to the contested notion of human rights, the social construction of difference, the importance of the constant repatterning of social experience in the light of historical and contemporary change, the nature of policy and the interface of all these with education. The theoretical importance of the proposition that policy is made (and subverted) at all levels in society (Fulcher 1989) may allow us to make some connections between the experiences and accounts of different contributors in this book and provide a powerful idea that will enrich cross-cultural research and analyses. It will be interesting to see how, for example, this relates to your reading of the book.

We acknowledge that the meanings attached to all these concepts will be very different across and within different contexts – if they exist at all. What is clear is that while we have been working closely on editing the same book and writing together, what we actually make out of this experience is enriching and different.

In their different contributions, authors have critically engaged with issues which they have raised in response to particular historical, cultural and socio-economic contexts. These include identifying the ways in which policies are variously made and implemented through practice and experienced as inappropriate, irrelevant or even strengthening discrimination and oppression.

We hope that you will find some important and useful insights and ideas in this book, and that these will stimulate interest, debate and an increasingly informed dialogue, both within your own society and, wherever possible, with members of different societies.

Note

An excellent and detailed overview of United Nations instruments is to be found in the book by T. Degener and Y. Koster-Dreese (eds) (1995) *Human Rights and Disabled Persons: Essays and Relevant Human Rights Instruments*. London: Martinus Nijhoff.

References

Fulcher, G. (1989) *Disabling Policies? A Comparative Approach to Education Policy and Disability*. London: Falmer Press. Republished in 1999 by Philip Armstrong Publications, 1 Collegiate Crescent, Sheffield.

Hall, S. (1995) New cultures for old, in D. Massey and P. Jess (eds) *A Place in the World?* Oxford: Oxford University Press.

Whitty, G., Power, S. and Halpin, D. (1998) *Devolution and Choice in Education: the School, the State and the Market*. Buckingham: Open University Press.

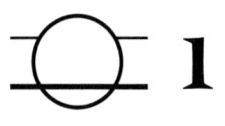 **1**

Disabled people's quest for social justice in Zimbabwe

Robert Chimedza and Susan Peters

Overview

In this chapter, we take up the challenge of creating a new cultural and transformative paradigm for justice and human rights through the example of the disability human rights movement in Zimbabwe. In two decades (approximately 1973 to 1994), disabled people in Zimbabwe went from institutionalization as the dominant form and structure of community, to national recognition as leaders in disability rights. They began in a position of powerlessness and complete dependence on patrons, advancing to a self-managed political organization in an amazingly short period of time. We look closely at the Zimbabwean people's struggle for place and identity in a society that has traditionally marginalized disabled people. Paradoxically, institutionalization of people with disabilities in Zimbabwe spawned the disability rights movement, just as colonization sowed the seeds of liberation and independence for the country as a whole. In the search for identity and place, the example of the Zimbabwean struggle for independence – not only in society at large but for people with disabilities – illuminates a process of community building through the educational praxis of conscientization. We argue that this quest for community is an essential building block for establishing social justice and human rights.

Introduction

In a thoughtful and provocative volume entitled *Disability and the Dilemmas of Education and Justice* (1996), Carol Christenson and Fazal Rizvi explore alternatives to what they see as the dominant distributive paradigm of justice in the world polity (and its correlate, human rights). The dominant 'distributive' paradigm purports to guarantee individual choice in a free market behaviourist and technocratic discourse. From this paradigm, rights are distributed/allocated based on individuals' productive or economic contributions to the nation state. Christenson and Rizvi propose a new counter paradigm that recognizes cultural rights within a broad redistributive framework. Whereas the distributive paradigm concerns itself with equality and social justice on the basis of wealth, income and other material resources, a redistributive paradigm addresses equality and social justice through focusing attention on the injustices that result from cultural disrespect, and is concerned with issues of identity, difference, cultural domination and recognition (Rizvi and Lingard 1996: 24).

In this chapter, we take up the challenge of making this new redistributive paradigm for justice and human rights explicit through the example of the disability human rights movement in Zimbabwe. We believe the Zimbabwe example holds promise for educational transformation in schools. At its base, this redistributive paradigm emphasizes the cultural and transformative aspects of human rights. We view these aspects as prerequisite to changing the economic and political factors that dominate the current view of human rights and the purposes of schooling. To accomplish the task of making this new paradigm explicit, we look closely at the Zimbabwean disabled people's struggle for place and identity in a society that has traditionally marginalized this group. We shall argue that disabled persons are excluded from societal rights (and thus traditional forms of education in schools) and that what is needed is a focus on cultural identity and individual empowerment.

In response to their exclusion from the right to education, as well as employment, social interaction and other forms of participation in society, a growing number of disabled people in Zimbabwe have developed unique forms of education to gain inclusion. They have learned to utilize education as a tool for liberation from oppression, versus 'schooling' as an instrument for perpetuating the political/social/economic status quo. The style this education takes is a form of praxis – a combination of reflection and action directed at structures to be transformed, not the least of which are schools. This praxis, arising from a critical number of disabled people's responses to exclusion, has created a quiet revolution. This revolution has been achieved not with mere verbalism or activism but with reflection and action directed at transforming societal beliefs and structures. It is not surprising to us that, faced with failure of society – and schools as a reflection of society – to accept people with disabilities, these disabled people have taken educational praxis upon themselves.

Disabled people's transformation of educational praxis reveals volumes about the failure of schools successfully to include marginalized individuals, and especially those with disabilities, who are the last to be included. Their attempts to liberate themselves from oppression through educational praxis outside of traditional schooling have much to say about the ways in which social justice gets carried out and about the as yet unrealized roles of schools in legitimizing individual differences and in achieving equal opportunity for all members of society. The authors of this chapter take this approach in order to inform educators of the possibilities and lessons learned, and to urge educators to apply educational praxis to school contexts.

It is interesting to note that disabled people's approach to educating their members in Zimbabwe contains a paradox. Namely, the institutionalization of people with disabilities and exclusion from schooling spawned the disability rights movement in Zimbabwe, just as colonization sowed the seeds of liberation and independence for the country as a whole.

In their search for identity and place, the example of the Zimbabwean struggle for independence – not only in society at large but for people with disabilities – illuminates a process of community building through conscientization, which is the embodiment of educational praxis. The Zimbabwean approach to revolutionary change through conscientization is a process that is eminently educational in nature. It demands transformation of society in general, and specifically schools as a reflection of societal goals, so that they can be renewed.

Conscientization is the basic concept inherent in educational praxis. Conscientization in the Zimbabwean context parallels and extends Paulo Freire's educational work in Brazil. Freire's notion of conscientization was appropriated in the 1970s by the liberation movement in Zimbabwe and subsequently appropriated by Zimbabwean people with disabilities in the 1980s. (For an in-depth discussion, see Peters and Chimedza 1998.) The act of conscientization has achieved solidarity and community in Zimbabwe. Essentially conscientization, or 'education for liberation', is the organized act of collectively educating with emphasis on Subject instead of Object, or the 'Other' (Freire and Macedo 1996). At its core, conscientization involves a search for identity and raised awareness/recognition of oppression necessary to transform the dominant distributive paradigm of human rights.

Educational praxis and its process, conscientization, in the Zimbabwean context have focused on the ability to combine the social, cultural, educational and political aspects of disability. From its onset, the disability rights movement in Zimbabwe began with individual self-awareness of social identities within Zimbabwean culture. As the movement gained momentum, disabled people's politics of representation exemplified the dictum: the personal is political. In this chapter, then, we argue that the Zimbabwean disabled people's quest for identity and community through conscientization is an essential building block for establishing a redistributive paradigm of social justice and human rights. However, contradictions and tensions involved in the process of their search for identity and place raise the question: how can we build community/society/schools that are open to contingency, difference and individual self-identity, but still allow disabled people to engage in a hegemonic project that reconstructs public attitude towards disability through the politics of solidarity?

The authors of this chapter believe that answering this question, with its universal underpinnings, will provide a vision and a tool for addressing human rights and education that could be applied to educational/school contexts across cultures. We begin, then, by discussing the historical contexts within which the seeds of social justice and human rights were sown in Zimbabwe.

In the following discussion of the historical context, we highlight the experiences of three disabled Zimbabweans: one woman and two men from the two dominant subcultures in Zimbabwe (Shona and Ndebele) who exemplify the goals of social justice and the successful pathways for attaining human rights in their society. These individuals are Ranga Mupindu, Lainah Magama and Joshua Malinga. The late Ranga Mupindu was the Executive Director of the National Council of Disabled Persons Zimbabwe (NCDPZ) until his death in 1995. Lainah Magama worked for the International Labor Organization as a programme expert on a project concerning disabled women's rights, and she was the chair of the women's programme in the NCDPZ. The third individual, Joshua Malinga, is one of the most renowned persons with disabilities in Africa, if not internationally. Joshua is a founding member of NCDPZ. He is the past chair and a founding member of Disabled Persons International (DPI), Secretary General of the Pan Africa wing of DPI, Secretary General of the Southern Africa Federation of the Disabled (SAFOD), councillor and past mayor of the city of Bulawayo (Zimbabwe's second largest city) and was the guest of honour who gave the opening address at the 1996 Paralympics in Atlanta, Georgia, in the United States.

These three disabled people come from adverse backgrounds and circumstances typical of disabled people in Zimbabwe. They have been chosen by disabled people in Zimbabwe as leaders of their organizations and spokespersons for their causes. We give their dialogues a prominent place in this chapter in order to reclaim the voices of disabled people as inherent to formulating a new redistributive paradigm of social justice and human rights. In doing so, we also bring our own experiences to bear as disabled persons and disability activists deeply involved in both US and Zimbabwean disability rights movements. (Note: all quotations by these three individuals in this chapter are derived from taped interviews that Chimedza and Peters conducted in 1994, 1995 and 1996.)

Zimbabwean cultural context

In two decades (approximately 1973 to 1994), disabled people in Zimbabwe have gone from institutionalization as the dominant form and structure of community, to international recognition as leaders in disability rights. They began from a position of powerlessness and complete dependence on patrons, advancing to a self-managed political organization in an amazingly short time. This self-managed empowerment is all the more remarkable considering the roots of social injustice and cultural disrespect that disabled people have faced in Zimbabwe.

To begin with, the birth of a child with disabilities in the traditional Shona and Ndebele cultures is viewed negatively. Often it is associated with witchcraft (Department of Social Services 1982), promiscuity by the mother during pregnancy (Addison 1986) and punishment by ancestral spirits. It is generally felt that one should not laugh at a person with a disability or the curse may be transferred to you (Barnatt 1992), and that pregnant women should not look at or associate with people with disabilities or they may give birth to a child with disabilities. Some disabilities are seen as being possessed by evil spirits. For example deaf people's speech defects perpetuate this perspective (Chimedza 1998).

These attitudes to disability were confirmed to us in the interviews we conducted. Commenting on the Zimbabwean people's attitude to disability, Ranga Mupindu gave the example of his own childhood experiences:

> There are many factors that made me critical of our culture, including conflicts within our culture. For example, my grandmother thought that to be secure I would need to be cleansed, and the experience was nasty. I remember even my mother telling me it was the only way. I was taken to a mountain and I was left overnight on the mountain on my own. They were to collect me the following morning. Traditional rituals were performed. It was expected that that was the way of helping me out. It was terrible.

Ranga goes on to say:

> The expectations of the people at home, even close relatives would always say something like, 'It was the spirit from the wife that caused the disability.' This attitude even threatened the marriage of my father and mother. They had to consult a traditional healer to say it was not their fault. Otherwise, it would have led to divorce. There are many divorces as a result of disablement in the villages.

Lainah Magama's experiences echo Ranga's powerful examples of negatively assigned cultural identity. Lainah was an only child and both her parents were in the medical profession. At the age of 18 months she contracted polio and became disabled. Although her father was a nurse in the medical profession, he could not accept it. To quote Lainah's words:

> My father did not quite accept the fact that his child had acquired a disability. He thought that having a child who had a disability was shameful. He decided that I should be put in an orphanage run by missionaries. When my mother said, 'NO,' he divorced her and asked her to leave with me, so we went to live elsewhere.

Attitudes to disability apparent in family reactions carried over into schooling. Ranga's experience is not atypical.

> At Jairos Jiri Center in Bulawayo one afternoon, there were two deaf guys who were pushing me around the Center in my wheelchair. There was a school nearby where people were enrolling . . . I took my birth certificate and produced it to the headmaster and I was enrolled. Then information reached the administration [at Jairos Jiri] that I was no

longer taking leatherwork – that I was going to the secondary school. I was summoned to the office to give an explanation of why I had gone out of my way to enrol myself in secondary school.'

(Excerpts from interview published in Peters 1995: 67)

Whereas Ranga and Lainah rose to be prominent members of society and leaders in the disability movement in Zimbabwe, their experiences of social and cultural degradation in school and family are typical for most people with disabilities in the country. They all have their own similar stories to tell. Further, in pre-independence Rhodesia (Zimbabwe's colonial name) the situation was bad enough for black people and worse for black people with disabilities. The only provision of services they got was through charitable non-governmental institutions and individual philanthropists such as Mr Jairos Jiri. This pattern of charity and cultural disrespect for the human identity of disabled people also played itself out in the institutional context at the larger societal level.

Institutionalization

It is difficult to discuss the institutionalization of people with disabilities in Zimbabwe and their quest for social justice without discussing the Jairos Jiri Association, for two reasons. First, it was Jairos Jiri who initially liberated many disabled people from hunger, starvation, illiteracy, disease and begging in the streets and brought them to his own house for care and educational training. This eventually grew to the Jairos Jiri Association as it stands today. Second, it was the oppressive system of institutional care and structure at the Jairos Jiri Association institutions that led people with disabilities to form a disability rights movement to stand for their rights, not only in the institutions that controlled their educational opportunities, but in society at large.

Jairos Jiri was a chief's son, of very little or no formal education. While working as a delivery boy for a bottle store in the city of Bulawayo, he was shocked by the number of people with disabilities he saw begging and in rags in the streets. Many came to beg at his place of work. Back in his village this would never happen. Family and the chief would always provide at least food for the survival of their disabled kith and kin. Moved by the plight of these people, Jairos Jiri began to take them one by one to his house in the townships. He gave them food, took them to the hospital, gave them shelter and provided training in work skills such as basket-weaving and leather-making. Against all tribulations of little finance, criticism from friends and local authorities, he worked very hard – resulting in the mammoth Jairos Jiri Association schools, sheltered workshops and training facilities that we see today (see Farquhar 1987 for more details of Jairos Jiri, the man and his work.) The Jairos Jiri Association was not the only organization with institutions that provided services and educational training to people with disabilities in the country. Missionaries and other volunteer organizations built institutions and schools for the care and education of people with disabilities. The basic model used was institutionalization in segregated places, with little contact with non-disabled people besides workers in the institutions. This institutional treatment magnifies and correlates the experiences at the family level.

> I should say that from my early beginning in the NCDPZ, the most frustrating thing that really moved me to be particularly involved in disability issues was criticism of the system of Jairos Jiri in our approach. This involvement was due to what was happening in Jairos Jiri, or what was still happening in some cases was a situation where disabled persons are not given any voice. That system really affected us to the extent whereby we could not even realise any job opportunities available for disabled persons in that association in top positions.
>
> (Ranga Mupindu 1994)

Ranga felt that there was too much nepotism in the institution – whether low-level positions or senior administrators. From his perspective, that really denied disabled persons the opportunity to be tried in responsible positions of authority.

> Even when we were at the centre that really showed without any doubts the fact that the association would not consider the talents of disabled people. The tendency was just to look at your disability and you would not be given a chance. The attitude was that the disabled persons should always remain disabled. They should not be given opportunities.

The experiences of the disabled people in the Jairos Jiri Association centres was not different from what disabled people in other institutions were experiencing. It seems to us that the model of educational service delivery to disabled persons in the country then came from the 'rehabilitation medical model' based on economic/productive approaches, and not from a cultural model of individual identity and recognition. We realize that many organizations internationally started from this point of rehabilitation. However, we note from Ranga Mupindu's statements that the institutions in Zimbabwe did not go the next step to empower disabled people and to involve them in the planning and management of their own lives and in societal issues.

The situation of employment for disabled persons is similar to their educational experiences. Lainah Magama struggled to graduate from college with a masters degree in urban and regional planning in the Philippines, and returned home to work in Zimbabwe. Despite her education, Lainah quit her first job after working for more than five years without any promotion at all. Lainah describes her situation then as follows:

> I took my first job just after independence, and people were still looking at race. I mean, the color of one's skin was still very important. It is still important now, but it is not that important. As a result, I had three things against me: I was black. I was a woman. I had a disability. Life was really

difficult for anyone with a combination of those three. With just a combination of two, it was bad enough. I stayed in that job for quite a while – for more than five years. At one point they told me I could not be promoted. At least my friend who was supervising me was told that I am not promotable because I was a woman and I had a disability.

In order to build on Lainah's and Ranga's personal testimonies, we now turn to the voice of Joshua Malinga. Because Joshua Malinga is a founding member of NCDPZ and has held many positions of leadership nationally, regionally and internationally, we use his views here as representative of some of the views that NCDPZ uses in its conscientization process. We believe the message he brings out represents the voices of disabled people in Zimbabwe. The position could have been the same even if we had interviewed any other member of the leadership in the NCDPZ (e.g. Alexander Phiri, David Zulu), because we know that is what they stand for. In our interview with him soon after the Atlanta Paralympics (1996), Mr Malinga took a broad stance, addressing five key issues that have influenced Zimbabwean societal response to disabled people: education, charity, self-governance, professional attitudes and public mass media.

Education

As with Ranga, Joshua spent most of his life at an institution at Jairos Jiri Center in Bulawayo. He hates institutionalization of any kind. He does not believe in special schools for people with disabilities either. He says that his happiest days as a student were the ones he spent at a regular local high school learning with non-disabled fellow students. He believes special education can still be taught to a child with disabilities in the regular classroom. For students with severe and multiple handicapping conditions, he believes their programmes could be separate but should be on the same site as the non-disabled students.

Charity

The Jairos Jiri Association where Joshua spent most of his early life is a charitable organization that provides shelter and some schooling, mostly in the form of training for low-skill level jobs. Joshua has seen many people with disabilities become objects of charity in these situations. The organizations to which they belong use them for fundraising. In some cases he has seen disabled people become beggars or remain permanently on social welfare and treated as destitutes. He strongly feels that disability is not an issue of charity nor is it a welfare issue. He argues that disability should be treated as a development issue that people plan and budget for as a right for disabled people. It should be part of the national agenda. Charity has never benefited disabled people because charity is not part of development.

Self-governance

Joshua is a leader in several organizations of disabled people. He is also a leader in the community at large. He argues that disabled people should be given a chance to run their own lives. He does not oppose the existence of organizations for the disabled, but is worried by their paternalistic approach. He thinks most of these organizations for the disabled would benefit people with disabilities more if they were run by disabled people themselves. As a result, he advocates for educating disabled people to take leadership positions so that they can run their own affairs. He believes disability is a multibillion-dollar business, yet the largest percentage of the money ends up paying non-disabled professionals and administrators who run the affairs of people with disabilities and do not give them the necessary training and education to take over those positions.

The professionals

Joshua argues that professionals (teachers, doctors, social workers, therapists) see disability as pathology. They are stuck in the medical model of disability. Using this perspective, professionals do not accept the disabled person for what he or she is. They become preoccupied in trying to remake the disabled person into a non-disabled one. This does not work. Joshua feels professionals should spend more time identifying and developing the abilities of the disabled person. For instance, he says he is very articulate in his speech and very good with figures, yet at the Jairos Jiri School he spent close to 50 per cent of his school time in the physiotherapy room. The professionals spent more time trying to make him walk, which he will never accomplish, than on his capabilities and talents. Their perspective refuses to accept disability as a difference between people just like one's 'race', colour of skin, religion, gender etc.

The public

Joshua believes that there is need for a lot of education of the public so that they accept people with disabilities as equals. His experience in Zimbabwe and internationally is that people with disabilities are treated as second class citizens. In his own country, negative beliefs and attitudes towards people with disabilities still exist in the community. Parents are shy and feel embarrassed to have a child with disabilities. Employers will not employ someone with a disability unless it is for charity or pity, or they are compensated for it. He believes disabled people should be employed in their own right as equal members of society. He calls for intensified education and high skill level job training to make this realistic.

Joshua is particularly annoyed with the mass media. He says the mass media portray people with disabilities negatively. Newspaper reports and television shows portray disabled people more as receivers of charity and welfare. The mass media shape the image that society eventually has of people with disabilities. They are a powerful socializing agent. Their negative portrayal of disabled people has great impact on how these people in the main are viewed by other people.

Finally, Joshua emphasizes that it is the responsibility of every person with a disability to stand for his or her rights, and organizations of the disabled should help their members to understand that. He argues that disability is no longer a civil rights issue. It is now a human rights issue. Not only civil societies, but all human societies, should respect disabled people as equals.

From these experiences, a picture begins to emerge of oppression against the cultural/human rights of disabled people. In the next section we describe their responses to this oppression, rooted in the basic human need for recognition as social beings with potential for productive contributions to the social polity. These responses form the broader contextual factors influencing disabled people's quest for social justice in Zimbabwe.

The quest for social justice: from conscientization to public policy

The seeds of reaction to oppression in family and institutions and the development of the redistributive paradigm of human rights began with one of the strongest felt needs of disabled people – socialization. At Nguboyenja (one of the Jairos Jiri centres) there was no entertainment and the inmates (as the disabled people called themselves) were punished if seen talking to members of the opposite sex. They were not allowed to go visiting in the nearby township without supervision from the workers. Faced with this oppressive form of cultural disrespect for the basic human right of social interaction, isolated from their families and removed from society, young people with disabilities formed a support system of their own. They developed strong ties with each other. It was through realization of their boredom that they formed an entertainment club called Kubatsirana/Ncedanani (which means to help each other, in Shona and Ndebele respectively). The club organized picnics and excursions to places of interest outside the institution. These activities provided an opportunity for the disabled people to come together and discuss their problems. Despite much opposition from the patrons and management at the centre, the club became registered as a welfare organization in 1975. It was at a time when the war of liberation and the political situation in Rhodesia made people think politically. As Ranga Mupindu pointed out, 'We would listen to Radio Mozambique, hearing revolutionary ideas. That is when we started seeing the administrators of the association as people who were not really having our interest at heart.' According to Crewe and Zola (1983), 'Significant social movement becomes possible when there is a revision; people looking at some misfortune see it no longer as warranting charitable consideration, but as an injustice which is intolerable in society.'

The disability rights movement in Zimbabwe organized through the process of conscientization. Excluded from traditional forms of education and socialization, disabled people formed their own unique forms of educational praxis. They learned to utilize education as a tool for liberation from oppression, versus schooling as an instrument for perpetuating the political, social and economic status quo. Through their socialization clubs, such as the one at Nguboyenja, and their mobilization programmes, such as the Rural Membership Development Programme, NCDPZ began to conscientize people with disabilities that their suffering was a result of the oppressive social system that did not treat disabled people as equal members of society. Disabled people were not to blame for their plight, nor was it a fault of their disabilities. The problem was with societal institutions that were negative to them and needed to be transformed. The approach was to change disabled people's level of consciousness and to make them see it as their right to have equal access to education, health, employment, recreation etc. It was also imperative to conscientize policy and decision makers and the public at large so that they realized how unjust the social systems were to disabled people. According to Ranga Mupindu, it is not enough for a Member of Parliament to present to Parliament the demands of disabled people out of pity, mercy or charity.

> What is needed is for the Member of Parliament to do so out of his own conscience that tells him or her of the genuine injustices disabled people are experiencing just as the war of liberation was a fight against an unjust system and not against individuals.

It was largely through the organized efforts of NCDPZ and the conscientization of its leadership and grass-roots members that the Disabled Persons Act of 1992 came into being. This organization saw the passage of this law as the beginning, not the end, of the quest for equal human rights. It used the law as a tool to direct attention to the plight of disabled people and as a weapon to provide teeth for their human rights. Strategies were employed to broaden and shift policy agendas from a focus on welfare and economic issues (distributive paradigm) to an acceptance as social equals, and recognition of themselves in their cultural identities (redistributive paradigm). The strategy that NCDPZ employed at the organizational policy level exemplifies the concept it used in the conscientization/educational praxis of its individual members: the personal is political.

NCDPZ sent two delegates (one disabled woman and one disabled man) from each of Zimbabwe's 45 provinces to its Second National Congress at Victoria Falls in November 1994. Working groups composed of delegates developed policy platforms in each of the following areas: government policy development, economic development, commercial projects, mobility rights, children and youth projects, social/cultural environmental issues, managing disasters (drought and famine) and women's issues. From these working groups, six priority areas were identified and resolutions put forth for vote by the entire delegation. The six priority areas were legislation and representation, socio-economic issues, gender issues, social and health reform, employment and education. (See the Appendix for details of these recommendations.)

As part of the strategy for the National Congress, all ministers of government attended at the behest of NCDPZ to present a governmental response and to engage in a dialogue with all delegates regarding what had been done since passage of the 1992 Act, and how they would address resolutions in future policy development. As a central part of this strategy, specific delegates had been democratically preselected from the working groups to address each government minister on political issues at a personal level and to present key specific recommendations. Two powerful examples include Farai Cherera, who talked about forced sterilization and involuntary abortions, and Ephraim Mafura, who described the hardships brought about by disabled people's exclusion from resettlement schemes and distribution of drought relief foods.

The President of Zimbabwe, The Honourable Robert Mugabe, also attended to listen to the ministry presentations and to hear issues raised by delegates. President Mugabe responded at length to the delegation with specific guarantees, including a promise for disability representation in Parliament, immediate adjustment of school fees (thus promoting universal access to education), disabled women's representation at the World Congress of Women in Beijing and a stop to sterilizing people with mental impairments. With regard to negative attitudes that lead to injustices, particularly in land distribution, health care, education and employment, the President recognized that 'awareness is not a one shot endeavour but a continuous exercise' (NCDPZ 1994).

Overall, this Congress exemplified the strategies that Joshua Malinga spoke of in our interview with him: proposing resolutions to achieve integration; promoting self-government and leadership of disabled people through their active participation in policy development; insisting that professionals (particularly government officials) develop enabling policies; and addressing public attitudes head-on through face-to-face dialogue with top government representatives.

Conclusion

Disabled people in Zimbabwe recognize that human rights and the quest for social justice require more than laws and political action, but ongoing conscientization of individuals – both disabled and non-disabled. Their work continues with a two-pronged strategy of national political forums and grassroots mobilization of individual members. In 1995, the First National Disability Board Seminar was held in Harare, Zimbabwe. The Board was created as part of the Disabled Person's Act of 1992 to oversee implementation of the right guaranteed therein. The National Disability Board Chairman, in his opening remarks, explained that:

> The prime objective of this seminar is to, among other things, sensitise [conscientize] the public, policy makers and implementers, service delivering systems, and the media on the needs of disabled people, and

policies and legislations related to disability . . . The seminar delibera-
tions should focus on ensuring disabled persons are enabled to exercise
their fundamental human and civil rights like any other citizen in the
country.

(Phiri 1995: 2)

This statement supports the notion of the redistributive paradigm we began
with in this chapter. In addition to these nationally organized efforts, leaders
in the NCDPZ and individual members whose consciousness has been raised
continue the day-to-day fight for social justice and a broad human rights
agenda at the grass-roots level. Their efforts are multifaceted: at the family
level to combat cultural practices such as the traditional cleansing rituals
Ranga Mupindu experienced; at the institutional level in places of employment, such as Lainah Magama's campaign to overturn discrimination; within
organizations such as Jairos Jiri to force a shift away from charity and disem-
powerment; and at governmental levels for parliamentary representation to
ensure a voice in policy development.

At all levels, disabled people's strategies in Zimbabwe exemplify the recognition that disability is not a personal tragedy or charity-based approach to
social policy, but a cultural endeavour that requires a broad redistributive
counter paradigm to the dominant technocratic/economic discourse. These
strategies are a process of conscientization that is built on community, but
open to contingency. Conscientization allows for individual voice, while it
engages in a hegemonic project that reconstructs public attitudes to disability
through the politics of solidarity.

The individual and collective insights of the authors and the voices of disabled people heard in this chapter give us powerful images of the degradation
that comes with being disabled in a society that dehumanizes and devalues
disabled people. Their personal testimonies have much to say about social attitudes and values and about the ways in which these values are transmitted
through family, institutions and schools. They reveal institutionalization and
segregation of disabled people as part of a socio-politically based distributive
human rights paradigm.

Above all, these experiences highlight the importance of individual iden-
tity/solidarity in community. For schools, as potential agents of social transformation towards acceptance of the human rights of disabled people, the
Zimbabwean approach to human rights means that educators must be challenged to accept rather than marginalize young people, to recognize their
right to a place and identity as full participating members in society and to
view them as more fully human.

Questions

1 Many developing countries such as Zimbabwe still have special schools and
institutions as their basic provision for providing education to disabled

people. In what way does this violate the disabled students' human rights? How could this problem be alleviated, considering that most developing countries have weak economies?

2 The struggle of disabled people in Zimbabwe for a place in education and employment can be seen in the interviews with Ranga Mupindu and Lainah Magama. What is the status of people with disabilities in education and employment in your own country? How does that compare with the examples from Zimbabwe?

3 How can teachers and other professionals help to bring about public attitude changes towards people with disabilities?

Appendix: NCDPZ Second National Congress Resolutions, 4 November 1994

Resolutions address issues in six priority areas: legislation/representation, socio-economic issues, gender issues, education, social/health issues, and employment.

Legislation/representation

Resolution no. 1
NCDPZ and all organisations of disabled people should vigorously support the implementation of all requirements set forth in the Disabled Persons Act of 1992 and suggest revisions where needed. This support includes:

(i) Ensuring the voice OF disabled people is heard as a majority voice and disabled people are appropriately represented by gender, disability type, and organisation on the National Disability Board.

(ii) Ensuring that staff to the National Disability Board conform to the same standards as (i) above.

(iii) Ensuring that adequate funding and other needed resources are provided by government for the effective performance of the National Disability Board.

Resolution no. 2
A Member of Parliament should be appointed by the President from an organisation OF disabled people who is him/herself a disabled person. The same recommendation holds for all levels of government structure, including district and provincial levels. These appointees should have as their goal, controlling and accelerating the pace of reform for people with disabilities.

Resolution no. 3
NCDPZ represents all disability groups and will continue to vigorously pursue such issues as sign language availability for the deaf, availability of Braille materials for the blind.

Socio-economic issues

Resolution no. 1
The Land Acquisition Act should be revised to include a clause accommodating disabled people and the National Disability Board should monitor its implementation.

Resolution no. 2
Affordable and accessible housing and sanitary conditions, and clean drinking water in both rural and urban areas must be made available to people with disabilities in residential areas – not to be concentrated on one area.

Resolution no. 3
The establishment of new institutions for disabled persons must be discouraged and existing ones must be investigated to establish the purpose they are meant for.

Resolution no. 4
The tax allowance of 500 dollars and other grants-in-aid including the SDF (Social Dimension Fund) and a mobility allowance should be increased to an acceptable level or established, and income taxes should be introduced on a sliding scale. Distribution of money for development projects should be controlled by organisations of disabled people.

Gender issues

Resolution no. 1
Continue development and encouragement of women in leadership positions within NCDPZ and include their concerns in all decision-making processes.

Resolution no. 2
Sponsor educational programs to target parents and teachers in order to raise their awareness and provide skills necessary for disabled boys and girls to develop to their maximum potential and to be fully integrated in all aspects of community life.

Education issues

Resolution no. 1
Every disabled child shall have the right to an education regardless of ability to pay. Those assisted by the SDF (Social Dimension Fund) must not suffer delays in payment.

Resolution no. 2
Appliances shall be given to all those who need them regardless of ability to pay.

Resolution no. 3
Education is the key to quality life and should include both formal and informal educational opportunities that enhance the socio-cultural experiences of disabled people.

Social and health issues

Resolution no. 1
AIDS affects everyone and especially disabled women and men due to societal attitudes and marginalisation. People with disabilities must be included in all aspects of AIDS education including planning, decision making, seminars, workshops, health services, and home based care programmes.

Resolution no. 2
All disabled people have a right to choose their own method of family planning. The practice of forced sterilisation and involuntary abortions must be stopped.

Resolution no. 3
Work towards improving services, facilities and training for people with multiple/severe/mental disabilities including appliances, classroom assistants, scholarships and grants-in-aid and maintenance.

Resolution no. 4
Support programmes for youth, especially sports and recreation, through development of a youth programme in NCDPZ with specific objectives.

Resolution no. 5
Drought relief and natural disaster relief efforts must not exclude people with disabilities.

Employment issues

Resolution no. 1
Government should provide incentive to employers to hire disabled people, such as reducing taxes to companies who employ disabled people, subsidising salaries of unskilled disabled workers, and awarding prizes to companies with the best hiring record for disabled people. Government should set an example by hiring a minimum of 10 per cent disabled people as a total of all employees in all government offices.

Resolution no. 2
Those disabled people who are working, but their salary is below the poverty data line, should still receive some assistance from the Social Dimension Fund.

References

Addison, J. (1986) *Handicapped People in Zimbabwe*. Harare: NASCOH.

Barnatt, S.N. (1992) Policy issues in disability and rehabilitation in developing countries, *Journal of Disability Policy Studies*, 3: 45–65.

Chimedza, R. (1998) The cultural politics of integrating deaf students in regular schools in Zimbabwe, *Disability and Society*, 13(4): 493–502.

Christenson, C. and Rizvi, F. (1996) *Disability and the Dilemmas of Education and Justice*. Buckingham: Open University Press.

Crewe, N. and Zola, E. (1983) *Independent Living for Physically Disabled People*. San Francisco: Jossey-Bass.

Department of Social Services (1982) *Report on the National Disability Survey of Zimbabwe*. Harare: Government Printers.

Farquhar, J. (1987) *Jairos Jiri – the Man and his Works*. Gweru: Mambo Press.

Freire, P. and Macedo, D. (1996) A dialogue: culture, language and race, in *Breaking Free: the Transformative Power of Critical Pedagogy*. Cambridge, MA: Harvard Educational Review reprint series no. 27.

NCDPZ (1994) *Report of the 2nd National Congress*. Harare: unpublished.

Peters, S. (1995) Disability baggage: changing the educational research terrain, in P. Clough and L. Barton (eds) *Making Difficulties: Research and the Construction of SEN*. London: Paul Chapman Publishing.

Peters, S. and Chimedza, R. (1998) Conscientisation and the cultural politics of education: a radical minority perspective. Unpublished manuscript.

Phiri, A. (1995) *Report on the First National Disability Board Seminar*. Harare: National Council of Disabled Persons in Zimbabwe.

Rizvi, F. and Lingard, B. (1996) Disability, education and the discourses of justice, in C. Christensen and F. Rizvi (eds) *Disability and the Dilemmas of Education and Justice*. Buckingham: Open University Press.

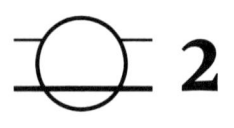 **2**

Human rights and the struggle for inclusive education in Trinidad and Tobago

Ann Cheryl Namsoo and
Derrick Armstrong

Overview

The struggle for 'human rights' has had enormous significance in the history of social policy in Trinidad and Tobago. Yet it should not be surprising that this struggle has been uneven, reflecting the complex array of interests and influences that have been in evidence in, and contested through, policy arenas. The history of education policy, for instance, reflects both the aspirations and the contradictions of this struggle. In this chapter we examine how struggles around educational policy and teacher professional education in Trinidad and Tobago have been informed by efforts to reconceptualize the meaning of 'human rights' in a post-colonial society.

Introduction

The education system in Trinidad and Tobago today has its roots in the former colonial system. While the general masses were excluded from education, local elites used a system of prestige schools to maintain their already established political and economic power. This system of elite schools laid the basis for a historic compromise between Church and State that has continued into the post-independence era, and has had significant implications for the quality of education made available to the general population. In this chapter it will be argued that this compromise has restricted the potential impact of education in the anti-colonial and post-colonial struggle for social justice based upon the principle of human rights. Instead, it has promoted the interests of traditional elites and of the rising black middle class, and has diverted resources away from the mass of the population towards the prestige schools. Moreover, the prestige school system creates conditions that advantage not only a minority of pupils but also that minority of teachers who work within this sector.

Attempts at educational reform in the post-independence era have been dominated by the intervention of international funding agencies such as the Inter-American Development Bank (IDB), the International Bank for Reconstruction and Development (IBRD or World Bank) and the International Monetary Fund (IMF). We will argue that such interventions are part of a wider agenda that is not necessarily concerned with inclusive schooling and which in practice has imposed further constraints on teachers and pupils.

The needs of teachers working within the 'non-prestigious' sector are inadequately met with the consequence that the educational disadvantage experienced by many pupils is compounded. It was in this context that non-governmental agencies like the Association for Special Education of Trinidad and Tobago (TASETT) and the Trinidad and Tobago Unified Teachers Association (T&TUTA) began to explore the development of teacher education programmes for professionals and para-professionals working with children who at some point in their development were experiencing difficulties within the education system. This led to a long-term collaboration with the Department of Educational Studies of the University of Sheffield for the provision of teacher education.

The T&TUTA/Sheffield programmes have been informed by a social justice perspective on educational disadvantage that has sought critical cross-cultural collaboration in the development of new initiatives, approaches and interventions in the field of 'special education'. The struggle for a social justice model of teacher education is one that must be based upon a theoretical and practical engagement with the politics of post-colonialism and upon the mutual analysis of the lived experience of educators and students. This, we argue, involves a critical unmasking of first-world perspectives on inclusion and an examination of how this impacts upon teacher professional education in the post-colonial world.

Historical background

The history of formal education in Trinidad and Tobago has been marked by the endeavours of the ruling elites to perpetuate their own social and economic power. Despite shared interests, the ruling colonial elites were from the earliest times divided along racial and religious lines between the non-English speaking Franco-Spanish, whose interests were represented by the Roman Catholic Church, and the British colonial power. A State system of secular schooling was developed by the British to challenge the control exercised by the Roman Catholic Church over education. Thus, the Queens Collegiate School (later Queen's Royal College) was set up and subsidized by the state with the explicit remit that there should be no religious education. The Roman Catholic Church responded by establishing its own 'prestigious' school, the College of the Immaculate Conception (referred to as St Mary's College) (Look Loy 1984).

This prestige system of denominational and state schools was to have a profound effect upon the development of education in Trinidad and Tobago, as resources were focused upon this sector at the expense of the general populace. As a Crown Colony, the system made provisions for the establishment of primary schools in each ward for the supply of free 'secular instruction' in moral and social matters. Yet in a report on public education (Keenan 1869) it was revealed that the total subsidy for primary education in the country came to £3450, while the subsidy to Queen's Royal College alone came to £3000.

Although the population continued to grow, no real attempts were made to offer equal opportunities to children of different ethnic and social backgrounds. Primary or 'elementary' education was slowly extended to the masses, but secondary education was largely denied. The Harris Report of 1851 had made it abundantly clear that 'it was useless to attempt more than to arouse, enlighten and render active the intellectual faculties and moral sentiments . . . so that the State may not suffer from the vices and errors which ignorance is likely to induce' (Braithwaite 1991: 23). The Keenan Report (1869) noted the inadequate provision of toilets, bad furniture and school design, the lack of organization, poor commitment of teachers and inadequate materials. During this period, the colonial government also made a decision to allocate public funds to the provision of secondary education. Interestingly, those students who benefited from this 'public-funded education' were not an accurate representation of the population of the country: fewer than one-fifth of the students were 'Coloreds' and none were 'Negroes' in a country which had a majority of 'Coloreds' and 'Negroes' (Alleyne 1995) By the beginning of the twentieth century, secondary education remained the preserve of the middle classes. According to the Gollan Commission, in 1915 there were 277 primary schools and only four secondary schools.

At this time, there were few opportunities for social mobility and the school system, far from creating openings for the emergence of a new black middle class, in practice reinforced the social and racial divides existing within the society. Government Reports of this period – Harris (1851), Keenan (1869) and Gollan (1916), all cited in Braithwaite (1991) – all focused on the differences of class, creed and colour among the races. Even in the selection of teachers, a racist benevolence was the guiding principle. Keenan, for example, though not overtly objecting to the fact that, with one exception, primary school teachers at that time were 'all persons of colour', felt that European female teachers should be persuaded to 'establish themselves in the colony' because of the (c)onsiderations of the weightiest moral importance'. He elaborated further by stating that although the staff comprised primarily mature persons, their level of 'solidity' and 'influence of character' was in no way comparable with that of English teachers of similar age.

By the 1930s, the total number of schools had increased to 288, of which the majority (244) were denominational. Yet education was still not compulsory.

Moreover, prior to 1950, each school was a law unto itself. The hiring and firing of staff was the responsibility of the management (usually religious) and the principal of the school. The principal, then known as 'head teacher', was also a leading figure in the region where he lived – to the villagers, he was greatly respected and the embodiment of all knowledge. Anyone seeking 'any advice on anything' went to the 'head teacher'. In fact, so much power was vested in this role that the school, regardless of its 'real' name, was called by the name of the head teacher, as in 'Mr John's School'. Each principal decided who would be accepted into 'his' school and who would not.

Principals of secondary schools set pre-qualification examinations for students who wished to be considered for entry into their schools, so it was not uncommon for students to be writing as many exams as there were schools in an effort to gain acceptance into at least one. The elitism of the system was reinforced by a fee structure of around TT$16 per term, which placed secondary schooling out of the reach of even middle-class families. The fact that there were only eight exhibition (free) places available each year meant that working-class families were totally excluded from secondary education.

The period prior to 1964 has been described by Braithwaite (1991) as 'one of educational stagnation'. Although there was an increase in the number of available primary schools to house the increasing primary school population, because education was not deemed appropriate for the masses there was only limited expansion in the secondary school system. This, according to Braithwaite (1991), reflected an elitist, exclusive concept of secondary education. Moreover, the school curriculum was strongly Eurocentric in nature. Although Keenan in 1869 had recommended the inclusion of books with lessons which depicted the life and experiences of the colony, it took another 63 years before books with some local flavour were introduced into the system. Despite this injection, paradigms were shifting very slowly and in the 1960s children in primary schools were still being taught that there were four seasons and that snow and Christmas went hand in hand.

Independence, far from loosening the influence of the denominational school sector, brought with it an intensification of the struggle between Church and state for the control of education. Although committed to universal education, the People's National Movement (PNM) government of Eric Williams was forced to accede to the wishes of the Church and preserve the denomination system of prestige schools for the middle classes. This compromise was enshrined in the 'Concordat' of 1961, a pre-independence agreement between Church and state that served only to transfer the elitist education system from the colonial era to the post-independence era. The denominational boards were the ultimate 'powerbrokers' and continued to maintain ownership, direct control and management of all denominational primary and secondary schools. Moreover, a common entrance examination was introduced to select those pupils who would receive secondary education. While 80 per cent of secondary pupils in the denominational schools gained their places by passing the examination, another 20 per cent could be chosen by the schools. This served to reinforce the position of the mainly white elite at the expense of the mainly black and East Indian poor.

Later attempts to reform the system and lessen the power of the denomi-national schools suffered a similar fate. The Draft Education Plan of 1964 led to the provision of secondary education for most children through the junior secondary and senior comprehensive systems. Double-shifting was a strategy developed for the junior secondary schools to satisfy the great demand for secondary education without incurring the expense of a major school build-ing programme. This doubled the normal capacity of the schools by assigning different groups of children to a morning shift and other groups to an evening shift. However, the denominational 'prestige' schools were allowed to remain outside the plan and in consequence the possibility of establishing a demo-cratic education system based on equality of opportunity was lost. Although the junior secondary system was designed to 'stimulate the development of more practical and realistic curricula than that offered by the traditional gram-mar school' (Alleyne 1995: 45), in practice it became a dumping ground for those who failed to gain admission to the much sought after 'prestige' second-ary schools, and problems arose with children having too much unsupervised time and reduced access to teaching time as compared to those attending non-shift schools.

The continuation of this dual system of schooling stands in sharp contrast to national policy pronouncements on education. The latter have employed much stronger rhetoric on 'human rights', as is evidenced, for example, by the most recent policy paper on educational development for Trinidad and Tobago, which declares the following beliefs:

That every child has an inherent right to an education which will enhance the development of maximum capability regardless of gender, ethnic, economic, social or religious background.

That a system of 'heavily subsidised' and universal education up to age 16 is the greatest safeguard of the freedom of our people and is the best guarantee of their social, political, and economic well-being at this stage in our development.

(Ministry of Education 1993: xvii)

Yet, in practice, little has been done to move forward from the rhetoric of such pronouncements towards their implementation. In part, as we have already argued, this resistance to change reflects the vested interests of the denomi-national school system. However, the relationship between the Church and the state is only one part of the story.

Since political independence in August 1962, educational policy has been increasingly influenced by international funding agencies such as the IBRD, the IDB and the IMF. At one level, these agencies can be understood as pur-suing a reform agenda aimed at regenerating economic efficiency. However, at another level this loan support engulfs the country in a manipulative 'debt trap' which seems to run parallel to the political and economic control wielded by the colonial government. Evidence of this was seen during the 1980s, when the country had to undertake severe structural adjustment programmes that were prescribed by the IBRD and the IMF to 'cure' its international debts and balance of payment deficits. This resulted in severe cuts in government allocations to the social services and to education services that were perceived as not contributing directly to the short-term economic growth of the economy.

From a reform and regenerative perspective, the stated aims of the current Basic Education Project (1995–2001), which is co-funded by the government of Trinidad and Tobago and the IBRD, include: improvement of educational quality at the pre-school and primary levels through the training of teachers, and provision of textbooks, library books and other resources; increasing access to education by constructing and expanding early childhood centres, primary schools and a few secondary schools, especially in rural areas; strengthening the management and institutional capabilities of the education sector at all levels by supporting the reform and decentralization goals of the Ministry of Education; and providing principals and teachers in primary schools with skills that will enable them to plan quality programmes more efficiently in their schools.

The reform agenda of this Basic Education Project is an ambitious one. It recognizes how democratizing the educational system is important to the development of an economic infrastructure capable of taking the country forward in a rapidly changing international economic context. The production of an elite, though perceived to be necessary, is not sufficient in the highly competitive environment of a globalized economy. Thus, in a report on the financing of education in Trinidad and Tobago (World Bank 1996: 7), it is argued that although Trinidad and Tobago

> is successful in educating a small number of elite students who are second to none; . . . it is less successful in bringing the masses to a level of high performance . . . [Moreover,] the low rates of student participation in the study of science indicated a relatively low stock of future scientists and engineers. All of these indicators boded poorly for the country's new economic development strategy of reducing its reliance on petroleum exports by encouraging foreign investment and developing labor intensive industries; a low skilled but relatively high cost labor force is not competitive on the international labor market.

The Bank has been particularly critical of the dual system of schooling that has traditionally favoured the prestige schools. The latter have the ability to tap into more diverse resources, including religious sources, and can supplement their recurrent and capital spending through their connections with the business and professional communities. Yet, because 'the resource endowment differs enormously from school to school . . . The unaccounted for differential in inputs is a likely reason behind the large variability in learning outcomes' (World Bank 1996: 15).

Despite these criticisms, the reforms recommended by the World Bank in practice leave the advantages of the prestige schools unchallenged, focusing instead upon an expansion of basic education (particularly access to pre-primary education) and the universalization of junior secondary education (non-prestige three-year secondary schools). This is an option that is acknowledged to be possible because of the medium-term demographic future of the country rather than because of any commitment to the extension of educational opportunities to all children as a right (World Bank 1996: 47). The reticence of the Bank to encourage any fundamental restructuring of the education system is further evidenced by its dismissive rejection of a variety of other reforms. For instance, on the issue of the abolition of double-shift schooling at the junior secondary level, the Bank maintains that 'available international evidence does not find any negative impact of double-shift schooling' (*ibid.*: 45). The relationship between improvements in learning and lower pupil–teacher ratios is rejected on the basis of comparisons with South Korea and Taiwan, which, it suggests, indicate that 'the apparent correlation between pupil-to-teacher ratio and student achievement might be spurious' (*ibid.*: 46). Increasing teachers' salaries is ruled out on the grounds that only 40 per cent of studies on school effectiveness have found any correlation between this measure and improvements in learning outcomes. Unfortunately, no indication is given of the studies that have been reviewed, and therefore it is impossible to say whether any of these related to situations comparable with that existing in Trinidad and Tobago.

In consequence, despite some rhetorical pronouncements on equity and human rights, the World Bank's intervention has failed to address the fundamental inequities that have dominated educational policy and practice since colonial times, and have perpetuated the interests of minority elites over the mass of the population.

The agenda of the Bank in supporting educational reform in a country like Trinidad and Tobago has to be understood within the wider context of the international economic and political situation. In the first place, despite a decline in total government expenditure on education between 1985 and 1994 of 26 per cent in real terms, notable increases have occurred in capital expenditure, attributable to the provision of government financing for external borrowing from the IBRD (World Bank 1996). In addition, although minor equipment accounts for the smallest proportion of national expenditure, enforced cuts in this area have had serious consequences for the maintenance of the educational infrastructure of the country.

There have also been serious doubts expressed about the viability of the educational reforms in decentralization and curriculum-based assessment which are being funded by the World Bank. Too often, such programmes are based upon dogmas imported from the 'First World' that are unrealistic in the conditions prevailing in the developing world. In practice, such policies operate both financially (through interest repayments on debt) and ideologically (through the new orthodoxies of marketization and competition) to impose economic controls and political obligations, while ironically restricting genuine development opportunities.

Teacher professionalism, educational policy and human rights

It is clearly impossible to understand the development of educational policy in Trinidad and Tobago outside of the colonial and post-colonial contexts within which such policy has been contested. This struggle has been characterized by a history of compromises between powerful interests – particularly the interests of Church and state, and latterly the state and international financial institutions. Yet it would be an oversimplification to consider the history of education in Trinidad and Tobago only in terms of the power struggles of elites or as a response to the external demands of colonial and post-colonial power brokers. It also reflects an intense struggle for the soul of the nation.

The role of education in colonial society was principally directed towards perpetuating the political and economic dominance of elite groups. In practice, it was also a tool to be used by different elites in their struggles against each other for power within the society. This struggle, articulated through the policy of dual control in education, nurtured what D. W. Rodgers (1973) saw as 'the newsmongering . . . backscratching, opportunist type of teacher who will sell his soul and his mother for a mess of pottage.' Despite this, a quite different struggle, the struggle by teachers for the recognition of their status as professionals, has played an important role in linking improvement in educational opportunities to the broader demands for democratic citizenship based on a recognition of human rights.

Under colonial rule, recruits to the teaching profession were frequently 'persons who for one reason or the other failed to succeed in the United Kingdom and were venturing forth to seek their fortune in the colonies' (Alleyne 1996). By 1916, the issue of teacher quality was being taken more seriously. The report of the Education Commission of that year premised its call for improvements in the quality of education on the dual strategy of increasing teachers' salaries and changing the system of school inspection. However, the main impetus for professional recognition for teachers followed upon the trade union and anti-colonial agitation of the 1930s. At the core of these struggles was the right of the teacher to publicly criticize and challenge the educational policies of the colonial administration (Lavia and Garcia 1998).

As a colonial society, the social organization of Trinidad and Tobago was founded upon the inequality of its citizens. The education system was inextricably tied into the practices and struggles taking place around colonialism. Thus, it both perpetuated the power of elites and offered a site upon which that power was contested. Education played a central role in the struggle to reconceptualize the meaning of human rights in the anti-colonial movement and in post-colonial Trinidad and Tobago. In particular, teachers challenged the elitism embedded in the system, basing their challenge on the fundamental democratic principle that educational opportunities should be equally available to all children and that the existence of a skilled professional body of teachers made this attainable. Improving professional skills, qualifications and terms and conditions of service may be seen as different, but necessarily linked, strands of the same argument.

By contrast, resistance to teacher professionalism has shown itself to be a strategy for resisting the democratization of education, and a strategy that continues to this day. It is for this reason that the World Bank's opposition to increases in teacher salaries (a view that has seriously restricted the options available to government for over a decade) has had such a reactionary impact upon educational opportunities. Likewise, the division of schools into prestige and non-prestige has created divisions between teachers which militate against a unified profession committed to common ideals and outcomes. Denominational prestige schools tend to attract better qualified staff because principals have the authority to 'hand-pick' their staff and the conditions of work in this sector are viewed as being more physically and psychologically attractive. In consequence, the elitism of the prestige schools is continually reinforced.

The struggle for professionalization and the democratization of education were central concerns leading to the formation of T&TUTA in 1981 and are enshrined in its constitution. The traditional trade union struggles over conditions of service are linked to the enhancement of professional standing, something reflected in the portfolio of the First Vice President, who has responsibility for this aspect of the Association's work. T&TUTA's commitment to professional education has led to significant initiatives in this field, including the setting up of a study circle programme in schools across the country, the running of staff development workshops and, perhaps most significantly, the introduction of a special education training programme for teachers.

The Special Education Programme and the struggle for the right to education for all

One of the most important initiatives undertaken by T&TUTA has been its 'Special Education Programme'. This programme was established with the following principles:

1 ... Every child is entitled to an education that will enable him/her to achieve his/her optimum potential.
2 ... A non-categorical approach to understanding and teaching individual students.
3 ... A belief that most students are best taught all or part of their schooling programme in the regular class.
4 ... A commitment to the idea that educators, families and communities all share in the responsibility for appropriate education of children.

(T&TUTA 1991: 1)

The significance of this programme is that it has placed teachers at the forefront of the struggle for educational change based upon principles of social justice.

The focus of special education in Trinidad and Tobago had initially been on the one thousand or so children with physical and/or sensory impairments and children exhibiting behaviour problems who were placed in the country's ten special schools. Thus the Education Act of 1966 makes reference to the establishment of a system of public education within which 'there may be provided special schools suitable to the requirements of pupils who are deaf, mute, blind, retarded or otherwise handicapped.' The Education Plan of 1968 referred to the need for remedial work for 'students who were failing'. This was reinforced in 1976 by a modification of Act 4 of the Constitution of the Republic of Trinidad and Tobago recognizing the rights of a parent or guardian to 'provide a school of his own choice for the education of his child or ward.' However, little was done either to address the needs of disabled children in the mainstream sector or to provide access for children excluded from any sort of educational provision.

In January 1979, a 'visiting team on the handicapped' was invited to Trinidad by the Partners of the Americas, with support from the Ministry of Education and Culture and the Organization of American States. Among their 17 recommendations were the following:

1 . . . that the Minister of Education and Culture establish at a high level of responsibility the position of Coordinator of Special Education as an integral part of Ministerial affairs (to) coordinate, develop and inspect programs in both regular schools and special settings.
2 that the Ministry of Education begin developing services for handicapped children in regular schools.
6 that the teacher training curriculum be modified so as to prepare regular teachers to deal more effectively with the special needs of handicapped children in the regular school.
7 the expansion of training programs in the University and teacher training facilities to fully prepare qualified special education teachers and supportive professional personnel.

(Winschell 1979: 6, 7)

In its response, delivered in 1980, the government recognized the need for the establishment of a Special Education Unit within the Ministry of Education to coordinate the delivery of special education and related services in the country. The unit was established in 1981 with responsibility to the Director of School Supervision for all matters pertaining to Special Education. Among the agreed upon functions of the unit are:

(a) developing policy on education, care and rehabilitation of the Handicapped within the community . . .
(c) providing services for handicapped children in the existing Special Schools by:
   (i)   further training of teachers and ancillary staff now employed in the Special Schools in order to upgrade their skills . . .
   (iv) introducing an integrated special education programme for the phasing-in of education of the mildly handicapped into the normal public schools system;

(v)   organising of programmes for the training of teachers in skills necessary for the provision of special remedial services to mildly handicapped children in normal schools;

(Pilgrim 1989: 1, 2)

Yet, to date, the post of the coordinator of the unit has never been filled. A visually impaired stenographer was appointed to work in the unit, but nine years later the post had still not been confirmed. A Special Advisory Committee was also set up at this time to provide guidelines to the Minister on matters pertaining to special education. This committee did prepare a draft list of guidelines but changes have not yet been made to the Education Act.

The St Clair King Report of 1982 (Government of Trinidad and Tobago 1982) reviewed education in both junior and senior secondary schools, and the recommendations contained therein crossed another dimension in the educational history of the country. They suggested that there was 'need for the provision of remedial work at all levels of [the] education system' and that 'a centre for the training of teachers in remedial education should be established' (p. 60).

During the period 1981–4 the University of Manitoba, in conjunction with the government of Trinidad and Tobago and funded by the Canadian International Development Agency (CIDA), had organized a series of professional development workshops aimed at teachers working with children with special educational needs (Chee Wah 1998). These workshops attracted a large group of teachers (approximately 1100) from the regular schools. The interactive methods used ensured a deeper awareness of the problems that existed in the classroom and the need for more specialized information and support services. Yet the programme also encountered problems. The workshops focused upon sensitization rather than upon rigorous training, and as such did not adequately prepare teachers for working to improve the quality of education in the classroom.

The Marge Report (1984) estimated there to be approximately 28,500 disabled children within the mainstream primary sector whose educational needs were not being met. It was acknowledged that it was economically unrealistic to expand the special school sector to cater for the unmet needs of these children and thus it was proposed that mainstream schools should gradually be adjusted to meet the needs of disabled children. The Marge Report identified the need for approximately 736 professionally trained special educators to provide educational support for disabled children within the mainstream. It also recommended the setting up of diagnostic prescriptive centres in each educational district, comprising specialist staff who would support the work of teachers in the mainstream. Although the government acknowledged the importance of the Marge Report by including the general findings and recommendation in the Education Plan (1985–90), it still proceeded to relay mixed messages to the population. While seeming to give a firm commitment to providing educational opportunities for those seen as having special educational needs, the authors of the plan hastened to add that the country 'must proceed with caution and seek alternatives which are educationally and socially acceptable, but which are not demanding on the public purse' (Ministry of Education 1985).

Some of the educators who had been part of the CIDA experience, although recognizing weaknesses of the CIDA projects, were none the less able to capitalize on its strengths and began to develop locally directed programmes of teacher education for teachers working with disadvantaged children in the mainstream sector. Spurred on by the concerns of the Marge Report, they set up an association for the professional development of persons working with children with special educational needs (TASETT) and combined forces with other interest groups to host workshops and micro-seminars throughout the country, write position papers and develop other strategies to enhance teacher professional development.

This marked the beginning of a new wave in teacher education in the country. Members of the T&TUTA Special Education Committee, TASETT and the Trinidad and Tobago Association for Retarded Children continued to voice their opinion that teacher education, particularly in special education, had been a neglected area in Trinidad and Tobago. This group of advocates felt that, if given the chance, they could use less money than that allocated to the CIDA project (approximately $1 million) and provide quality teacher education to a large enough group of teachers, which would result in them being awarded 'proper' certification that could be recognized internationally. Thus, the main impetus for change came through the work of the Special Education Committee of T&TUTA and TASETT, and their efforts to address the shortage of trained teachers in this area.

New training initiatives were established in collaboration with the University of Sheffield (UK). Beginning with certificate and diploma programmes in special education, these programmes have since expanded to include masters' programmes in special and inclusive education, educational studies and vocational education, as well as a doctoral programme. At its inception, the project was destined for success – the process of a collective struggle contributed to the momentum and vitality of a shared vision. This vision was part of a self-liberating movement where teacher-participants were encouraged to become reflective practitioners in the process of self-empowerment. The pioneering group (course participants as well as the management committee) recognized that long sought after change in education was not coming from the technocrats and the bureaucrats of the Ministry of Education but from the creativity and effort that was generated by the struggle for social justice and rights. Thus arose a revolutionary idea of changing schools and by extension the education system from within. With the new tools of education came liberation for some, and children who were probably 'faceless bunches' in the schools were now recognized and included in the processes of change and learning.

Conclusion

The history of colonial and post-colonial struggles for educational reform in Trinidad and Tobago illustrates both the complexity of the politics of change and the enduring character of these conflicts. We have argued that the interests of colonial elites continue to be represented through the division of educational provision into 'prestige' and 'non-prestige' sectors. In the post-colonial period the education system has allowed a new black middle class to access some of the privileges once held by whites alone, but, ironically, gaining access to these privileges for some has reinforced the educational disenfranchisement of many others. Under the dual system, selection is founded upon the requirement for rejection; success is founded upon the necessity of failure.

The 'modernization' of education, based upon the selective principle, has reconstituted the anti-colonialist ideals of 'freedom', 'human rights', 'equality' and 'social inclusion' in terms of market place choices. The privileges of the powerful become the 'needs' of the powerless. The day-to-day struggles of the poor and the oppressed for dignity are fought out in the lives of those children, parents and teachers who contest the forces of social exclusion in their fight for the right to education. Teachers have played a leading role in this fight. It has not been without its contradictions; nor has it always been working towards a common purpose. Professionalism may easily transform into the oppression of 'expertise' through the colonization of knowledge. Yet the story of teacher-led professional education programmes in Trinidad and Tobago has shown how, through the collective action of teachers, the rights of citizenship can be contested as a reality and not simply as an ideal.

Questions

1 It might be argued that the notion of human rights stems from a 'First World' perspective of how the world and the peoples of the world must be and should think. If this is so, then the application of the concept would be quite manipulative. How does culture impact upon human rights issues?
2 If education is one of the basic human rights, how much is required until the right is fulfilled? If there is an appropriate cut-off point, then how and by whom is this to be determined, or should it be provided indefinitely?
3 If inclusive education is based upon the rights of the learner to citizenship, how could a social justice perspective on teacher education inform the struggle for that principle?

References

Alleyne, M. (1995) *Nationhood from the Schoolbag: a Historical Analysis of the Development of Secondary Education in Trinidad and Tobago*. Washington: Organization of American States Interamerican Educational Series.

Braithwaite, R. (1991) *Moral and Social Education*. Trinidad: Paria Publishing Company Ltd.

Chee Wah, B. (1998) Some teachers' perceptions of the CIDA Special Education Project 1987–1990 in Trinidad. Unpublished MEd thesis, University of Sheffield.

Government of Trinidad and Tobago (1966) *Laws of Trinidad and Tobago – Education, Act 1, Chapter 39: 01*. Trinidad and Tobago: Government Printery.

Government of Trinidad and Tobago (1974) *Draft Plan for Educational Development in Trinidad and Tobago*. Trinidad and Tobago: Government Printery.

Government of Trinidad and Tobago (1976) *Constitution of the Republic of Trinidad and Tobago, Act 4, Chapter 1, Part 1*. Trinidad and Tobago: Government Printery.

Government of Trinidad and Tobago (1982) *Report of Working Party on Education*, Chairman, St Clair King. Port of Spain.

Government of Trinidad and Tobago (1989*) Macro-Economic Policy – Medium Term (1989–1990)*. Trinidad and Tobago: Government Printery.

Keenan, P. J. (1869) *Report upon the State of Education in the Island of Trinidad*. Dublin: Alexander Thom.

Lavia, J. and Garcia, A. (1998) The history of teachers in the Caribbean, in J. Lavia and D. Armstrong (eds) *Teachers' Voices from the Caribbean*. Sheffield: Sheffield Papers in Education.

Look Loy, K. (1984) *The State and the Boards: Denominational Education in Trinidad and Tobago – a Position Paper*. Trinidad: Trinidad and Tobago Unified Teachers' Association.

Marge, M. (1984) *Report on the Survey of the Incidence of Handicapping Conditions in Children between the Ages of 3 and 16 in Trinidad and Tobago, Commissioned by the Ministry of Education*. Republic of Trinidad and Tobago, Sponsored by the Organization of American States.

Ministry of Education, Government of Trinidad and Tobago (1985) *Education Plan 1985–1990*. Republic of Trinidad and Tobago.

Ministry of Education, Government of Trinidad and Tobago (1993) *Education Policy Paper (1993–2003)*. Report of the National Task Force on Education (White Paper).

Pilgrim, E. (1989) The Special Education Unit. Unpublished report of the Ministry of Education of Trinidad and Tobago.

Pilgrim, E. (Chairman) (1990) *Report of the Collation and Evaluation Committee for the Development and Implementation of a National Special Education System for Trinidad and Tobago*. National Consultation on Special Education, Ministry of Education of Trinidad and Tobago.

Rodgers, D. W. (1973) *Chalk Dust*. Trinidad and Tobago: D. W. Rodgers.

T&TUTA (1991) *Draft Policy Proposal – Special Education*. Curepe: Trinidad and Tobago Unified Teachers Association.

T&TUTA/TASETT Special Education Project (1989) *Course Booklet for Professional Studies (1989–1991)*. Curepe: Trinidad and Tobago Unified Teachers Association.

Winschel, W. F. (1979) *Final Report OAS Technical Multi-National Project: Special Education and Rehabilitation*. New York: Central New York Partners of the Americas.

World Bank (1995) *Trinidad and Tobago: Basic Education Project*. Staff appraisal report no. 14865-TR. Washington, DC: World Bank.

World Bank (1996) *Trinidad and Tobago: the Financing of Education*. Report no. 16216-TR. Washington, DC: World Bank.

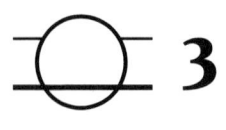 **3**

Headlights on full beam: disability and education in Hong Kong

John Lewis

Overview

This chapter explores differences in the ways disability and failure at school are conceptualized in Western and Eastern societies. Particular reference is made to the former British colony of Hong Kong, where strong elements of European and Chinese cultures have converged to influence the shape of public policy responses to disabled people. It is shown how the colonial period installed a conservative mid-twentieth century Western model of special education in Hong Kong, based on notions of personal deficiency, segregation and rehabilitation. Reasons are suggested why Hong Kong's policy makers persist with a 'medical' model of disability and continue to expand segregated schooling at a time when the rest of China has adopted a policy of inclusive education. It is suggested that the post-colonial period will bring opportunities for policy change, and care must be taken that these initiatives are not subverted by traditionally orientated interests.

Introduction

> If the public schools can be considered as a vehicle for the advancement of a just society, then special education should be viewed as its headlight.
>
> (Hong Kong's Board of Education 1996: 2)

How segregated schooling is viewed by policy-shaping groups such as the Board of Education is important for Hong Kong, because special education remains the major local education policy response to youngsters identified as disabled. The call for special education to be considered as lighting the path for the local school system in its pursuit of justice is an optimistic one, especially as in other places segregated schooling has not been a liberating experience for disabled children. In the past decade or so, countries such as the USA, the UK and Australia have sought to implement policies of inclusive education, in part because of concerns that traditional special education practices may have limited the life chances of disabled youngsters and restricted their human rights in the process. This chapter looks at the ways in which the concepts of human rights and disability are perceived by Western and Eastern cultures, and how they are translated into social policy responses, particularly in the field of education in Hong Kong.

Hong Kong is a Special Administrative Region of the People's Republic of China. It is made up of 235 islands and a small corner of the Chinese mainland known as Kowloon and the New Territories. Most islands are uninhabited, but the large main island known as Hong Kong, and parts of the mainland attachment, are some of the world's most densely populated areas. It was not always so. At the time of annexation by the UK in 1841, Hong Kong was populated by about 5000 people scattered throughout some 20 villages, and a further 2000 or so fishermen used the numerous harbours as shelter. The origin of the transformation of Hong Kong into a bustling modern commercial and financial centre can be traced to when the British assumed colonial sovereignty over the area as part of the UK's campaign to maintain its influence and opium trade with China. From 1841 until mid-1997, Hong Kong was ruled over by a series of British governors, and became increasingly important as the West's main commercial gateway to China. It also became famous for its highly competitive and free-wheeling form of capitalism, its hard-working labour force and, until quite recently, its hands-off style of government. As a Special Administrative Region of China, Hong Kong enjoys a great deal of autonomy, and the pre-existing public policies in areas such as health, education and the law – which are quite different from those prevailing throughout the rest of China – continue to be largely respected by the motherland.

Two important and distinct cultural forces have played key parts in shaping Hong Kong's modern social identity and public policy arrangements. The first has been contributed by the powerful Western colonial presence of the UK for the past 150 years, and the second by the largely Chinese immigrant population from mainland China. At the end of the Second World War, Hong Kong had a population estimated at only about 600,000, but this now stands at approximately 6.5 million, of whom about 98 per cent are ethnic Chinese, with origins mainly in Southern China (Cameron 1991). While other ethnic groupings are represented, this continual juxtaposition of values from West and East has been a major influence in determining the nature of Hong Kong's way of life, and complex elements of both cultures have continually permeated government processes, including the way social policy issues are defined, analysed and responded to. This includes the intertwined areas of disability, human rights, justice and education – areas where the Board of Education expects special education to illuminate the path ahead.

Great care must be taken when interpreting differences between Eastern and Western cultures. For example, neither is a single identity: a singular Western culture clearly does not exist, just as a singular Eastern culture does not exist. Furthermore, although the great bulk of Hong Kong people share a common cultural identity with Chinese mainlanders, China itself is made up of numerous diverse minority cultures. There are also important differences which have emerged between those Chinese who reside in Hong Kong and those who live on the mainland – especially over the past 50 or so years. These differences have been prompted by a number of factors. The Hong Kong Chinese have had their erstwhile cultural practices confronted and often suppressed by 150 years of a domineering foreign colonial administration, and subjected to Western belief systems strongly reinforced through instrumentalities such as the schools and courts. Local Chinese have also enjoyed a great amount of freedom to travel overseas, whether for holidays or, as has often been the case, to study. These circumstances are quite different from those experienced by those in mainland China, where for much of the twentieth century the country has been comparatively closed, with its citizens having restricted opportunities to travel abroad and little contact with outsiders.

The dissimilar circumstances that have prevailed in Hong Kong and China for the past 150 years or so have contributed to differences in how the respective populations have constructed certain realities – including those concerning human rights, education and disability. There are also significant differences between how these concepts are perceived in the West and the East.

Conceptualizing human rights and disability

Clarifying the manner in which the state might interact with its citizens in order to define, promote and maintain aspects of human rights such as equality and justice has been a major endeavour of Western societies at least since the times of Plato and Aristotle. Reflecting this interest, many Western countries have sought to guarantee certain rights to their subjects by specifying them and writing them into their constitutions. Many of these have drawn heavily on the Christian belief that, in the eyes of God, all people are equal (Byrnes 1992). The notion that rights are something that individuals possess as a birthright was vigorously pursued internationally following the end of the Second World War, culminating in 1948 with the adoption by the United Nations of its Universal Declaration of Human Rights. The use of the word 'universal' here implies a sweeping worldwide acceptance of an agreed type of relationship that all individuals have, or should have, with their state. However, clear differences exist between how the West and East perceive both the concept and the importance of human rights. Although the concept of personal autonomy is basic to much of the West's understanding of human rights, it receives a very different emphasis in traditional Chinese culture – in both mainland China and Hong Kong.

Although the idea of human rights is understood and acknowledged in Chinese culture, it is transcended by notions of personal obligation, obedience and duty. Human relationships for the Chinese have been guided for many centuries by the teachings of Confucius (552–479 BC) and other prominent scholars who emphasized the obligations that individuals have to each other in order to achieve the desired goals of peace, harmony, stability and a good society (Chen 1992). These norms prescribe:

> how children should behave to their parents, living or dead, as well as to their ancestors. It makes stringent demands: that one should provide for the material well-being of one's aged parents, perform ceremonial duties of ancestral worship, take care to avoid harm to one's body, ensure the continuity of the family line, and in general conduct oneself so as to bring honour and avoid disgrace to the family name . . . filial obligations . . . are overriding in importance, rigidly prescribed and are binding from the time one is considered old enough to be disciplined until the end of one's life.
>
> (Ho 1996: 155)

These obligations of filial piety are extended to the state, which might be considered as part of an extended family, and so the common good is valued more than what is good for the individual.

Thus the Western tradition regarding human rights can be characterized as one that focuses on personal autonomy and personal choices, whereas the Chinese emphasis is on personal obligations and selflessness – differences that may be characterized as individualism versus collectivism. The recent public struggles against authority by disabled people in the West in order to claim their perceived rights to an integrated life in areas such as education, housing, transport and work may seem inappropriate behaviour from an Asian viewpoint, which nevertheless does stress the moral duty of the state to care for all of its 'family' members. Cheng (1998: 3) explains the difference in this way: individualistic Western societies are expected to meet the needs of individuals, otherwise they are not good societies. By way of contrast,

> Collectivistic societies work the opposite way. Individuals are only part of the society and are well catered for only if they live in a sound society. Hence, individuals should honour the needs of the society. They should either submit individual needs to the needs of the society, or to consciously adapt the needs of the society to the individuals' needs.

Within this cultural climate of conformity, obedience and duty, there are many dour aspects to the way in which disability is conceptualized and responded to in Chinese societies – including Hong Kong. This is well illustrated by the way in which disability is expressed in written language. A common Chinese way of writing 'disability' is carried out by combining two characters: the first character in isolation translates as 'broken' and the second as 'useless'. Thus the concept of a disabled person is infused with notions of uselessness and defectiveness. Youngsters who are perceived as disabled (or broken and useless) in Chinese communities are often seen as bringing shame to their parents, who may consider they are being punished for past wrong deeds. As a result, disabled children may be hidden from the community or even from relatives, particularly if the handicap is pronounced and obvious.

Disability in a Chinese family is also commonly viewed as a burden. Sons are expected to support and care for their parents in their old age, so a son who is not likely to be able to complete this expectation because of his disability is seen as a serious cultural encumbrance. There is also a likely economic hardship because it is common in Hong Kong families for both parents to be employed and to work long hours – often six days a week. If a child has needs which require day-to-day supervision and care, this usually has to be paid for by the family.

In such a context, the idea that disabled people may have human rights is not a prominent one, and government initiatives to provide services such as special schools, mental clinics and play centres sometimes result in hostile public demonstrations in the localities for which they are planned. Cheung (1998: Chapter 7.1) explains that Chinese attitudes to disabled people are also dominated by the idea that they should be recipients of charity or welfare, and it is not uncommon to find disabled adults begging in some Hong Kong streets – a practice acceptable in Chinese culture. However, disabled children are expected to attend school where special arrangements are provided.

Schools and failing students

In the West, failing students have commonly been perceived as being deficient in some way: perhaps low in intelligence, or beset with some other individual pathology such as learning disabilities, dyslexia or attention deficit disorder. These and other personal conditions are generally believed to limit performance, and if the condition is thought serious enough, a student may be considered more or less permanently disabled and unlikely ever to achieve standards considered normal. In such a case, a child may be removed from the regular class and placed in a special school.

Although Chinese culture recognizes endowed differences, these are not generally viewed as being restrictive, but something to be overcome through greater personal effort and better environments. For example, students who get bad school grades are likely to interpret this as resulting not from a lack of individual ability, but from not making enough effort. Stevenson and Shin-ying Lee (1996: 136–7) explain that 'success is dependent on hard work and hard work reduces or eliminates any constraints imposed by differences in ability.' It is common for Hong Kong students doing poorly at school to be encouraged by their parents to study late into the evening; if grades do not subsequently improve, then even more effort is thought to be required, so they are encouraged to get up early in the mornings for additional study. It is also quite common for poorly performing students to participate in extra classes after the regular school day has finished. There is a Chinese saying that many parents pass on to encourage their student children to greater effort: 'With hard work, even an iron bar can be refined to a needle.'

The belief here is that the problem of students failing to make the grade at school is not so much a matter of individual deficiency, but a situation to be overcome by increased personal effort. Chan found evidence that this idea is acquired and reinforced early in life. Mothers ranked effort as more likely to contribute to their primary school child's academic success than factors such as ability, interest, difficulty of the work, help from home, study methods, help from teachers or luck. The young students also ranked effort as the highest factor influencing success (Chan 1992).

Nevertheless, despite increased efforts to overcome poor grades, some students continue to perform badly and fail to satisfy both their family's expectations and the education system's requirements. Hong Kong's school system is highly competitive and numerous examinations and other selection processes filter students out along the way. Biggs (1996: 5) observes that 'At all stages, the curriculum, teaching methods, and student study methods are focused on the next major assessment hurdles.' Failure at any of these hurdles is dealt with sharply. Schooling is compulsory for children between the ages of about six and fifteen years, and about 85 per cent start earlier by attending academically orientated kindergartens (Cheng 1997). Much of the teaching focus in primary schools is on the secondary school placement allocation, which assigns those leaving primary year 6 (P6) to a secondary school. These schools are arranged into five 'bands', each catering for about 20 per cent of a supposed ability range. Thus, band 1 schools take the top 20 per cent of students, band 2 schools the next 20 per cent and so on. Cheung (1998: 7.3) explains that it is common for the 'banded' secondary schools to stream their students even further, so that the top 40 students will be placed into one class, the next 40 in another class and so on. Only about 30 per cent of the age cohort are selected for study in secondary years 6 and 7 (S6 and S7), from where about 50–60 per cent are then admitted to higher education (Cheng 1997). Cheung (1998: 7.3) comments:

> In Hong Kong, students who can obtain good results in examinations are regarded as the winners while those who do less well are regarded as losers. Thus some students and their parents would be very resistant to accept students with special needs in their schools who are regarded as a hindrance to their children's academic excellence and consequently their future prospect.

Those youngsters categorized by professionals early in life as having particular forms of disability will not enter this system at all, but be enrolled in special schools instead. Others may be guided into special schools or special classes at later stages of their schooling, particularly if they come under notice for a lack of satisfactory academic performance. The rigorous system of public and internal school examinations is supplemented by other gate-keeping mechanisms, such as the 'Observation Checklist for Teachers'. This is administered to all children in their first year of school, and is designed to identify suitable candidates for subsequent part-time withdrawal into resource classes due to learning difficulties. A broad range of other special education settings awaits those seen as unable to profit from the regular school arrangements.

Disability, special education and underpinning beliefs

Fundamental to Hong Kong's educational response to disabled young people is the provision of a range of special schools based on personal and categorical deficits. These schools are typically well organized and staffed with energetic teachers. These settings are supplemented by an extensive network of part-time withdrawal classes in both primary and secondary schools for students considered to have learning disabilities, and an array of support services provided by specialists such as educational psychologists, physiotherapists, occupational therapists, speech therapists, social workers and school nurses. In 1998 there were 73 special schools arranged into eight categories of disability catering for the perceived needs of approximately 8000 students. Figures for 1995 indicate that at that time an additional 6195 students, mainly between their third and sixth years of primary education, were segregated for part-time instruction into 489 resource classes located in 304 primary schools. At the same time, more than 85 per cent of primary schools offered some form of remedial teaching, and about 14 per cent of all primary school pupils attended some form of remedial teaching group (Board of Education 1997: 35–6). Part-time withdrawal classes are also conducted in 99 secondary schools, and 14,404 students, or about 10 per cent of the enrolment, participated in 1995 (Board of Education 1996: A46).

The categories used to describe special schools and their students are similar to mid-twentieth century British practice, as are the processes for selecting students, general curriculum arrangements and the use of day centres and sheltered workshops for disabled students when they become adults. Similarly, Hong Kong's provision of part-time withdrawal classes in regular schools for those academically weaker students considered learning disabled resembles the use of the withdrawal-style opportunity (or auxiliary) classes that were common in many parts of Europe and the USA by the early twentieth century (Kanner 1969; Lewis 1987).

All Hong Kong's special schools are managed by charities or community-based groups through subsidies provided by the government – the government has not provided any special schools of its own. The reason for this situation might partly be explained by the long acceptance of links between charity and disability in traditional Chinese culture, although in mainland China the overwhelming majority of special schools are provided by the government. In any case, educating Hong Kong people, whether disabled or not, was apparently not a high priority for the British colonial administration, as compulsory schooling was not introduced until the 1970s – 100 years after it was introduced into some of its Australian colonies. Postiglione and Lee (1997) have observed that even at this late stage it was introduced in response

Table 3.1 Special schools in Hong Kong, 1998

Category	No. of schools	Schools with residential services
1 Blind	2	2
2 Deaf	4	2
3 Physically handicapped	7	2
4 Maladjusted	7	6
5 Mentally handicapped	42	11
6 Hospital school	1	One school conducts classes at 16 hospitals.
7 Practical school	3	2
8 Skills opportunity school	7	0
Total	73	25

Source: Communication with Education Department (1998); Board of Education (1996: 35).

to criticism from the European Economic Community that the prevalence of cheap child labour in Hong Kong was providing an unfair economic advantage in the international market place. Within this context, the schooling of disabled children may have been considered a lesser priority and something best left to those who had an interest in it.

A number of researchers have pointed out that there are negative consequences of voluntary agencies being involved in the provision of disability services. For example, Drake (1996) has described how in Britain it reinforces notions of disability as a personal tragedy, justifying segregation and dependence. However, in Hong Kong the commanding role local voluntary organizations play in special education arrangements remains unexamined and generally regarded as unproblematic. The current categories of special schools provided are summarized in Table 3.1.

The arrangements and beliefs underpinning the educational provision for disabled students in Hong Kong are firmly rooted in what is often termed the 'medical model'. In education, this view contends that a student's failure to make expected educational progress is due to a disability, deficit or weakness located within the failing individual. It is called a medical model because its ideas and responses draw on many of the characteristics long employed by the medical profession: individuals thought to have problems are typically examined by specially designated professionals who diagnose the condition and make recommendations regarding remedial treatment. Oliver (1996: 32) summarizes the medical model as one that first 'locates the "problem" of disability within the individual and secondly it sees the causes of this problem stemming from the functional limitations or psychological losses which are assumed to arise from the disability.'

Because of the medical perspective's central belief that the cause of the problem is located within the individual, within the context of schooling it is the student who is the focus of both the diagnosis and the treatment. This medical view of disability can be observed in the Education Department's definition of students in need of special education (Education Department 1994):

Children are considered to have special educational needs if they cannot derive full benefit from the curriculum provided for children of their age cohort and/or who cannot be catered for adequately in the ordinary educational setting. Children with one or more of the following characteristics can be considered as children with special educational needs: visual impairment, hearing impairment, physical handicap, mental handicap, maladjustment and learning difficulties.

Hong Kong's special schools and network of part-time withdrawal classes for remedial instruction in the subjects of Chinese, English and mathematics are considered by the Board of Education (1996: 11–12) to 'form a network of diagnosis, classification, referral, consultation and remedial attention for those in need.' This commitment to the traditional Western belief that students fail because of some individual deficit is not consistent with the traditional Chinese belief of inadequate personal effort. It has also led to the virtually unquestioned and unchallenged adoption of an increasingly broad range of Western terms to describe diagnosed pathologies, including 'special education needs', 'remedial', 'the unmotivated', 'specific learning disabilities', 'mentally handicapped', 'autistic', 'learning disabled' and 'maladjusted'. Corbett (1995) has argued that the development and use of terms like these ultimately seeks to define, label, control and devalue people with disabilities. However, categorical terms such as these are common currency in Hong Kong's education system, teacher training programmes for special education and the reports of numerous government advisory bodies.

In recent decades, Western disability literature has increasingly interrogated and challenged the assumptions underpinning the medical model of disability (Mercer 1981; Barton and Tomlinson 1984; Biklen 1985; Christensen 1996), including its policy practices, such as categorization (Finlan 1994; Oliver 1996) and segregation (Tomlinson 1982; Abberley 1987; Gartner and Lipsky 1987; Fulcher 1989; Stainback *et al.* 1990). Such questioning has stimulated the emergence of alternative models of disability, which propose different policy responses, including those deployed in the education system (Tsui 1993). For example, a social model of disability is concerned with the processes and forces within society which assign disability roles to people, and the consequences of these roles. Oliver (1996: 32) observes that the social model:

> does not deny the problem of disability but locates it squarely with society. It is not individual limitations, of whatever kind, which are the cause of the problem but society's failure to provide appropriate services and adequately ensure the needs of disabled people are fully taken into account in its social organisation.

However, despite such a long and strong Western presence, alternative models of disability such as this remain largely unfamiliar in Hong Kong, and public policy responses remain largely focused on remediating perceived individual deficiencies through government supported instrumentalities with an orientation of segregation, welfare, social services and rehabilitation (Llewellyn 1982; Tsui 1993; Board of Education 1996; Rehabilitation Advisory Committee 1996). This overwhelming reliance on a medical view of disability has meant that over the years policy makers have resorted to establishing more and more special settings and creating more and more categories of disabled students to fill them. As a result, the percentage of students enrolled in special schools when compared to the total school population has increased from 0.73 per cent in 1971 to 0.89 per cent in 1995 (Yung 1997: 18).

Reasons for a lack of alternative viewpoints about disability

A number of factors can be identified that have contributed to the lack of debate in the local disability domain. Importantly, MacNeil has pointed out that precisely because Hong Kong has been a colony and not a nation, it has been difficult for Chinese people to express their own cultural identity, because 'the ideology of imperialism suppresses local attachment' (MacNeil 1992: 97). Within this political context, it is therefore not surprising that the 'correct' way of doing things – including the conceptualization and response to disability – would be largely determined by those who ruled, rather than those who were ruled over. Although traditional Chinese beliefs about disability are still strong in Hong Kong, the public policy instrumentalities established to deal with it are essentially Western duplicates underpinned by Western thought. Interestingly, devoid of a British colonial presence, the system of education in mainland China has adopted and implemented policies which strongly support the inclusion of disabled students rather than their segregation (Chen 1996; Lewis *et al.* 1997).

There has also been a lack of wide academic interest and research activity in the field of disability and special education in Hong Kong. This inactivity, across many aspects of education, was noted during a comprehensive review of the local school system by Llewellyn in the early 1980s, and that author subsequently called for an improvement in the scope and quality of educational research (Llewellyn 1982). However, local studies into disability and under-achievement at school have commonly remained written from within the traditional medical viewpoint, and are frequently descriptive rather than analytical. Furthermore, research contributions which examine local disability issues from disciplines such as sociology, philosophy, history or economics are very rare or even non-existent. The result is that the local medical model of disability lacks a critical literature and is virtually isolated from international debates – a situation that limits the information and choices available to policy makers, people with disabilities, parents, student teachers and others. The narrowness of local research is illustrated in a review by David Chan of 58 issues of Hong Kong's education and education related journals published in the ten years from 1986 to 1995. He found very few articles on intervention research, evaluation studies of student placement, or even those which examined teaching strategies. He concluded that 'Special education services in Hong Kong have not been well planned or co-ordinated on the basis of sound knowledge from research findings' (D. Chan 1996: 1).

This narrow range of available ideas has sometimes been exacerbated by the government's own policy-making processes, which take place within a political structure that Cheng (1997) has described as a consultative autocracy. As the British monarch's representative, the Governor had complete authority over policy during the colonial period, and various advisory mechanisms were established in order to offer him guidance. A similar situation has remained in place with the return of Hong Kong to China, except that the Governor has been replaced by the Beijing-approved Chief Executive. Important current advisory bodies and others involved in education policies, including those concerned with disability, are groups such as the Education and Manpower Branch, Education Department, Board of Education and the Education Commission. Others, such as the Health and Welfare Branch and the Rehabilitation Advisory Committee, also give advice on disability and special education matters. However, the plethora of advice available has not elicited competing conceptualizations of disability, but opened up potential problems of inter-departmental rivalry, the reinforcement and non-questioning of existing policy fundamentals, duplication of effort and a lack of overall coordination and focus. Difficulties have also been noted in the composition of some advisory bodies. For example, Llewellyn (1982) observed that policy advisory committees have sometimes been unable to address long-term policy issues because their memberships were prone to pursue the narrow agendas of their own vested interests.

Access to advisory mechanisms is of particular importance in Hong Kong because it lacks a fully representative government structure, meaning that through the system of government advisory committees 'the civil service both proposes and disposes policy' (*The Economist* 12 September 1998: 30). However, people with disabilities are not always well represented on government sponsored disability advisory committees, and those with memberships well connected with the medical, special education and charity fields could be seen to have a stake in maintaining the existing arrangements and preserving their own privileged positions. It is a noticeable feature of disability politics in Hong Kong that grass-roots organizations composed of disabled activists, their families and supporters have yet to achieve a strong presence. This is in contrast to many Western countries, where the formation of reformist-orientated disability groups has often been nurtured by governments, who have then sought their assistance in understanding the needs and wishes of disabled people, with the aim of addressing issues of human rights, formulating progressive policies and organizing self-help and advocacy mechanisms. However, Hong Kong's advisory processes remain largely dominated by prominent community figures, disability professionals and charity-linked personnel. As a result, these committees, and hence the government, have often lacked access to first-hand advice as to the problems encountered by disabled people and their families. They have also often been restricted in their access to contemporary research outside a medical viewpoint, isolated from contemporary overseas thinking and not made detailed comparisons with approaches taken by disability services in other countries. For example, it is surprising that in the lead up to reunification with China in 1997, Hong Kong-based reviews did not explore why the local education bureaucracy was persisting with the expansion of segregated schooling at the same time that China was limiting its own segregated settings and extending its already considerable commitment to inclusive schooling (Chen 1996; Lewis *et al.* 1997). In response to this isolation from overseas policy debates and lack of comparative studies, David Chan (1996: 3) lamented that 'the lessons derived from . . . overseas countries . . . can be immensely valuable in guiding our practice in special education.'

However, as it enters a new non-colonial era and a new millennium, the traditional and familiar headlights of special education are on full beam.

Conclusion

The basic differences in the ways in which people from the West and the East have constructed notions of disability centre on matters such as causation, human rights and the importance afforded to individual differences. Although traditional Chinese beliefs regarding disability are still evident in Hong Kong, the actual educational arrangements for disabled children overwhelmingly reflect a Western medical view established during 150 years of colonial rule. Within the confines of a relatively closed and non-representative political and policy-making structure, a limited critical literature, the dominance of voluntary agencies, a lack of alternative discourses about disability and a dearth of comparative studies, the traditional Western practices of rehabilitation and the placing of disabled people into segregated forms of schooling and work have flourished. Furthermore, the range and percentage of children falling under the ambit of special education continues to grow. By focusing the cause for a lack of school progress on the individual student in this way, the removal of an increasing proportion of students from Hong Kong's mainstream classes is legitimized, and attention is drawn away from alternative explanations of school failure, such as possible weaknesses in the schools, their curriculum, the education system or even the nature of society itself. Yet who gets called disabled in Hong Kong and how this relates to determining the winners and losers in the highly competitive socio-economic infrastructure remains largely unexplored.

However, future changes in disability policy are probable, particularly now that Hong Kong is once again part of China, from where political, intellectual and cultural forces are increasingly likely to challenge many of the colonial legacies – especially those out of step with national policy. Mechanisms which created, justified and nourished segregation before the change of sovereignty, now have an opportunity to play a progressive and unifying role in facilitating inclusive policies and practices in Hong Kong. This would usually entail a deliberate broadening of policy direction. For example, the training of local special education teachers, which has long promoted disability as a medical construct and serviced the categorically arranged special education settings, could assist the broadening of community knowledge by exposing future teachers to thinking about disability from viewpoints derived from disciplines such as sociology, history, philosophy and economics. This is already established practice in Chinese universities.

The danger here for Hong Kong is that with community interest in inclusion already becoming evident, special education may endeavour to maintain its traditional expert role in the field of disability by redefining an inclusive discourse into its own conventional and medically orientated framework. A particular danger would be if special education doctrines were taught to student teachers destined for regular schools in the belief that 'inclusive education means doing special education in the regular school'. In this way, inclusive education would become the new name for special education. This has happened in other countries, where special education has sometimes seen inclusion as a vehicle for expanding its influence, resulting in the labelling of even more children as disabled and increased segregation (Tomlinson 1982; Gartner and Lipsky 1987; Fulcher 1988, 1989; Lewis 1993). It has been observed that disability professionals come under pressure to restructure alternative understandings of disability into old frameworks in this way for reasons such as an unwillingness or inability to understand the difference between segregating and inclusive discourses, territorialism, personal ambition, arrogance, fear of change, a desire to preserve their existing jobs and status, and opportunism (Fulcher 1988, 1989; Semmens 1993).

Those with policy and administrative roles within the disability field in Hong Kong are fortunate in that they have the opportunity to draw from the experiences of a wide range of other countries that have sought in recent decades to reform policies limiting the life chances of disabled people. Not to take this opportunity would severely hinder the likelihood of an already overdue improvement. An opening up of the debates around disability in Hong Kong and an increase in positive choices for disabled people will need to involve a fundamental reassessment of the prevailing medical model, an appraisal of the role of voluntary agencies and expert-driven services, the establishment of more broadly based advisory mechanisms, a connection to international contemporary thought, an increased acknowledgement and valuing of Chinese cultural perceptions of disability and the creation of alternative service delivery mechanisms. It will therefore require new ways of thinking and new people. Most importantly, disabled people will need to be engaged in determining their own futures.

Questions

1 In what ways do Western and Eastern notions of human rights and disability differ? How can these differences be observed in Hong Kong's school system?
2 One of the legacies of the long colonial administration in Hong Kong is a system of education for disabled children that largely mirrors mid-twentieth century British thought and practice. In the emerging post-colonial era, should these arrangements remain the same, or should they be changed? Give reasons for your opinion. If you think that they should change, what should the new arrangements look like and how could they be achieved?
3 Do you agree with the Hong Kong Board of Education's statement that 'If the public schools can be considered as a vehicle for the advancement of a just society, then special education should be viewed as its headlights'? Give reasons for your opinion.

Acknowledgement

This chapter was written with the kind assistance of three dear friends and colleagues – Stella Chong Lau, Kwok Kuen Chan and Julianne Y. C. Lo – who through a volatile process, which included laughter and tears, taught me much about Chinese culture and much about myself.

References

Abberley, P. (1987) The concept of oppression and the development of a social theory of disability, *Disability, Handicap and Society*, 2(1): 5–19.
Barton, L. (ed.) (1996) *Disability and Society: Emerging Issues and Insights*. Harlow: Longman.
Barton, L. and Tomlinson, S. (eds) (1984) *Special Education and Social Interests*. London: Methuen.
Biggs, J. (ed.) (1996) *Testing: To Educate or Select?* Hong Kong: Hong Kong Educational Publishers.
Biklen, D. (1985) *Achieving the Complete School*. New York: Teachers College Press.
Board of Education (Hong Kong) (1996) *Report of the Sub-Committee on Special Education*. Hong Kong: Government Printer, May.
Board of Education (Hong Kong) (1997) *Report on Review of 9-year Compulsory Education*. Hong Kong: Government Printer, March.
Byrnes, A. (1992) Equality and non-discrimination, in R. Wacks (ed.) *Human Rights in Hong Kong*. Oxford: Oxford University Press.
Cameron, N. (1991) *An Illustrated History of Hong Kong*. Hong Kong: Oxford University Press.
Chan, D. (1996) Special education in Hong Kong: the need for research that informs practice, *Educational Research Journal*, 11(1): 1–6.
Chan, J. (1996) Chinese intelligence, in H. M. Bond (ed.) *The Handbook of Chinese Psychology*. Hong Kong: Oxford University Press.

Chan M. (1992) The relationships between mothers' and children's attributions for academic achievement. Unpublished master's thesis, University of Hong Kong.

Chen, A. (1992) Human rights in China: a brief historical review, in R. Wacks (ed.) *Human Rights in Hong Kong*. Oxford: Oxford University Press.

Chen, Y. (1996) Making special education compulsory and inclusive in China, *Cambridge Journal of Education*, 26(1): 47–57.

Cheng, K. (1997) The education system, in G. A. Postiglione and W. O. Lee (eds) *Schooling in Hong Kong*. Hong Kong: HKU Press.

Cheng, K. (1998) Special education in Chinese society: a cultural perspective, *Hong Kong Special Education Forum*, 1(2): 1–9.

Cheung, C. T. (1998) The development of an integrated education system in Hong Kong. Unpublished MEd thesis, Sheffield University.

Cheung, F. (1996) The assessment of psychopathologies in Chinese societies, in H. M. Bond (ed.) *The Handbook of Chinese Psychology*. Hong Kong: Oxford University Press.

Christensen, C. (1996) Disabled, handicapped or disordered: 'What's in a Name?', in C. Christensen and F. Rizvi (eds) *Disability and the Dilemmas of Education and Justice*. Buckingham: Open University Press.

Corbett, J. (1995) *Bad-Mouthing: the Language of Special Education*. London: Falmer Press.

Drake, R. (1996) A critique of the role of traditional charities, in L. Barton (ed.) *Disability and Society: Emerging Issues and Insights*. Harlow: Longman.

Education Department (Hong Kong) (1994) Curriculum for School Aged Children with Special Educational Needs, in *Hong Kong – a Brief on Curriculum Planning*.

Education Department (Hong Kong) (1997) *A Guide to the Operation of Resource Classes in Ordinary Primary Schools*, 2nd edn. Intensive Remedial Services Section.

Finlan, T. (1994) *Learning Disabilities*. Westport, CT: Bergin and Garvey.

Fulcher, G. (1988) Integration: inclusion or exclusion in Roger Slee (ed.) *Discipline and Schools*. London: Macmillan.

Fulcher, G. (1989) *Disabling Policies?* London: Falmer.

Gartner, A. and Lipsky, D. (1987) Beyond special education: towards a quality system for all students, *Harvard Educational Review*, 57(4): 367–95.

Ho, D. (1996) Filial piety and its psychological consequences, in H. M. Bond (ed.) *The Handbook of Chinese Psychology*. Hong Kong: Oxford University Press.

Kanner, L. (1969) *A History of the Care and Study of the Mentally Retarded*. Springfield, IL: Charles C. Thomas Publishers.

Lewis, J. (1987) So much grit in the hub of the educational machine, in B. Bessant (ed.) *Mother State and Her Little Ones*. Melbourne: PIT Press.

Lewis, J. (1993) Integration in Victorian schools: radical social policy or old wine?, in R. Slee (ed.) *Is There a Desk with My Name on It?* London: Falmer.

Lewis J., Chong-Lau, S. and Lo, J. (1997) Disability, curriculum and integration in China, *European Journal of Special Needs Education*, 12(2): 95–106.

Llewellyn, J. (1982) *A Perspective on Education in Hong Kong*. Hong Kong: Government Printer.

MacNeil, W. (1992) Righting and difference, in R. Wacks (ed.) *Human Rights in Hong Kong*. Oxford: Oxford University Press.

Mercer, J. (1981) Sociological perspectives on mild retardation, in W. Swann (ed.) *The Practice of Special Education*. Oxford: Basil Blackwell.

Oliver, M. (1996) *Understanding Disability*. New York: St Martin's Press.

Postiglione, G. and Lee, W. O. (1997) Schooling and the changing socio-political setting: an introduction, in G. Postiglione and O. L. Wing (eds) *Schooling in Hong Kong*. Hong Kong: HKU Press.

Rehabilitation Advisory Committee (1996) *Hong Kong Review of Rehabilitation Programme Plan*. Hong Kong: Health and Welfare Branch, Government Secretariat.

Semmens, R. (1993) Implementing policy: some struggles and triumphs, in R. Slee (ed.) *Is There a Desk with My Name on It?* London: Falmer Press.

Slee, R. (ed.) (1993) *Is There a Desk with My Name on It?* London: Falmer Press.

Stainback, S., Stainback, W. and Forest, M. (1990) *Educating All Students in the Mainstream of Regular Schools*. Baltimore: Brookes.

Stevenson, H. and Sin-ying Lee (1996) The academic achievement of Chinese students, in Michael H. Bond (ed.) *The Handbook of Chinese Psychology*. Hong Kong: Oxford University Press.

Tomlinson, S. (1982) *A Sociology of Education*. London: Routledge and Kegan Paul.

Tsui, H. F. (1993) Special education in transformation: a call for renewal of education as a whole, *Chinese University of Hong Kong Educational Journal*, 21(1): 43–51.

Yung, K. K. (1997) Special education in Hong Kong: is history repeating itself?, *Hong Kong Special Education Forum*, 1(1): 1–19.

 **4**

Human rights and inclusive education in China: a Western perspective

Patricia Potts

Overview

In this chapter I shall discuss the meaning and value of human rights and inclusive education from both Western and Chinese perspectives. Although I shall also refer to international contexts for Western and Chinese perspectives, I shall not look in detail at how far rhetoric and diplomacy filter and refract domestic debates for overseas consumption. There are many relevant issues for whose discussion there is no space here: China's relationship with Tibet, the influence of multinational corporations, the globalization of information technology, the length of time it has taken for the UK to pass the Disability Discrimination Act of 1995 or China's rationale of 'One country, two systems' in relation to Hong Kong. I am also aware of the difficulty of portraying the complexities and internal variations of contrasting perspectives, whatever the permitted word length.

I shall argue that concepts of rights and inclusion in education have different meanings in different cultural and political settings but that, despite the significance of recent educational reforms, the stereotypic individualism of the West and collectivism of China both present obstacles to the development of education systems in which all students are valued equally and responded to equitably.

Human rights: a Western perspective

I began with the assumption that human rights are universal. For example, everyone shares an equal right to food and shelter. However, as soon as I extended my list to health, education and justice, my idea of an indisputable 'human right' dissolved, as I realized that there could be an infinity of interpretations. Moreover, not only are health, education and justice inaccessible to many people in the world, food and shelter are also denied. In practice, it seems that there is no such thing as an inalienable human right.

I had intended to contrast a timeless ethic with the idea of varying civil rights, defined as codes developed by particular societies. But the context for the acknowledgement of human rights is as social as the context for the elaboration of civil rights. Even if human rights derive from a higher-order principle, that of the guarantee of life itself, they are invoked in particular times and places for particular reasons. Opponents in domestic or international conflicts utilize human rights arguments because their superior moral force should prevail over particular legislation or cultural custom. A theory of universal human rights is sometimes useful.

Central to the idea of human rights is that they should not need to be fought for. They cannot be given or taken away. In practice, of course, people's experience of mutual respect for their common human rights varies hugely. Struggles for survival cannot always be separated from struggles to secure civil rights. Within and between countries, protecting human rights and codifying civil rights entail challenging the legitimacy of power from across boundaries of class, culture and nationality.

In England, the first major challenge was resolved when the aristocracy secured the king's signature to Magna Carta in the thirteenth century. A later challenge came from a rising land- and capital-owning middle class:

> The new thing in the England of the sixteenth century was that devices that had formerly been occasional were now woven into the very texture of the industrial and commercial civilisation which was developing in the later years of Elizabeth, and whose subsequent enormous expansion was to give English society its characteristic quality and tone. Fifty years later, Harrington, in a famous passage, described how the ruin of the feudal nobility by the Tudors, by democratising the ownership of land, had prepared the way for the bourgeois republic.
>
> (Tawney 1924: 180)

The political power of land-owning classes was reinforced by the secularization of the law following the Reformation and the establishment of the Church of England. Individualism was associated with the demise of absolute authority, spiritual and temporal, with political pluralism and with free-market economics.

Four hundred years later, there are still debates about human rights in Britain. A Bill was published in October 1997 introducing legislation to incorporate into British law the provisions of the European Convention for the Protection of Human Rights and Fundamental Freedoms, a treaty of the Council of Europe drawn up in 1948. Up to now, the argument has been that the provisions of the Convention were adequately safeguarded within the British system. This is not the view of the Labour government:

> It is plainly unsatisfactory that someone should be the victim of a breach of the Convention standards by the State yet cannot bring any case at all

in the British courts, simply because British law does not recognise the right in the same terms as one contained in the Convention . . .

> We . . . believe that the time has come to enable people to enforce their Convention rights against the State in the British courts, rather than having to incur the delays and expense which are involved in taking a case to the European Human Rights Commission and Court in Strasbourg and which may altogether deter some people from pursuing their rights.
>
> (Home Office 1997: 4, 6, 7)

In the West, the theory is that personal rights and freedoms, secured in law, will be protected by institutional frameworks which cannot be overridden without redress by anyone.

Human rights: Chinese perspectives

In the exhibition room of a primary school in central Shanghai one board reproduces words uttered by President Jiang Zemin. He said, 'the problem of disabled people is a problem of human rights.' What did he mean by this? What does it signify that these words are prominently displayed in a mainstream school?

What are the frameworks that inform and express Chinese ideas about human and civil rights? In a discussion of post-compulsory education in what he sees as a rapidly changing society, Cheng Kai Ming reflects back on the ideological education of young people in China in the 1950s, and compares this with the internalized norms of traditional culture:

> The notions of individual needs and individual choice which are so fundamental to educational ideas in the west were simply absent in China. In a way, any emphasis of individual needs might be seen as reactionary to the socialist ideology. Individualism was never taken in its neutral sense. It is constantly a word for criticism . . . Education in the Chinese socialist ideology was to eliminate individualism rather than to cater for individual needs . . .
>
> The ideology of submission to national needs is also in keeping with the traditional culture where individuals honour the community. In traditional Chinese societies, each individual is part of a social hierarchy, is conscious of his or her own position in this social configuration and acts accordingly . . .
>
> This helps to explain why the strict mode of manpower planning so readily took root in China after the 1949 revolution. Indeed the entire notion of socialism in Mao's framework is a combination of Marxist ideas and traditional Chinese thought.
>
> (Cheng 1994: 65–6)

China's official position on human rights is presented in English in a State Council Information Office booklet of 1991. It covers: the right to subsistence;

political rights; economic, cultural and social rights; rights in law; the right to work; freedom of religious belief; the rights of minority nationalities; family planning; disabled people and participation in international human rights activities. Coming two years after the military suppression of the student-led democracy demonstrations in Tiananmen Square, this booklet must be seen as indicating sensitivity on the question of human rights, a response to the enduring condemnation of the international community. The focus is not on human rights as universal imperatives but on how 'countries differ in their understanding and practice of human rights' (State Council of the PRC 1991: ii).

China's view of herself as a developing country is integral to her arguments about human rights:

> China has gained independence, but it is still a developing country with limited national strength. The preservation of national independence and state sovereignty and freedom from imperialist subjugation are, therefore, the very fundamental conditions for the survival and development of the Chinese people . . . The people's right to subsistence will still be threatened in the event of a social turmoil or other disasters. Therefore it is the fundamental wish and demand of the Chinese government to maintain national stability, to concentrate their effort on developing the productive forces . . . persist in reform and opening to the outside world and . . . secure a well-off livelihood for the people throughout the country so that their right to subsistence will no longer be threatened.
>
> (State Council of the PRC 1991: 7–8)

The Constitution of the People's Republic of China states that all power belongs to the people. Legislation therefore represents their interests and is supported by them. Conflicts of interest that could be resolved by publicly negotiated shifts in the balance of power are unintelligible within this rhetoric, for it is the people, not individual persons, who enjoy human rights. The consequences of this position illustrate the huge gap in the understanding of human rights between China and the West.

For example, it is argued that China's particular social and economic conditions require policies for the 'control of population growth and improvement in quality of the population' (State Council of the PRC 1991: 69). In 1993 a draft Law on Eugenics and Health Protection was announced by the official Xinhua news agency. Hostility from overseas commentators resulted in a new English title, the Maternal and Infant Health Care Law, and it came into effect in June 1995.

> This draft law aims to prevent new births of inferior quality people and heighten the standards of the whole population. It promotes sterilisation, abortions or celibacy for people with hereditary, venereal or reproductive ailments, severe psychoses or contagious diseases . . . Its effects and the willingness of doctors and psychiatrists to put it into practice cannot be assessed. Such policies are another manifestation of priorities that place

the good of the collective higher than the wishes or rights of the individual.

(Pearson 1995: 53–4)

In the West, measures to prevent 'inferior' births would now seem abusive to
some people and contrary to the acceptance of disability and other kinds of
difficulty as ingredients in the diversity of ordinary life. In China, however,
improving population 'quality' is seen as essential to the modernization of the
country. Discussing the tensions between China's coexisting policies for the
protection and for the prevention of disability, Emma Stone argues that
the perspective of the affluent 'North' has to be rejected in favour of one
which appreciates the position of the countries of the 'South':

> Malnutrition and poverty are the principal causes of impairment in the
> South . . . It is clearly impossible to separate impairment from the politics
> of underdevelopment . . . In the Chinese government's view, prevention
> is not diametrically opposed to the equalisation of opportunities, and the
> protection of disabled people's rights and interests. Prevention, protec-
> tion and integration go hand in hand and are regarded as appropriate
> steps for a modernising, westernising, power.
>
> (Stone 1996: 480, 481)

Wei Jing Sheng, the pro-democracy Chinese dissenter released from prison
in China in 1997 and now living in the United States, discusses the relationship between human rights and the Chinese Communist Party. He is neither
sympathetic to official Chinese arguments nor to Western writers' appreci-
ation of the complexities facing China:

> Each person is nothing more than part of an undifferentiated and ideal-
> ised mass. This does nothing to further democracy . . . The Chinese have
> struggled for democracy for 100 years, but the true nature of humanity,
> the individual person, has been overlooked . . .
>   Democracy is fought for real people with all their failings. We differ
> from the Communist Party in recognising that when we fail to guarantee
> another person's human rights we undermine our own rights in the
> process . . . The killers in Tiananmen Square were soldiers. They could
> only do what they did because they failed to recognise that in suppress-
> ing the rights of others they were also destroying their own . . .
>   The need to change people's way of thinking is at the heart of our
> struggle for democracy. So far, we haven't achieved this. The Communist
> Party keeps tight control of culture . . . Our traditional notion of virtue
> has been destroyed; the virtues of modern western civilisation have not
> been established. We live in a state of 'no thought', a moral and intellec-
> tual vacuum . . . This is what I mean by 'intellectual dependency'. With-
> out even being aware of it they do the ruler's thinking for him . . . That
> kind of dependent thinking is deeply engrained.
>
> (Wei 1998: 31, 34–5)

For Wei Jing Sheng, there are no mitigating circumstances, such as China's exceptionally large population or the excessive deprivations suffered during imperialist times. Though sharing some of these criticisms, a different assessment of the values of Chinese Communism is given by a man who was a senior Red Guard in 1966, when he was 20:

> As I said, I have no regrets about my part in the Cultural Revolution. To thoroughly repudiate the movement politically is valid. I have no disagreement. But as a mass movement one cannot simply negate it, one cannot draw a simple political line. How to understand it? Well, let me give you a few of my own thoughts. I think the Central Committee is in a bind because China has never really escaped feudalism – by this I mean specifically the mentality of the people. One thing I clearly learned in my countryside experience was that the old system of connections still dominates everything. It's not what you do but rather who you know or who you're related to. It's like a giant web. Once you get caught up in it, you will never be able to disentangle yourself. That's why it's so hard to carry out reforms. For the sake of stability, the Central Committee totally repudiated the Cultural Revolution, and this was necessary . . . But I feel that the red Guards should not be repudiated. They should be analysed from a historical perspective . . .
>
> There's another thing you've got to understand. All our lives we were brought up to believe that the Party was always right and, of course, Chairman Mao was the Party. Our generation is still dedicated and patriotic in our goal to reform China. We're the most reliable group in China, not like the old people who oppose anything new or the young who chase every rainbow. The most important thing comrade Mao Zedong gave me is class affinity. No matter what happens I will never become a degenerate or a criminal, not even in times of strife. However, there's something this kind of education gave me that I'll always hate. I was conditioned to blindly follow the leadership and never to think for myself. Mao was like old Lord Ye who professed to love dragons but surely didn't want one to visit. Mao told us to put down slavery and dogmatism, but look what happened when we took him literally.
>
> (Feng 1990: 99–100)

A Chinese friend and colleague echoed the Red Guard's story when he said to me: 'China is governed by men, not by laws.' He was referring not only to the absolute power exercised by imperialist or communist rulers but also to the hierarchical structure of Chinese society as a whole. Confucius advised that people, rulers and subjects alike, should be guided by an ethic of proper behaviour rather than by laws. One consequence of the subordination of the law to social custom was that it was impossible to know in advance whether or not a particular action would be defined as criminal. Another consequence was that, without a formal system of redress, personal relationships became paramount and the protection of rights and interests had to be accomplished through social connections. A third consequence was that dissent would be acutely threatening:

> Unless the issue is one on which the dictatorship is willing to compel obedience, any actor whose compliance is needed for a decision to take effect can block it. It is as if everyone had a veto. Collective decisions have to be near-unanimous to have a chance of being implemented . . . Under the ancient and modern dictatorships and their myths of unity lies a combination of conservatism and a kind of anarchy. All this has little to do with the basic acceptance of the rules of limited social conflict that is essential if any democratic structure is ever to be effective.
>
> (Jenner 1992: 186)

China's formal system of criminal law was drawn up in 1979.

Inclusive education: a Western perspective

Support for inclusive education entails a commitment to increasing participation in and reducing exclusion from the educational mainstream. This definition implies that there will be diversity within rather than between educational settings and that students will be valued equally, regardless of their level of attainment, cultural background, gender, disability or social class. Inclusive education seeks to overcome barriers to education which may be the result of isolation, prejudice, poverty or difficulties in communication, mobility or social relationships. Support for inclusive education implies a rejection of the view that difficulties in learning are the result of personal deficiencies, in favour of a view of the nature of difficulties in learning as arising from social relationships between learners, teachers, curricula and the resources available to provide support. Systems which rank students according to their level of attainment and place a high value on competitive selection reinforce exclusionary rather than inclusionary pressures.

The task of moving towards greater inclusion in education involves rights issues because access to education is a human right and because people share an equal right to full membership of mainstream social and educational communities. In the UK, the Education Act of 1996 does not recognize the force of these arguments, and there are students who face compulsory segregation. A contradictory orthodoxy has developed in which inclusion in the mainstream is common for some groups, while exclusion is increasing for others. There are some students who seem, because of their level of attainment or their social problems, to have forfeited their right to belong in the mainstream. The question of rights is subordinated to questions which are seen as professional or technical, with the social and political meanings attached to assessment and resourcing systems being denied.

Since the exposure in the late 1970s of the inhumanities suffered by disabled children, young people and adults living in residential institutions, civil rights and self-advocacy movements have grown and strengthened in Britain (see Oswin 1978; Ryan and Thomas 1981; Shearer 1982). Parents' organizations and alliances between them and organizations of disabled people have also flourished. They draw on the current rhetoric of the 'entitlement' of all students to a full curriculum and appropriate resources for learning support to argue for inclusion in mainstream educational settings.

To set the scene for their detailed case study of processes of inclusion and exclusion in one community high school in the north of England, Tony Booth, Mel Ainscow and Alan Dyson have reviewed policy and practice since the 1944 Education Act. The context for inclusive schooling in the late 1990s is an increasingly competitive system, in which practices derived from the principles of comprehensive schooling that were elaborated in the 1960s are being systematically dismantled in attempts to combat failure and raise educational standards (see Booth and Ainscow 1998: 196–203).

Inclusive education: Chinese perspectives

Senior education authority officers in Shanghai told me that, for them, support for inclusive education is an indication of their prosperity, civilization and scientific approach to research. While the main problem for teachers was described as the identification and assessment of students' abilities, implying a medical view of difficulties in learning, these educators also acknowledged the influence of environmental factors and teaching styles, implying a more social view.

Reflecting on my discussions with Chinese educators and my observations in some Chinese classrooms, the concept of 'inclusive education' seems to be defined both as welcoming more students who experience difficulties in learning into mainstream classes and as developing a more professional approach to the education provided in special schools. In the context of the exclusion of numbers of children from any sort of educational provision until recently, it could be argued that both kinds of development represent greater inclusion, however inconsistent building up the segregated sector seems to be. And after all, this is only what is happening in the UK.

It could be that, in talking about 'inclusive education', I and my Chinese colleagues were referring to different concepts or that my English could not be accurately translated into Chinese. I have been visiting Chinese kindergartens, schools and universities for ten years now, and have had an ongoing conversation with some colleagues for most of that time. It seems to me that there is a good understanding of Western rhetoric and terminology and that educators realize what kind of transformation of the existing system an inclusive approach entails. It may also be the case that, as I have discussed elsewhere (Potts 1998), people value inclusive and exclusive approaches at the same time.

One context for the development of inclusive education in China is the 1986 law on compulsory schooling, nine years in urban areas and six in rural areas. The drive for universal basic education encompasses disabled children. One Chinese educator estimates that the effect of this law has been to raise the enrolment of disabled students, of whom it is calculated that there are more than eight million in China, from 6 per cent in 1986 to 60 per cent in 1994, mostly in mainstream primary schools (Yeung 1998).

Another context is the higher profile of disabled adults since the establishment in 1988 of the China Disabled Persons' Federation by Deng Pufang, disabled son of Deng Xiaoping, which is a national network and provides a range of services. Since 1988, China has set out five-year work programmes for disabled people, and the Law of the People's Republic of China on the Protection of Disabled Persons was adopted in 1990. It is still more or less impossible for a disabled person to train as a teacher, however. On a visit to a teacher training college where students were preparing to work in special schools, I asked if any of the students were blind or deaf. The answer was: 'All our students are normal.'

A third context is the pressure of international rhetoric, from the time of the International Year of the Child in 1979 and the International Year of Disabled People in 1981, which came soon after China opened her door to the West in the late 1970s. The United Nations Convention on the Rights of the Child (1989), the UN Standard Rules on the Equalization of Opportunities for Persons with Disabilities (1993) and the UNESCO Salamanca Statement (1994) all press for the acknowledgement of educational rights (see Wertheimer 1997). Officially, China rejects what she sees as interference from other countries on issues of human rights, but educators I have talked to want to participate in these international movements.

There are contexts that work against the development of inclusion in China. These include the highly selective nature of the mainstream, in which the focus, from primary school onwards, is on university entrance examinations, although only a small proportion of students will go on to higher education. Primary and secondary schools are organized in similar ways, with large classes and specialist teaching. Vocational and academic curricula are not delivered to students in the same institutions. Parents are not formally involved in the education of their children, as they are in the UK, and there are no strong parents' organizations through which to express their views. In a recent study of provision in Shaanxi Province, Roger Merry and Zhao Wei (1998: 211) found that 'the emphasis on defining special needs in terms of official categories to be managed within a separate special education system means that there is little deliberate integration of children with special needs into mainstream schools.'

Nevertheless, I have seen a range of developments in Chinese schools and universities which seem to me to represent significant changes. There are children and young people in special schools now who, ten years ago, would have been at home or in welfare institutions. There are children identified as 'mentally retarded' in mainstream classes. I have seen students working in small groups, with their teachers moving round the room to talk to them in turn and encourage their participation in what they described to me as a skills-based approach, designed to stimulate more problem-solving and independent thinking among their students. I also saw classes with 20 students rather than the usual 40 or more, 'experimental classes' taking advantage of the falling rolls in some inner-city areas.

Experienced practitioners in some urban areas now have access to part-time professional development courses at universities. These include two-year certificate programmes and three-year undergraduate programmes. Many universities have extensive departments of adult education, which organize part-time courses and distance learning. However, the existence of part-time study in a subject department, with the award of a respected qualification at the end of the course, is a major innovation, even if on a small scale at the moment, which has been made in response to the urgent need for the upgrading and updating of teacher training. Distance learning versions of these professional courses – for example, for teachers of pre-school deaf children at Nanjing Normal University – make it possible for some teachers from rural as well as urban areas to pursue their training while continuing to teach. The consequences of bringing practitioners into universities and of facilitating national networks may gradually transform teacher education.

In thinking about how far these changes reflect a process of inclusion as I have defined it, however, there are continuities to set against them which remain powerful. First, the system of assessment by competitive examination has not been reformed: students seen as 'mentally retarded' are exempted from having to reach certain standards. I have read criticisms of the examination system, not on the grounds that it cannot respond to the different kinds of progress made by different students, however, but because, at the moment, girls seem to be doing too well (Ying 1998). Second, while it is easier now for local education authorities to develop their own curricular materials, and I saw a range of media used in their presentation, it remains the case that all students in a classroom undertake the same task; I did not see any differentiation of task or materials in response to the increasing variety of students' abilities and interests and the pace of the lessons I saw was fast. Learning support consists of subject teachers spending additional time with students, often after school, to help them catch up. Third, while I saw classes in which most of the students made a contribution and in which teachers obviously encouraged this, I never saw a student ask his or her own question. The participation of students was not on their terms. While it was clear that the teachers I observed are committed to including students who experience difficulties in learning and that they approach their work with warmth, its foundation is a principle of assimilation rather than one of responding to diversity.

However, there are signs that factors outside education may effect another transformation. Vocational high schools were first established in 1980. Their curricula are geared to expanding sectors of the labour market and their graduates secure employment outside the state allocation system:

> For the first time in the socialist society, young adults are given the liberty to exercise their individual choice rather than suppressing their individual desires . . .

There is a change of ideology, which is reflected in the textbooks. Starting from 1991, a subject called 'Career Guidance' has been added to the
secondary curriculum. In the textbook for the ninth grade in Shanghai,
the notion of state allocation has totally disappeared . . . There is . . . a
whole chapter discussing how young adults could 'understand one's own
characteristics' . . .

The notions of individual choice and individual needs, which are prevalent in western philosophies, for the first time become a necessary notion
in the education of youth in China . . . In a recent report, the compiler
[began] by saying: . . . 'By way of all these systems that undermine individual autonomy, the society might have attained some state of order and
stability. However, people's activeness and innovation, which may bring
about wealth as well as progress, are lost' (China Youth, 1992, pp. 1–2).

(Cheng 1994: 68–9)

If taking advantage of changes in the job market involves encouraging personal preference within a vocational education system whose status is rising
in relation to academic education, the ideological costs are offset by economic
gains. Order within an unpredictable and divisive market economy can be
restored in other ways. For example, a unifying sense of nationality is being
encouraged through a current campaign to strengthen the dominance of
'putonghua', the vernacular of the north of China, what we in the West know
as 'Mandarin' Chinese:

China's common language putonghua has not yet managed to eliminate
all the divisions preventing people from communicating with each other
in different parts of the country . . . Such confusion happens very often
among people who pronounce putonghua using their local dialects . . .
This diversity of language has caused people much inconvenience . . .
Businessmen from northern China are afraid of negotiating with those
from the south, fearing a misunderstanding could cost them millions.
They prefer fax machines to the telephone . . . By the middle of the 21st.
century, putonghua will be popularised and the language barrier will
have been removed . . . Priority is given to education . . . Those unable to
speak putonghua are unlikely to gain a teacher's qualification.

(Guo 1998)

This assertion of homogeneity might be consistent with assimilating more
students into the educational mainstream but it could not be consistent with
a process of inclusion which values diversity. Curricular choice could provide
a model for increasing differentiation within as well as between both courses
and institutions, but for this to happen it would have to become acceptable for
decision making to occur from the bottom up and well as from the top down.
The enormity of the cultural shift that this would represent can be glimpsed
in an article describing the Chinese government's plans for the celebration of
the fiftieth anniversary of the People's Republic of China in Beijing on 1 October 1999:

Migrant workers, mostly jobless men from the provinces, will be driven out of the city from the middle of 1999 to make way for the festivities. A western diplomat said the leadership had earlier re-activated a secretive Crisis Management Leading Group within the Central Committee to handle challenges to the administration by dissidents and laid-off workers . . .

A party source said Mr. Jiang and his politburo colleagues had ruled out any relaxation over the verdict on the student movement of 1989, officially characterised as 'counter-revolutionary turmoil'.

(Lam 1998)

Conclusion

China and the West are officially committed to the view that access to education is a right. However, dominant ideologies in both China and the West support the development of specialized provision alongside the educational mainstream. Inclusive education is not seen as the right of all students, even where it is increasingly perceived as a positive goal for some groups.

In the West, rights can be seen as a record of past conflicts, charting the reduction of absolute, unelected power. In China, rights are non-negotiable. Conflicts of interest between groups of people are denied: the 'people' are indivisible. Power struggles cannot be publicly acknowledged or resolved. The possibility of the abuse of power cannot be raised, except by those at the top. The position of both China and the West, however, is informed by an understanding that the assertion of civil rights is associated with bourgeois revolutions. In Britain this makes the middle classes the particular friends of the government; in China they are the particular enemies.

Neither Western nor Chinese values guarantee a democratic education system based on the values of social inclusion. If the obstacles seem to be greater in China because of the absence of political freedom and the rule of law, then the efforts of some educators to introduce the values of social justice into their schools must be seen as significant. In Western countries where there is official support for inclusion and freedom of choice, there is less excuse for educators to perpetuate educational inequalities.

President Jiang's words in the primary school exhibition room may mean something or nothing: a concrete acknowledgement or a bland slogan. As a Westerner, it seems impossible to tell.

Questions

1 How central to a comparative approach is the explicit examination of our own perspective and the consequent use of the first person to develop a critical voice ?

2 If equivalence of meanings cannot be assured across different languages,

how can cross-cultural research illuminate rather than avoid the inevitable misperceptions?

3 What are the implications of a comparative approach for the identification of relevant sources of information and for the presentation of research reports?

References

Booth, T. and Ainscow, M. (eds) (1998) *From Them to Us. An International Study of Inclusion in Education.* London: Routledge.

Cheng, K. M. (1994) Young adults in a changing socialist society: post-compulsory education in China, *Comparative Education,* 30(1): 63–72.

Feng, J. C. (1990) *Voices from the Whirlwind. An Oral History of the Chinese Cultural Revolution.* Chinese edition, Beijing: Foreign Languages Press. English edition, New York: Random House.

Guo, N. (1998) Language barriers tumble in putonghua campaign, *China Daily* 12 September: 1.

Home Office (1997) *Rights Brought Home: the Human Rights Bill,* Command number 3782. London: HMSO.

Jenner, W. J. F. (1992) *The Tyranny of History. The Roots of China's Crisis.* London: Penguin.

Lam, W. W. L. (1998) Leadership puts priority on stability, *South China Morning Post* 25 September: 10.

Merry, R. and Zhao, W. (1998) Managing special needs provision in China: a qualitative comparison of special needs provision in the Shaanxi region of China and England, *Compare,* 28(2): 207–18.

Oswin, M. (1978) *Children in Long-stay Hospitals.* London: Spastic Society.

Pearson, V. (1995) *Mental Health Care in China. State Policies, Professional Services and Family Responsibilities.* London: Gaskell.

Potts, P. (1998) 'A Luxury for the First World'. A Western perception of Chinese attitudes towards inclusive education, *Disability and Society,* 13(1): 113–24.

Ryan, J. and Thomas, F. (1981) *The Politics of Mental Handicap.* Harmondsworth: Penguin.

Shearer, A. (1982) *Disability, Whose Handicap?* Oxford: Blackwell.

State Council of the People's Republic of China (1991) *Human Rights in China.* Beijing: Foreign Languages Press, Information Office of the State Council.

Stone, E. (1996) A law to protect, a law to prevent: contextualising disability legislation in China, *Disability and Society,* 11(4): 469–84.

Tawney, R. H. (1926) *Religion and the Rise of Capitalism.* Harmondsworth: Pelican (1964 edn).

Wei, J. S. (1998) The taste of the spider, in U. Owen (ed.) Gagged for it. 50 years of free expression, *Index on Censorship,* 27(3).

Wertheimer, A. (1997) *Inclusive Education: a Framework for Change. National and International Perspectives.* Bristol: Centre for Studies on Inclusive Education.

Yeung, L. (1998) Life's devotion to the less fortunate, *South China Morning Post,* 8 September: 16 (interview with Dr Chen Yun Ying, Director of the Special Education Division of the China Central Institute of Educational Research in Beijing).

Ying, Z. (1998) Exam system needs reforming, *China Daily* 5 September: 4.

 **5**

Rights and disabilities in educational provision in Pakistan and Bangladesh: roots, rhetoric, reality

M. Miles and Farhad Hossain

Overview

This chapter reviews historical developments, notions of rights and attitudes towards disabled children underlying educational provisions in Pakistan and Bangladesh. Traditional schooling focused on rote learning by boys of wealthier families; yet some evidence exists of alternative pedagogy, girls' education and casual integration of disabled children. Knowledge of special educational methods accumulated slowly from the 1840s in private schools, but government support has always been weak. The number of disabled children casually integrated always greatly exceeded that of children receiving separate special education. Most children have had no formal education at all, but benefited from a strong and continuing right to socialization within their extended family, rather than rights understood as an individual's claims on the state. Most children are still born into a familial and local network of mutual obligations with a strong Islamic underpinning, different from but not necessarily inferior to current Western middle-class notions of individual rights and entitlements. Secular Western evangelists and Asian urban elites still offer or impose their own cultures and concepts for the 'improvement' of the masses, but seldom assess the collateral damage caused by their attempted ideological hegemony.

Introduction

This chapter reviews historical developments, notions of rights and official attitudes towards disabled children underlying current educational provisions in Pakistan and Bangladesh; and enquires whether European 'human rights' and 'inclusive' approaches to disability, difference and education have had or should have relevance to educational planning and the social ethos in which planning takes place.

Pakistan's East and West wings opened in 1947 with a combined population of 70 million, when India was partitioned. East Pakistan comprised largely the area formerly known as East Bengal. Its geographical separation from West Pakistan by 1000 miles of Indian territory was reinforced by linguistic, cultural and political differences, which led to a successful struggle to become the independent nation of Bangladesh at the end of 1971. Despite their differences, the two countries have many comparable features. In 1999 their largely Muslim populations are both in the 130–150 million range and each growing by some four million per year, having quadrupled since 1947. Through more than two millennia, both have participated in northern Indian history, languages and cultures. Both have economies dominated by agriculture and globally ranking in the poorest quartile, and an unsettled recent political history in which military men have been prominent. Pakistan's gross national product in recent years, around US$ 460 per capita, has been roughly double that of Bangladesh, and a much smaller proportion of its population falls below the poverty line (30 as against 80 per cent). Pakistan and Bangladesh are not *very like* one another; but they are probably more like one another than like any other country.

Both have a rich cultural heritage. Among wealthy and poor, more and less educated people, there remains some folk memory that ancestors once built, crafted or wrote great works of architecture, art and literature; they commanded respect and lived decent lives under just laws, they had enough food and could enjoy some leisure, at least in some periods of history. This memory or belief serves to keep alive the idea that Pakistanis and Bangladeshis may yet construct societies in which the present admittedly gross inequalities, injustices and indignities suffered by substantial parts of their populations will be much mitigated. The hope remains among some that this can be achieved without their cultural distinctness being lost; that they can become 'modern' without becoming disastrously 'Western'. Against this hope, the covert but powerful messages beamed by Western global media to both countries tend to be: 'You are poor, you are backward, your culture is useless, your religion is ridiculous. If you want to become modern you must learn Western ways; then, slowly, you can grow up. Your grandchildren may be like little Europeans and Americans.' The present study of rights, disabilities and schooling must therefore begin with the historical-cultural roots from which South Asians might shape a future where their grandchildren of whatever ability or disability can enjoy human rights as Asians understand them, and continue to be proudly and recognizably Asian.

Traditional schooling: innovations with infants and girls

Traditional schools in Bengal are described in literature dating back to 1600 or earlier. Pedagogy centred on the teacher, rote memorization and painful punishments. Das Gupta (1935) found such descriptions, from centuries earlier, similar to the picture in the 1930s. Sixty years on, Hossain (1994) found little change in rural schools – a situation unfavourable to the revolution of school ethos required for 'inclusion' of disabled children. Yet there were occasional innovations. Adam (1835) remarked on a Calcutta private school with neither rote learning nor beatings. The benefits were recognized of allowing children to 'acquire a considerable knowledge of Bengalee before they began to learn English' (*ibid.*: 13). British officers found some *female* education 'in all parts of the Punjab' among Hindus, Muslims and Sikhs: 'the existence of such an education, almost unknown in other parts of India, is an encouraging circumstance' (General Report 1853: 67). The Bengal government adopted parts of the kindergarten approach in 1901, in an optimistic and ultimately unsuccessful effort to modernize and revitalize existing indigenous schools (*patshalas*) (Shahidullah 1984). Similar efforts in the Punjab also fell into the gulf between planners' ideals and rural school realities. (Sanderson and Parkinson 1931: 9).

Diversification of public interest in disability

Formal special educational efforts in Bengal were recorded as early as 1840 at Calcutta, where blind orphans used Lucas's embossed script to read in an ordinary school. In fact, 50 years of work with disabled children took place in ordinary settings before special schools started (Miles 1997). A school for deaf pupils began in 1893 (Calcutta School 1895), and by 1904 there were two for blind children (Progress of Education 1904). At Kurseong, just outside East Bengal, 1918 saw the opening of The Children's House, following Montessori's famous *casa dei bambini*, training 'those children who through physical and mental defects are unable to profit by the instruction given in an ordinary school' (Annual Report 1919: 5). Psychology teaching began at Calcutta University in 1916, then at Dacca (Dhaka) in the early 1920s. Dacca Training School staff were pioneers of intelligence testing in the 1930s (Malin 1968). A case study of special education concerned a Bengali boy at Calcutta whose individual programme was 'in the form of play-work': detailed records were kept, and the psychologist commented that 'where ordinary system of schooling is of no avail, training by modern psychological methods proves efficacious' (Sinha 1936). In East Bengal a school for deaf children opened at Barisal in 1911; then between 1916 and 1939 similar schools began at Dhaka, Chittagong and elsewhere (Banerji 1949/50). A detailed study of language, speech and thought forms in Bengali children focused on sign languages used unofficially by deaf pupils (Banerjee 1928). Case studies on speech disorders appeared later at Lahore (Latif 1938). In what is now Pakistan, the earliest formal disability rehabilitation centres were a government 'blind school' at Lahore, opened in 1906 (Makhdum 1961: 19), and in 1923 the Ida Rieu School for 'blind, deaf, dumb and other defective children' at Karachi. Pressure from parents of deaf children in the 1940s resulted in the formation of a

Deaf and Dumb Welfare Society at Lahore in 1949, and a special school opened soon afterwards (*ibid*.: 6–7).

Eugenics fallout

While European missionaries and their Indian colleagues developed formal disability services, a more malign Western influence arose from eugenics literature. Pillay (1931: 110), discussing rural welfare problems, believed 'insanity, feeble-mindedness and idiocy' to be hereditary, and 'the only way to eradicate them is by preventing those now affected from parenthood.' He linked the threat of venereal diseases with 'moral imbeciles, idiots and similar other diseased or tainted persons' (*ibid*.: 163). Bhattacharyya (1939: 13), surveying Indian special education, feared an 'abnormal growth' in the number of 'imbeciles', and found the 'education and segregation of this class' a matter of national importance. The Ranchi Mental Hospital superintendent called mental deficiency 'a social evil of tremendous proportions', and advised provincial governments to 'sort out all grades of defective children from existing schools by the help of the School Medical Officers and establish special schools for them' (Annual Report 1939: 8). Fifty years later, a prolific Pakistani social commentator still bases his views of 'feeble-mindedness' on Goddard's eugenic literature of 1914, suggesting that the question still arises: 'Would it not be better quietly to put them out of their misery?' (Quddus 1990: 265–70).

Exclusion or casual integration

Bengalis attending Persian schools, and millions of Sindhi and Punjabi children in the period before independence, memorized parts of Sadi's *Gulistan*, including a tale of vain efforts to educate a slow learner (Gladwin 1988: 225). In another tale, a teacher's own sons outshine the king's son. To the king's complaint, the teacher responds, 'the education was the same, but the capacities are different' (*ibid*.: 233). In real-life schools, slow-learning boys were often integrated with their peers, only to be ejected when the teacher lost patience. Generations of South Asian students were thus assured of the futility of trying to 'educate the ineducable'. Yet members of India's Central Advisory Board of Education had a different vision (Post-War 1944: 76–82). Whatever its drawbacks, IQ testing had shown them that imperceptible gradations of mental ability existed across the spectrum. They saw that many pupils would need 'special education only for a limited period', after which they should rejoin the mainstream. Less intelligent children might have 'other attributes which will enable them to play their part as independent and useful citizens.' Even if they might do some work separately, it was 'essential that throughout the school life they should have opportunities of mingling freely with their brighter fellows and of sharing with them such work and pleasures as all children enjoy' (*ibid*.: 77). The Board foresaw that an early investment would save later remedial costs.

There is evidence that thousands of children with mild to moderate disabilities had long been casually integrated in ordinary schools with no special attention or resources. Leitner (1882: Part I, p. 19), surveying indigenous schools in Punjab, was pleased to find no whole-class teaching 'retarding the industrious for the sake of the dullard'. Each boy went at his own pace, though the 'dullard' was at greater risk of caning. Integration of blind students was reported from the Deoband training institute for mullahs in the 1870s (*ibid*.: 79). Leitner named various blind men as notable schoolteachers, among scores of other teachers with disabilities. An energetic English headmistress at Lahore in about 1872 undertook the integrated education of a young blind girl, Asho, who later became a capable teacher of blind adults (Hewlett 1898: 50). Soon after Pakistan's independence in 1947, a more extensive integration of children with visual impairments began in a middle school at Pasrur (Grant 1963).

Children with various impairments and disabilities continued to be part of the normal enrolment throughout the primary cycle, and the introduction of compulsory education would later reinforce this. Rauf (1975), who studied schooling at Lahore from the 1950s to 1970s, realized that even secondary school classes contained both prize winners and 'the repeaters, the dullards, the laggards and the backward' (p. 202). Later studies and reports confirm that children with appreciable levels of learning difficulty continue to sit in ordinary classrooms without any special attention being paid (Miles 1985; Zaman 1990; Begum 1991).

Government policies

In the early 1950s, when East Pakistan had minimal special services, only 40 per cent of all school-age children received any education, and the best of school buildings were 'tin sheds with bamboo walls and earth floors' (Huq 1954: 49, 57). Ordinary primary schools experienced drop-out rates of up to 90 per cent, a colossal wastage which persisted into the 1960s. Attention to disabled children was therefore an extremely low priority. By 1957, planners could manage merely a nod towards special needs:

> However desirable these services or activities may be, none of them is immediately essential to the basic programme of education. To attempt them nationally at the present time would require great expenditure, and diversion of trained personnel which would inevitably slow down and weaken the more urgent process of establishing the basic school system.
>
> (First Five Year Plan 1957: 587)

The Commission on National Education Report (1960) found that government should be responsible for the 'training of teachers who will serve in institutions for the handicapped' run by private philanthropists (p. 251). It was not until the 1980s that the governments of Pakistan and Bangladesh would begin more seriously to *contemplate* equalizing the educational opportunities of disabled children. Actual progress remains minimal for disabled children in ordinary families. Some resources have been allocated to a modest number from the urban middle classes.

Equalities of value? Basic rights?

Tradition depicts South Asian schools as being reserved for fit and capable boys of wealthier families, who rote-learned textbooks under threat of painful punishment, before becoming the ruling class of the next generation. Yet, as noted above, pedagogical approaches with some child-centred, play learning (valuing, discovery) basis flourished in odd niches, disappeared and resurfaced elsewhere, at least as early as the 1830s. Some teachers here and there imparted knowledge to children's minds without resort to hitting their bodies. In some places, boys with disabilities were in school, either in a group or along with capable and well-to-do boys. Some poor boys were in school, with average and well-to-do boys. Far less often girls were in school, including some with disabilities. These exceptions to the traditional picture, and their increasing frequency during the past 150 years, suggest that counterparts of recent ideas of justice, fairness and opportunity have long been present to challenge privilege and exclusion.

To what extent, then, do such ideas have indigenous roots? Historically, South Asian visions of 'peace and plenty' have required a strong and righteous ruler administering just laws given by god or gods, and thus keeping a balance between rich and poor, strong and weak. In Islamic Asia, the nostalgia persists for 'a perfect leader (a perfect representation of the laws of God) and a perfect constitution (the Medina constitution)', believed to have existed in 'the utopia of original Islam' (Inayatullah 1996: 122). Yet the idea of equalizing, abolishing the distinctions between caste or class, removing privilege and raising the humble, hardly entered the picture. Even less has the idea been expressed of upgrading the valuation of disabled people. Certainly, a few disabled people had good status because of their family, or their particular talent (temporal or spiritual); but the disability 'itself' was perceived negatively – it is hard to find exceptions to this rule. The only positive aspect was that it challenged other people to act in a righteous way – and sometimes they rose to the challenge. The vision of a rightly functioning Muslim community does include such a challenge. Thus Wadud could point out that beyond *Adl* (justice) in the Islamic social order, there was *Ehsan*: 'a condition wherein an individual lagging behind in spite of his best efforts gets his deficiency made good by others to restore the disturbed balance of society. This is not by way of charity but as a matter of right' (Wadud 1986).

Wadud was writing neither about disabilities nor to impress Westerners – he was lamenting the lack of a truly Islamic social order in Pakistan. His statement suggests some convergence between 'a matter of right', i.e. a Muslim community acting rightly, and the 'rights, not charity' demand of Western disabled activists. Yet Wadud's perception is perhaps more holistic. Charity (*zakat*) is still enjoined upon individual Muslims as a basic pillar of Islam. Traditional community arrangements for administering *zakat* were designed to minimize the stigma of need, for the community acts both to benefit the individual and to put right a flaw within itself. By comparison, the slogan 'rights, not charity' and more aggressive versions appear to wash away the personal element of concern, and to overlook the economic fact that states raise funds by taxation, and minority rights are funded by majority tax hikes.

Recent decades have seen some international resurgence of confidence in Islamic history and religious values, among different Muslim groups. Traditionalist and radical fundamentalist groups have attracted most publicity, often engendering fear and ridicule. Less obvious, but perhaps with better long-term prospects, have been various modernizing movements based on the belief that there can be no ultimate contradictions between the essential messages of Islam and the development of knowledge – provided that care is taken in communications from each 'side'. Such movements are also keen that Islamic insights should be seen to contribute to modern knowledge; and that the 'moral high ground', e.g. of international discourse on rights, bioethics and social issues (including disability), should not remain the exclusive property of post Judaeo-Christian philosophers. A major difficulty in doing so, as noted by Hasan (1995: 25), Pakistan's senior disability thinker, is that ethical and social issues are 'not a discourse that forms part of the mainstream thought process in those [Muslim] societies or even within the medical profession.' The dominant voices have been those of reactionary clerics, whose instinct is to damn rather than discuss. Noting that historically Islam has had far more freedom for individual thought and autonomy of decision than is now generally credited, Hasan believes that the free-thinking movement will grow.

A graver difficulty in providing viable Islamic inputs to international debate lies in the Western domination of language (i.e. English) and media (i.e. the press, satellite TV, the Internet and educational publishing), and the ideological imperialism that uses the media to obliterate or marginalize cultural and conceptual notions differing from the latest European mezzo-brow trends. (That most other religious and philosophical viewpoints also fail to make much impact in mass media and dumbed down pseudo-academic media can be little comfort to serious Muslim thinkers.) In the Western world of education and disability, new terms are rapidly manufactured, consumed, discarded and dumped in a used condition on 'Third World' countries. Asian educational policy makers still trying to discover whether 'normalization' and 'special needs' have any meaning for children in their cities and rural schools now meet Western advisors nudging them onwards to 'differentiation' and 'inclusion' (see, for example, the confusions apparent in Khan 1998). The advisors seldom admit that the terms and the debate are opaque to many of the Western school teachers supposedly implementing the 'latest Western' policies, or that these policies are both experimental and in some quarters hotly contested. These games should, and do, generate some scepticism about Western educational exporting; yet few policy makers are willing to repudiate both the games and the aid packages bound up with them.

Pakistan

As a large country with a vast cultural history, Pakistan has many conflicting images. It is an Islamic republic; but Muslim modernizers, traditionalists and radicals differ sharply over how such a state should function. It is 'Third World' in terms of economy, health, education, life expectancy, women's rights and opportunities. Yet several million Pakistanis live 'modern' lives full of electronic gadgets and amusements, while the various forms of rural society are highly evolved and densely layered with relationships and nuances. Rural–urban polarization is severe, and there are gross variations between different regions of the country. Pakistan is 'ex-colonial' and still seeking, after 50 years, an independent national culture and stable polity; yet there is much that is distinctively Pakistani in styles and customs of everyday life.

Theoretically, all Pakistani children have a right to education, whether able-bodied and able-minded or not. In practice, half of Pakistan's children begin primary education, and half of these children drop out before completing the cycle. Among the non-starters, girls and children with disabilities are disproportionately represented. The educational 'right' to which all Pakistani children, able-bodied or disabled, ordinary or special, girls or boys, are entitled in practice, and which almost all do receive, is that of socialization and activity within their extended family network, their immediate neighbourhood and the religions and cultures of Pakistani society. Expectations, choices and opportunities vary greatly between all these children, sometimes as a result of disability or difference, sometimes through gender, social and economic class, urban or rural situation, regional location or other factors. Yet these wide variations are a traditional feature of life, and are not necessarily perceived as problematic or 'unfair'.

The rich and extensive socialization of young Pakistanis is nowhere written down as their 'right'. The willing hands, voices and domestic activities of mothers, grandmothers, aunts and older sisters are assumed to be there for all the needs of infancy and childhood, and (for girls) through young adulthood. The often heavier hands, voices and activities of men are fully present in Pakistani boys' lives from the age of five or six, and continue until they have their own grandchildren. Pakistani children have an uncontested 'right' to be present in family activities, because (other than a tiny urban elite) no one has invented childhood or adolescence as a separate condition that demands its own space, possessions and timings, or follows separate rules. Thus the right of Pakistani children to form and develop relationships with three or more generations – grandparents, parents, siblings and the often in-between generations of cousins – is enshrined in practical daily living, though hardly noticed as such. This 'right' carries with it the *assumption* of obedience by younger to older, which becomes the *obligation* of obedience whenever a question of choice arises.

For most Pakistanis, the only time these fundamental child-rights of participation with, socialization by and informal education from the persons of extended family relationship might consciously be recognized would be if they were confronted by an alien system of family and child-rearing. To see a child (aged, say, between 5 and 12) who has a single sibling or none, and lives in a house where grandparents, uncles or aunts are seldom or never seen, where the parental timetable seldom coincides with the child's, where few activities are carried out jointly between child and parents, where domestic helpers have been replaced by machines and where the child has its own jealously guarded room, possessions and programme of activities would seem strange, disturbing and deeply unbalanced. It might be hard to articulate the idea that such a child had been deprived of some fundamental human right – especially if the child were Western, well fed, well clothed and immersed in dialogue with the colourful screen of an expensive electronic apparatus. Yet it would be clear that some deeply engrained family experiences, amounting to mutual rights, would be severely threatened by any social movement towards the alien system just described. 'Virtual socialization' of their children via the Internet is not yet an appealing prospect for the older generation.

The mutual rights and obligations enshrined in the traditional Pakistani family, having much similarity with traditional family patterns in many countries present and past, constitute a resilient pattern that has reproduced itself over centuries while accommodating substantial external shocks and social changes. There is little or no room in it for the 'right of the individual' to have private space, to choose to believe something different from those around or to repudiate the network of relationships and obligations acquired at birth. Such 'rights' are perceived as forms of madness; and the Pakistani who learns that such rights are enshrined in 'Western society' is hardly surprised when mass media project images of deeply troubled Western societies. The 'madness' is acutely felt between the generations living in Pakistani households where grandparents migrated to Europe or America, parents grew up in two socio-cultural worlds but children are culturally 95 per cent European or American. For 'Pakistani' one might substitute many other nationalities during the past century. Traditionally, for the poorer and rural masses, the lot of each person was, and perhaps still is, thought to come from Allah. Wisdom consists in accepting this lot, and making the best of life within one's modest means. The Prophet Muhammad reportedly said that 'The son of Adam has a right only to the following: a house in which he lives, a garment with which he conceals his private parts, dry bread and water' (reported by 'Uthman, transmitted by Tirmidht). While continuing to give lip-service to such ideas, substantial parts of both urban and rural society in recent decades have been confronted with the reality of social mobility. This has arisen through the export of labour to the Gulf states and Europe, and the development of an 'artificial middle class' characterized by conspicuous consumption by indi-

vidual families, but without the civic and institutional investment traditionally associated with the middle classes (Hafeez 1991; Inayatullah 1996).

Services in Pakistan

Data from Akbar (1989), Richter (1996) and government sources suggest the
following growth of formal educational services for children with disabilities:

Year	1947	1960	1970	1980	1988	1996
Special schools	3	10	28	66	158	210

The number of children benefiting (or at least attending) in 1988 was thought
to be 10,373, and 12,475 in 1996. In federal government special schools, some
2760 are currently enrolled; and the programmes of the Directorate General of
Special Education consume a slender 0.3 per cent of the national education
budget (Khan 1998). A school survey (Miles 1985) found that 825 (1.9 per
cent) children with appreciable impairments were pointed out by school staff
without any special training or sensitization, in 103 ordinary primary and
secondary schools in the North West Frontier Province with a total enrolment
of 43,416 pupils. During the past 15 years, no significant factors are known
that would have reduced the proportion of disabled children casually integrated; so taking a more conservative 1 per cent level among some 20 million
Pakistani children currently in ordinary schools, there would be 200,000 children with noticeable impairments. Thus the number of disabled children casually integrated in ordinary schools is likely to be at least 16 times (and might
be 30 times) greater than the number in special schools, with virtually no extra
help or resources made available to them or to their teachers. As against this,
there are very roughly 40 million children of school age, among whom there
will not be fewer than a conservative 2.5 per cent having some moderate to
serious impairment, i.e. at least one million such children. Thus it appears that
the great majority do not attend school of any sort (along with some 19 million non-disabled school-age children who are not in school).

When young disabled people pass the age for schooling, there are even
fewer services or facilities available to them. Against this background of sparse
formal services, the secretary of Pakistan's Disabled People's Federation
reported that:

> The parents and relatives consider the disabled as an economic liability
> and curse of God. Government functionaries take them to be nincom-
> poop parasites. For the general public they are a nuisance. The disabled
> themselves are unaccepted by society, lose confidence in their faculties,
> lose self-respect and consider themselves fit for dependence upon others
> and beggary.
>
> (Malik 1988)

These are bitter words; but an earlier survey of attitudes to disabled people
(Miles 1983) supports Malik's experience. Although the spectrum of Pakistani

self-reported attitudes was similar to that found among Western populations, the majority were of the 'fear' or 'pity' type. A progressive minority felt that 'something should be done' for disabled people, e.g. 'there should be a place for them' (perhaps a residential colony?). However, a majority of respondents reacted favourably when ideas of integration and positive discrimination were suggested. The survey suggests that attitude change and service development are mutually interdependent.

Different directions?

Apart from the substantial difference of economic resources and political priorities, there are significant sociological and philosophical factors that might cause Pakistan to develop its services for disabled children in directions not taken by Western nations. Pakistan is still a profoundly religious country – not in the sense of Islamic fundamentalism, which is hardly popular; nor that most Pakistanis are 'good Muslims', which is debatable; but in that ultimately law and right and meaning in life are widely believed to derive from Allah. Children are thought to be born not so much as little individuals with personal rights, but as parts of an extended family network within a wider community of mutual duty and obligation. The duty and entitlement of support and care is traditional and religious, rather than being laid down by the state. There is a theoretical 'equality' of persons before Allah; but that is quite different from the idea of constructing a society where 'individuals are equal before the law'. Of course, the latter idea impinges on urban Pakistan, as it moves further from the idealized *Gemeinschaft* (traditional, communal society) towards *Gesellschaft* (conglomerated society of rational, chosen association). Yet notions of individual rights and equality that may seem self-evident to Westerners often look flimsy and artificial in Pakistan, where mass media naturally highlight the more ludicrous outcomes of these Western pursuits.

Of course, this picture is contested by Pakistan's accelerating urban rat race, endemic corruption within the education system, the parvenu/Dubai syndrome and the paralysing sense of peripheralization among those Pakistan 'brains' that have not already drained to the West. Yet while Western technology and knowledge is coveted, the family life and social conduct of Westerners, as communicated in the media or reported by expatriate Pakistanis, are deeply unattractive. It is by no means obvious that disabled European children and adults have more satisfactory lives, apart from differences attributable to technology and modern medicine, than disabled Pakistanis. When there is serious abuse, the means for detecting it and relieving the victim are certainly better organized in Western Europe than in Pakistan (Miles 1996a). However, Western groups campaigning for their personal 'rights', in competition with other vociferous groups, appear in the mass media with an image (possibly distorted) of childish rebellion and misery, the opposite of mature Muslim behaviour. The 'liberty' and so-called 'independence' prized by

Westerners are hardly the goals of Pakistanis who perceive their security and identity to rest in their family and community under Allah.

Bangladesh

The youngest of the South Asian independent nations, Bangladesh has the highest population density in the world, apart from a few small island states. Since 1971, the country has undergone political vicissitudes, moving from one-party rule to military regimes, to a democratic transition period. While some advances have been seen in the sectors of education, health, nutrition, demographic balance, child care, gender disparities and income distribution, Bangladesh is still one of the world's economically poorest countries. The highly adverse population–resource ratio (Haq 1997: 42) suggests that short- to medium-term prospects of significant economic improvement are weak.

Much of what has been stated for Pakistan is also valid for Bangladesh. In the collectivist environment of the traditional Bangladeshi rural society and family, the notion of 'responsibility' was readily understood and practised by ordinary people, without reasoning or articulation as such. In such a situation, people with disabilities or their families did not think about 'rights', except for hoping for some nearby medical assistance to cure the disability or relieve suffering. The result in urban areas has been that 'an attitude of dependency and humiliation developed among them. Social taboos made them evils in society' (Timm *et al.* 1993: 136). Integration to rural society as a disabled person has so far not been an issue, although society has long had, and still has, many prejudices about disabled people. Among the Garo tribes of northern-eastern Bengal in the nineteenth century there was reportedly, 'in most villages, a lame or blind person, incapacitated from other work, who invokes the deities, and offers sacrifices for the recovery of sick persons.' (Watson 1832). This pragmatic, if slightly cynical, matching of capacity with occupation may suggest something of the calculating rustic approach to religion, rather than any special consideration for including disabled people in the life of the community. The deities must be given their due, for what it is worth, but there is no point in wasting an able-bodied man on the job, when a blind or lame one can just as well chant the prayers, sprinkle the blood or whatever.

Until comparatively recently, people had little to do with the state, beyond paying taxes to the authorities and negotiating official property transfers or land settlement. Responsibilities related to disability were far distant from the state, and were taken care of by the family and local community. The notion of 'right' has a recent origin in modern Bangladeshi civil society. Ordinary public life in Bangladesh is full of its own cultural components, i.e. symbols, heroes, rituals, of which the value system is composed. The culture of its largely (87 per cent) Muslim population has developed with influences from Hinduism and Buddhism over centuries. 'Disability' is seen as calling for 'care', which belongs in the realm of religious merit – it is a matter of fulfilling personal responsibilities, rather than according people 'rights'.

The rich folk heritage of Bengali ballads contains numerous references to disability, mainly blindness, from which it is clear that the burden of care and responsibility is assumed to fall very largely upon *women* relatives. The translated collections by Sen (1926–32) often depict blindness (in a helpless male) as an opportunity for female devotion, self-sacrifice and nobility of soul. The Ballad of Kanchanmala, for example, opens with an elderly widower carrying his blind baby son, of whom he is keen to disencumber himself. Kanchanmala, aged nine, is promptly married to the blind baby by her father's arrangement, to avert an evil omen. A suitably heart-rending tale ensues (*ibid.*: II(i), 79–116), in which the blindness is first cured and then returns; but either way, it is assumed that a disabled person is helpless and some handy female should provide the necessary lifelong care.

Some modernization of ideas has taken place, at least at a superficial level, i.e. provided that it does not conflict with traditional cultural practices and religious beliefs. Thus the jargon of 'rights' is familiar to intellectuals, it may be used in political oratory, it is part of the package with which people feel that Bangladesh is transiting from the traditional to the modern. Yet a high degree of fatalism still operates in public life, a fatalism that is stronger and more basic than the notion of 'right'. State capacity to provide health care and education services to the ordinary people is weak, so the issue of services to disabled people remains a non-priority. Officially, some rhetoric of rights can be wheeled out to accompany a very modest scattering of disability services; but in practice the recipients of such services belong to well-to-do families, which could afford to buy services from private providers anyway. Government initiatives are distant from ordinary disabled people, and they fail to overcome the deep-seated cynicism and mistrust between the mass of the population and the formal establishments. Popular disbelief tends to be vindicated by studies such as that by Muhammad Hossain (1994), which reveals 'an appalling discrepancy between the intended effects and the practical outcomes' (p. 167) of efforts to modernize rural education services and thus to provide children with their 'right to education'. Hossain documents in detail the formalism, 'punishment-centred bureaucracy', 'dysfunctional supervision', conflict, alienation and red-tapism engendered by the modernization drive (pp. 172–7). He contrasts these features with the traditional system of trust, mutual assistance and personalization of all transactions in rural Bangladesh. Perhaps Hossain is a little idealistic about the latter; yet his long, carefully formulated education report certainly suggests that government schemes to 'modernize' services for disabled people in a depersonalized 'rights-based' fashion could create as many problems as they solved. Paper-based 'disability rights', backed (almost inevitably) by a mere fraction of the structural and attitudinal changes and resource provisions needed to give them substance, would increase the gulf between rhetoric and reality while relieving families and communities of even the 'charitable obligation' they at present feel, however half-heartedly, to give disabled children some help. For substantial numbers of have-nots, even what little they have would thus be snatched away and replaced by a fine-sounding slogan.

A recent review of social welfare legislation by Halim (1993) notes existing government legislation concerning leprosy (dating from 1898) and mental retardation (1912). Both Acts are full of measures to regulate and control these disabled persons, but during the past century have provided little or nothing by way of positive rights or entitlements. Halim in fact prepares his reader for this outcome, by first noting that the 'informal network of family, relatives and friends is a major provider of social help in Bangladesh.' He admits, however (p. 112), that under current economic pressures 'they are increasingly unable to fulfil their traditional role.' (Jain noted this problem as long ago as 1916 – the extended family is taking a long time to die). Basic necessities of life, decent job opportunities and social security in case of illness or disablement all in fact appear as government goals for its citizens in the Constitution of the People's Republic of Bangladesh, corresponding with articles in the Universal Declaration of Human Rights (1948). Yet the government is under the same economic constraints as the ordinary family when it comes to fulfilling its obligations.

There is a big gap between all these slogans and the practicalities of life in Bangladesh, not only in the case of disabled people but where it concerns the rights of all people – in particular the children of the poor, who suffer a variety of gross, ongoing abuses, described by the social anthropologist Blanchet (1996). The new slogans of bilateral, multilateral or NGO aid agencies – e.g. empowerment, policy advocacy, sustainability, conscientization, parents' mobilization on behalf of disabled children, community participation – tend to widen the gap and simply confuse local people, rather than building understanding of disability issues. 'Social model' rhetoric, insisting, for example, that 'the problem is not in the disabled person, it is society that has a problem', is incomprehensible to the vast majority of people who have always thought, still think and feel they have good reason to think that losing one's eyesight, for example, is an unmitigated personal disaster. There can be no objection to people developing such models and terminology in countries wealthy enough to sustain decades of effort in constructing and adapting public environments to be user-friendly to all sorts and conditions of humanity. But foisting these advanced notions on to an impoverished country where a majority of children are stunted for lack of adequate nutrition (UNICEF 1998) displays some arrogance about the practical realities of development.

Services in Bangladesh

Educational provision for disabled children is limited. The government runs 13 institutions in which 820 students (410 hearing impaired, 360 visually impaired and 50 mentally handicapped) are studying. These are all residential schools, each with a further 20 day students (Haqq 1994). NGOs are providing 27 institutions, with 1000 children and 720 adults getting education and vocational training. There are government and NGO integrated programmes for visually impaired and for mentally handicapped children, with resource teachers assisting about 80 ordinary schools. Some community-based rehabilitation (CBR) and outreach projects are also functioning, and there are national and local NGOs representing the major disability categories. The NGOs suffer from the usual problems, e.g. aid dependency, weak planning, weak managerial capacity, lack of quality in services, incapacity for scaling-up to serve larger populations (see Miles *et al.* 1996; Aminuzzaman 1998). Some of their difficulties arise from trying to follow the changing policies of Western disability aid agencies during the past two decades. Since the Year of the Child (1979), some aid organizations have first supported NGOs building special schools; then decided that the emphasis should be on special units attached to ordinary schools; then that NGOs should not provide services at all but should be campaigning for government provision of integrated education, but if NGOs do provide services, that they should be some sort of CBR, and (more recently) that whatever is done must be led by people with disabilities; next, that what is really needed is 'inclusion', involving a total reconceptualization of what education is about. (It can be anticipated that deaf organizations will now complete the circle by demanding separate special schools, as some have begun to do in Europe.) For there to be any hope of success, the introduction of each of these twists and turns probably required from 20 to 50 years, as well as strong political, parental and professional motivation, none of which has been present.

Reflections

Comparisons of Pakistan and Bangladesh can only be impressionistic without far more space and detail. However, a single item of data suggests real divergences of national policy and outlook, and ultimately of priorities for the people's welfare. In the early 1990s, Pakistan spent 10 times as much on defence as on health and education combined. Bangladesh spent 1.6 times more on health and education than on defence (UNICEF 1998). Every country has a right to its national pride and its own particular brand of ideological baloney; but it is clearly preferable that these luxuries be not indulged so far as to obstruct the pragmatic provision of services that can make a difference to the lives of real children and adults.

Western missionaries for rights, inclusion, disabled people's empowerment etc. cannot be stopped from spreading their messages across the globe, along with such other essential Western benefits as cola drinks, brunchburgers, pornographic videos and democracy. Indeed, as one South American bishop remarked when Paulo Freire promised to try to stem the southward flood of North American evangelists, 'Let them come. They may be the only *gringos* we get the chance to educate.' Certainly, Asian educationists should not be prevented from inspecting whatever is on offer in the global supermarket. However, two modest precautions might reduce the damage of inappropriate importing.

1 Efforts should be made to provide historical perspectives and ideological context, so that prospective clients can more easily see how and where the goodies were cooked up, and get a sense of how they fit, or fail to fit, in the long-term trends of Western societies.
2 The development of histories of social responses to disabilities and to people with disabilities in Asian countries should enhance their planners' cultural confidence, providing solid 'home ground' on which to stand and from which they may appraise more realistically the offers of Western enthusiasts (Miles 1996b).

European nations developed formal disability services slowly from the early nineteenth century onwards, within the means of their economies, without the censorious gaze of wealthy foreign monitors, and with decades of ongoing debate about methods and strategies. Whatever 'mistakes' they now, with the hindsight of history, may appear to have made seldom looked or felt like mistakes but seemed the best compromise at the time between idealism, realism, resources and knowledge. By contrast, economically weaker countries at the dawn of the twenty-first century have a plethora of modern knowledge, techniques and conflicting advice offered them, but lack the space, time and freedom to experiment and learn for themselves away from the dominating voices and slogans of Western mentors and funders, latter-day Ladies Bountiful, very few of whom have any appreciable experience of living and working on local salaries in the countries they are so eager to guide. Some recent Euro-American ideological trends have emphasized equality of personal value and equal educational opportunity, with a wide range of professional and community resources available, so that appropriate differentiation can be achieved. Where these are politically and economically affordable and where communities can raise their sights to embrace such trends, they are no doubt admirable. They are much less inspirational when forced down the throats of people who are having trouble feeding and clothing their own children, or providing their population with the most basic health and education services. For example, although senior Pakistan psychologist Riaz (1994) finds the Western integration gospel quite appealing as a prospect for Pakistan's future, 'in general it seems irrelevant to the present situation. Whatever may be the strengths or weaknesses of the present educational system, more than half of the pupils drop out after a year or so of schooling.' Ignorance of such basic realities is particularly unpalatable when the countries responsible for propagating the wonderful slogans are (rightly or wrongly) perceived as major contributors to the socio-economic disarray of the countries on the receiving end of all this well-meant advice.

Antonio Cassese (1990), in the chapter 'Are human rights truly universal?', skilfully describes some of the real divergences between alternative world philosophies, ideologies and religions. Nevertheless, some convergence is predictable in public sentiments about 'rights', as global communication, the Internet and so on expose large numbers of English-literate people to international currents. Yet any fruits of such a convergence are unlikely to appear quickly. There are powerful reactionary movements developing everywhere, in which people are desperate to maintain their identity and avoid being swamped by global, usually Western, culture. Such movements exist in South Asia, fighting both external influences and modernizing elites. Amidst these embattled groups, there are comparatively few peacemakers.

A small signpost towards peace and lateral thinking appears in a cherished story of the *Tablighi* movement, a mission for spiritual deepening. The story concerns a village simpleton, who joined a band of religious devotees and

> wandered with the group from place to place asking everyone to repeat the *kalima* to help him since he had never been able to learn it. His merit rested in being a stimulus to the piety of those thus constrained to articulate the attestation and offer him help. [The *kalima* is the basic Muslim statement of faith].
>
> (Metcalf 1996: 56)

It was a *Tablighi* maxim that all were welcome on their religious missions, the contribution of each one was valued and was never corrected or contradicted. Indeed, Metcalf (1996: 59) admires the *Tablighi* conviction that 'anyone can learn, that one learns by doing, and that the lives of "ordinary" people can be profoundly transformed.' Such tolerant, peripatetic, homespun philosophers and their socially valorized simpletons are as far as they could possibly be from the national defence budget, the Internet or the Western disability activists baying for their rights. If 'modernization' means wiping out the gentle ones, perhaps the price is too high.

Questions

How should aid programmes to Pakistan and Bangladesh take into account the following issues?

1 Whatever fine phrases issue from politicians, the Director of Education looks for 'improvement schemes' that can realistically be introduced and practised with reasonable effectiveness by the *average and below average* teachers constituting 85 per cent of the workforce; costing less, or at least no more, than the present system; producing pupil results measurable by ordinary, objective means (i.e. written tests and exams); not inflaming parents, religious teachers or any large or influential constituency; reducing, or at least not encouraging, the corruption, nepotism and canvassing that accompanies all staff postings; and delivering, within two or three years, benefits substantially outweighing the disruption involved in implementing the scheme.

2 'Equalization of opportunities for disabled persons' is extremely low on the list of development priorities in Bangladesh and Pakistan. People may agree that it is a nice idea, but it is hardly ever a 'felt need' even among disabled

people (the mass of whom are likely to be more interested in security of food and shelter, followed by training and employment).

3 For reasons of language and administrative competence, Western aid interventions intended for 'the poorest' almost always have to be mediated by urban, educated, national counterparts – who traditionally have regarded 'the poorest' as being beyond realistic redemption. Evaluators often report that aid programmes have benefited mainly the middle classes, who have the capacity to absorb a variety of aid inputs (whether or not the inputs were intended for them).

Acknowledgement

Cordial acknowledgement is due to Professor Waqar Ahmad for useful comments on a draft of this chapter.

References

Adam, W. (1835 and 1838) *Reports on the State of Education in Bengal* (ed. A. Basu, 1941). Calcutta: University of Calcutta.

Akbar, R. M. (1989) A survey of special education facilities for the handicapped children in Pakistan. Unpublished MA thesis, Allama Iqbal Open University, Islamabad.

Aminuzzaman, S. (1998) NGOs and the grassroot base local government in Bangladesh. A study of their institutional interactions, in F. Hossain and S. Myllylä (eds) *NGOs under Challenge – Dynamics and Drawbacks in Development*. Helsinki: Ministry for Foreign Affairs, Finland.

Annual Report on European Education in Bengal, for the Year 1918–19 (1919) Calcutta: Bengal Secretariat.

Annual Report on the Working of the Ranchi Indian Mental Hospital, Kanke, in Bihar, for the Year 1937 (1939) Patna.

Banerjee, H. C. (1928) The sign language of deaf-mutes, *Indian Journal of Psychology*, 3: 69–87.

Banerji, S. N. (1949/50) Sixty years with the deaf in India, *The Deaf in India*, I(1): 3–9; I(2): 3–18; I(3): 26–7.

Bhattacharyya, K. (1939) A statistical survey of education of the infirm in India, *University of Calcutta, Journal of the Department of Letters*, 31: 1–56.

Begum, K. (1991) Identifying learning difficulties and adoption of remedial measures for primary school children, *Teacher's World* (Dhaka), 14(2): 1–7.

Blanchet, T. (1996) *Lost Innocence, Stolen Childhoods*. Dhaka: University Press Ltd.

Calcutta School (1895) *American Annals of the Deaf*, 40(1): 79.

Cassese, A. (1990) *Human Rights in a Changing World*. Cambridge: Polity.

Das Gupta, T.C. (1935) *Aspects of Bengali Society from Old Bengali Literature*. Calcutta: University of Calcutta.

First Five Year Plan, 1955–60 (1957) Karachi: Government of Pakistan.

General Report upon the Administration of the Punjab Proper, for the Years 1849–50 and 1850–51 (1853). Calcutta.

Gladwin, F. (trans.) (1988) *The Gulistan or Rose Garden by Musle-huddeen Shaik Sady.* Islamabad: Lok Virsa.

Grant, I. L. D. (1963) Integration at Pasrur, in I. L. D. Grant (ed.) *Handbook for Teachers and Parents of Blind Children in Pakistan.* Lahore: Ilmi Press.

Hafeez, S. (1991) *The Changing Pakistan Society.* Karachi: Royal Book Co.

Halim, M. A. (1993) *Social Welfare Legislation in Bangladesh.* Dhaka: Oihik.

Haq, M. ul (1997) *Human Development in South Asia.* Karachi: Oxford University Press.

Haqq, M. S. (1994) Policies and programmes concerning disabilities and people with disabilities in Bangladesh. Paper presented at Regional Seminar on Childhood Disability, Dhaka, 3–5 December.

Hasan, K. Z. (1995) The principles of medical ethics from an Islamic view point, in S. H. Zaidi, M. H. Jafary, U. Niaz-Anwar and S. A. Jawad (eds) *Medical Ethics in the Contemporary Era.* Karachi: Royal Book.

Hewlett, S. S. (1898) *They Shall See His Face.* Oxford: Alden.

Hossain, M. H. (1994) *Traditional Culture and Modern Systems. Administering Primary Education in Bangladesh.* New York: University Press of America.

Huq, M. S. (1954) *Compulsory Education in Pakistan,* Paris: UNESCO.

Inayatullah, S. (1996) Mullahs, sex and bureaucrats. Pakistan's confrontation with the modern world, in D. Bahri and M. Vasudeva (eds) *Between the Lines: South Asians and Postcoloniality.* Philadelphia: Temple University.

Jain, P. S. (1916) A preliminary note on pauperism in India, *Indian Journal of Economics,* 1: 351–68.

Khan, F. (1998) Case study of special needs education in Pakistan: the process of inclusion, *European Journal of Special Needs Education,* 13: 98–111.

Latif, I. (1938) Some aetiological factors in the pathology of stammering, *Indian Journal of Psychology,* 13: 103–15.

Leitner, G. W. (1882) *History of Indigenous Education in the Punjab since Annexation and in 1882.* Lahore: Republican Books.

Makhdum, S. A. (1961) *Special Education in West Pakistan.* Lahore: West Pakistan Bureau of Education.

Malik, S. (1988) Situation of the physically disabled in Pakistan. Report of DPI Asia/Pacific Leadership training seminar for women with disability. Islamabad, November 1987, Islamabad.

Malin, A. J. (1968) Psychological tests for retarded Indian children, *Journal of Rehabilitation in Asia,* 9(1): 32–3.

Metcalf, B. (1996) Meandering Madrasas, in N. Crook (ed.) *The Transmission of Knowledge in South Asia.* Delhi: Oxford University Press.

Miles, M. (1983) *Attitudes towards Persons with Disabilities Following IYDP (1981).* Peshawar: Mental Health Centre.

Miles, M. (1985) *Children with Disabilities in Ordinary Schools.* Peshawar: Mental Health Centre.

Miles, M. (1996a) Walking delicately around mental handicap, sex education and abuse in Pakistan, *Child Abuse Review,* 5: 263–74.

Miles, M. (1996b) Community, individual or information development? Dilemmas of concept and culture in South Asian disability planning in *Disability and Society,* 11: 485–500.

Miles, M. (1997) *Disability Care and Education in 19th Century India,* rev. edn. ERIC Document Reproduction Service.

Miles, M., Hossain, F. and Ringstad, B. (1996) Report of an external evaluation and assessment of the co-operation between the Society for Care and Education of the

Mentally Retarded, Bangladesh (SCEMRB) and the Norwegian Association for the Mentally Handicapped (NFPU) from 1982 to 1995. Unpublished. Obtainable from authors or from NFPU, Oslo.

Pillay, A. P. (1931) *Welfare Problems in Rural India.* Bombay: Taraporevala.

Post-War Educational Development in India (1944) Report by the Central Advisory Board of Education. Delhi: Government of India.

Progress of Education in India, 1897–98 to 1901–02 (1904) *Vol. I. Fourth Quinquennial Review.* London.

Quddus, S. A. (1990) *Social Change in Pakistan.* Lahore: Progressive.

Rauf, A. (1975) *Dynamic Educational Psychology,* 3rd edn. Lahore: Ferozesons.

Report of the Commission on National Education (1960) Government of Pakistan.

Riaz, M. N. (1994) Pakistan, in K. Mazurek and M. Winzer (eds) *Comparative Studies in Special Education.* Washington, DC: Gallaudet University Press.

Richter, L. (1996) Report to Radda Barnen, Stockholm, on a consultancy on disability in Pakistan. Unpublished.

Sanderson, R. and Parkinson, J. E. (1931) *Rural Education in England and the Punjab.* Calcutta: Bureau of Education, India.

Sen, D. (1926–32) *Eastern Bengal Ballads.* Calcutta: University of Calcutta.

Shahidullah, K. (1984) The new education in Bengal: the 1900 syllabus for the 'kindergarten' and 'lower primary' years and its problems, *Indian Economic and Social History Review,* 21: 215–47.

Sinha, S. (1936) Learning curve of a mentally deficient child, *Indian Journal of Psychology,* 11: 223–35.

Timm, R. W., D'Souza, J. and Siddique, M. H. (1993) *State of Human Rights 1993 Bangladesh.* Dhaka: Bangladesh Manobadhikar Samonnoy Parishad.

UNICEF (1998) *The State of the World's Children 1998.* New York: UNICEF.

Wadud, S. A. (1986) Why Islamic order could not be introduced, *The Pakistan Times,* Magazine section, 28 March.

Watson, A. (1832) Annotation, A. White (ed.) *Memoir of the Late David Scott, Esq.,* Calcutta.

Zaman, S. S. (ed.) (1990) *Research on Mental Retardation in Bangladesh.* Dhaka: Bangladesh Protibondhi Foundation.

 **6**

Inclusive education in Canada: a piece in the equality puzzle

Marcia Rioux

Overview

This chapter argues that at the same time that the struggle for inclusive education has been going on in Canada, there has been an active opposition to it. It outlines a number of the arguments that have been raised against inclusion and postulates that, more than arguments against inclusive education, these are arguments against human rights and equality. Analysing the implications of backlash generally provides a framework within which the author analyses education as an equality issue. The chapter concludes with international examples of education inclusion that counter the backlash trend.

Introduction

For many years, families, self-advocates, equality rights workers, educators and thousands of concerned individuals in Canada and indeed around the world have devoted themselves to the struggle for inclusive education. The allies have been found in many places – in courts, in classrooms, in Faculties of Education, in Human Rights or civil rights commissions, in employment equity initiatives, in government departments, in churches, synagogues and mosques, in specialized agencies of the United Nations (such as UNESCO) and in community development projects.

At the same time this has been happening, there have been some disquieting trends – there is, as there has always been, an active opposition to inclusive education. But that opposition now has an undertone that suggests that it is not so much about education as it is about an opposition to human rights and equality.

There are some indicators that suggest that children with disabilities are bearing the brunt of responsibility for collapsing education systems around the world. And inclusive education is becoming a lightning rod for those who oppose equality rights. What is the evidence that leads to such a conclusion?

First, there are thousands of students in the wealthy, industrialized nations such as Canada, streaming out of the schools and into the shopping plazas and gaming arcades long before the school day finishes; and they are dropping out before high school ends. They are understimulated and disengaged for reasons that the school systems seem unable to address. And the statistics indicate that different groups are disengaging in different ways. Students of minority groups, from marginalized and low-income families and from abusive families find schools places from which to escape. In some countries a pattern is emerging where children of the middle and upper classes are moving to privately run schools. This leaves fewer parents committed to creating a better curriculum in the state schools. In this environment, investing scarcer and scarcer public resources to make classrooms inclusive of children with disabilities is read by some as an unjustified investment when the system is failing the best and the brightest.

Second, there has been a call in many countries for more and more specialized classes to deal with a quantum increase of students with learning disabilities – some estimates suggested are as high as 40 per cent of students. There does not, however, appear to be any rational or scientific explanation for such dramatic increases in numbers. This suggests that factors other than an actual increase in the incidence of learning disabilities may underlie the increasing demand. It may be that specialized classes have become a way of dealing with overcrowded, overextended, ineffective learning environments. Special education provides, arguably, an avenue for a parent to get additional educational support and greater individualized instruction for a child. However, with increasing demand, the budgetary and political profile of special education is heightened. Children who use these services are a target for backlash from those who preach exclusion in the name of fiscal restraint.

Third, there are increasingly strong voices from some quarters about the impact of inclusive education on other children in the class. In an editorial written by Albert Shanker, then President of the American Federation of Teachers, he argued against the tyranny of inclusive education in the following way: 'Advocates demand that all disabled children be put into regular classrooms, regardless of their ability to function or benefit and regardless of the effect on other children in the class.' In his remarks he reflects what we hear from many people around the world who think some people are more able to learn and are more worthy of teaching than others. His is unfortunately not a lone voice.

A recent article from the *New York Times* magazine had a similar theme. Brent Staples, who writes editorials on politics and culture argued in that piece (1997) that special education classes with their limited classroom size and individualized attention are enviable, and any move towards inclusive education is foolhardy. He claimed:

Faced with skyrocketing costs and wildly uneven results, nearly two-thirds of the states are sketching out plans to limit special-education spending. Most hope to save money by pushing disabled children out of the small, specialized classes that many of them need to succeed and into crowded, ill-equipped classrooms where they will compete with non-disabled peers. The process – often called mainstreaming or inclusion – is being justified by the civil rights movement notion that segregation of any kind is damaging and that diversity is an indisputable social good.

(Staples 1997: 64)

He then went on to present all the reasons he could muster for why mainstreaming will not work. And he concluded by stating that:

Diversity is a noble ideal. But many disabled children would be marginalized and ridiculed in the mainstream . . . The central goal [of special education] was always to educate children who had traditionally been viewed as ineducable. Integration was an important but distinctly secondary objective.

(Staples 1997: 64)

Like others, he based his argument on the premise that education seeks the achievement of standardized measurable ends that are consistent with productive contribution to the paid economy. He did not recognize the core aims of education in Western civilization, which traditionally have been the promotion of the fullest development of the person's intellectual, moral, physical, aesthetic and cultural potential.

Fourth, and not exclusive of the others, is the stampede to establish standardized testing procedures for children in schools to ensure that they are receiving a consistent, uniform, minimum number of quantifiable skills in the classrooms of their nations. Provincial education policy initiatives of this nature have surfaced in the past five years. This is part of the prevailing mean-lean economic agenda that dictates rigid standards and testing, and efficiency measured by economic contribution. We come full circle with standardized testing. An apparently neutral measure, which has the effect of dividing children on the basis of particular intellectual qualities, is reasserted after years of efforts for inclusive education work to make such a measure less relevant in judging the quality and outcomes of education.

So, overall, there are millions of children around the world never getting into schools, including those children who live on the streets of some of the world's largest cities, such as Rio de Janeiro, Calcutta and Bogotá; there are school-age children finding ways of escaping the classroom to avoid its meaninglessness for them, such as we see in Toronto, Canada; there is mass labelling of school-age individuals as having learning disabilities; there is a popular myth that there are some children who cannot benefit from education; and finally – and not least of all – there is a prevailing economic agenda driving the education system.

Clearly, these are not problems of school systems alone, nor are they problems of inclusion, but are part of a larger picture, which we can perhaps understand in one way by looking at what is happening in the terrain of human rights generally.

Backlash

The backlash to inclusive education reflects a general backlash to human rights in everyday life as well as in law. Backlash has been defined by Seymour Martin Lipset and Earl Raab as 'the reaction by groups which are declining in a felt sense of importance, influence and power' (Lipset and Rabb 1970: 3). A jurist provided an explanation of resistance to human rights as

> analogous to a chronic virus which flares up from time to time when certain conditions are right. These conditions occur when specific efforts are made to improve the status of minority groups and women – efforts which are interpreted by backlash promoters as real threats to their own economic and social well being.
>
> (Mahoney 1996: 139)

Sometimes called the politics of resentment, backlash is similar to discrimination, except its range of antagonism is broad. Equality is as much the enemy as equality seekers themselves. All kinds of techniques are used to reimpose conditions of inequality and to place the blame for inequality on the individual and his or her incapacity. Equality-promoting initiatives and strategies are undermined by the backlashers to try to reverse any gains that might be made in approaching equality. Backlashers realize that control of the language of rights is an important strategy and so we see how a discourse of human rights is twisted to justify segregation and marginalization for people with disabilities. And so, in education, for example, exposing children to regular classes is attacked as a denial of needed individual attention and special education technology on the one hand. On the other, it is seen as a threat to the rights of the rest of the children to enjoy scarce educational resources and opportunities in the classroom. That is, those who oppose inclusion are not denying education but they are protecting children from the harassment and the lack of attention endemic in public schools.

Backlashers blame equality for other kinds of evils. Chipping away at private anxieties and collective political will, the presence of children with disabilities is seen as a problem contributing to the failure of the schools. The effect is to create widespread misconceptions that the child with a disability is educated at the expense of other non-disabled children and lowers the education standards. The disability movement is blamed for creating havoc with education, for undermining the merit principle, for pointless use of school time and for perpetuating the hoax that there is a purpose to educating children who will never have real jobs and contribute to the economy. The solution proposed is that disability rights advocates should lower their standards, a solution which is proposed by backlashers for others who seek equality as well.

This presentation of inclusive education as though it was about competing rights – the rights of non-disabled students and the rights of disabled students – sets up the argument commonly made for continuing a system of separate and unequal. But there has to be another conceptual formulation – one based on an interaction between the right to be different and the right to be the same. In that way it is possible to achieve a system based on a common citizenship, without distinction based on disability, but at the same time to acknowledge and celebrate the historical experiences and forms of personal identification that come from disability. Albie Sachs, a justice of the Constitutional Court in South Africa and well known for his work in the anti-apartheid movement, dismissed any suggestions that the two are in opposition this way:

> On the contrary [to being in opposition], the right to be the same in terms of fundamental civil, political, legal, economic and social right, provided that foundation for the expression of difference through choice in the sphere of culture, lifestyle and personal priorities. In other words, provided that difference was not used to maintain inequality, subordination, injustice and marginalisation, it represented a positive value in human society.
>
> (Sachs 1996: 15)

Access to education in Canada

In Canada, we are also getting caught in the equality backlash, and a recent education case makes it clear that there are still distinctions being made, and sought, between the kind of equality granted to people with disabilities and the kind granted to others. The legislative background to the case is that while all children have the right to an education under Canada's provincial Education Acts, and most provincial and district level policy permits individual schools and school districts to include students with disabilities in the regular classroom, it does not require them to do so. Lack of clarity in the legislation regarding inclusion gives school authorities the power to interpret their responsibilities regarding placement decisions, which results in children being placed, over their objections and those of their parents, in segregated special education schools or classes designated for children with disabilities. In this particular case, a school district in Ontario, Canada's largest province, decided that a child would be best educated in a special class.

Currently New Brunswick is the only province where the law (The New Brunswick Schools Act 1985) requires that every child be in a *regular* class in a neighbourhood school; if a particular child needs to be placed in any other situation the onus lies on the school to justify why the child cannot be in a regular class.

As well, Canada has the distinction of specific constitutional language guaranteeing equal benefit and equal protection of the law for all persons, including those with physical or mental disabilities. Section 15 of the Constitution Act of Canada provides:

(1) Every individual is equal before and under the law and has the right to equal protection and equal benefit of the law without discrimination and in particular, without discrimination based on race, national or ethnic origin, colour, religion, sex, age, mental or physical disability.

(2) Subsection (1) does not preclude any law, program or activity that has as its object the amelioration of conditions of disadvantaged individuals or groups including those that are disadvantaged because of race, national or ethnic origin, colour, religion, sex, age, mental or physical disability.

Because of its constitutional nature, this guarantee of equality rights applies to all levels of legislative authority in Canada. Its reach is broad, in that it applies to all Canadian law, including taxation, immigration, education, health care and even human rights protections. It is the highest law of the land and can thus be used to bring into question, and declare invalid, provincial statutory provisions such as those in provincial Education Acts.

For the past decade Section 15 has provided an important process for defining and clarifying the rights of citizens. It has provided a context in which the discourses as well as the legal and policy considerations of disability have taken on the equality rights perspective. Covering both substantive and procedural rights under Section 15(1) and permitting affirmative action-type programmes in Section 15(2), the *Charter of Rights and Freedoms* is a powerful tool for redirecting the understanding of disability as an individual deficit or as a medical condition, attributable to medical or biological abnormalities, to the notion of disability as a social status. In addition to the Charter, each provincial and territorial jurisdiction in Canada has a *Human Rights Code*, which provides protection from discrimination based on, among other characteristics, physical and mental disability.

In addition to human rights legislation, which applies to all educational facilities in the province or territory, each provincial and territorial jurisdiction also has an *Education Act* or *School Act* governing the provision of education at elementary and secondary levels. These Acts, while they vary in their language, all contain specific provisions regarding the education of disabled students, and most provide for universal access to education, irrespective of disability.

Eaton v. Brant County Board of Education

In 1997, the Supreme Court of Canada heard an appeal in the case of Emily Eaton, a school age girl with cerebral palsy, whose parents had sought to have her educated in a regular classroom in the neighbourhood school near Brantford, Ontario. Her parents had always sought inclusive education, believing it was Emily's constitutional right to be educated along with her peers. However, the neighbourhood school denied her that access, and the case eventually ended up in the Ontario Court of Appeal (*Eaton* v. *Brant County Board of Education* (1995), 22 O.R. (3d) 1, at 21 (Court of Appeal)). In that ruling, the Court found that the Ontario Education Act and particular regulations attached to the Act were unconstitutional under the equality rights provisions of the Canadian Charter of Rights and Freedoms, in that they did not require that school boards protect Charter equality rights of children with disabilities to be educated with their peers in the regular education environment. Justice Arbour, writing the judgement for the court, rejected the arguments of the Special Education Tribunal, which had argued that Emily could not be accommodated in a regular class. She found that

> Inclusion into the main school population is a benefit to Emily because without it, she would have fewer opportunities to learn how other children work and how they live. And they will not learn that she can live with them, and they with her.

On the basis of this and additional arguments that pedagogical theories can be inherently exclusionary and on that basis questionable, she found that

> In short, the *Charter* requires that, regardless of its perceived pedagogical merit, a non-consensual exclusionary placement be recognised as discriminatory and not resorted to unless alternatives are proven inadequate.

However, Emily did not find her way into the regular classroom on the basis of this judgement. The Board of Education appealed the case to the Supreme Court of Canada, which was less certain that constitutional equality guarantees had been compromised in the decision of the Special Education Tribunal. In fact, Justice Sopinka, writing the judgement for the Supreme Court, found, unlike the Court of Appeal ruling, that integration can be either a benefit or a burden, depending on whether the individual can profit from the advantages that integration provides (para. 69). The Court was convinced by the evidence presented by the tribunal that integration was not possible for Emily, nor that it served her well. It ruled without hearing evidence about the years of Emily's successful integration in a separate school.

Justice Sopinka also argued that the stereotypes which often underlie discrimination on the basis of race or sex did not apply in this case, in effect because people with disabilities *really do* have characteristics that make them different from others. This, he argues, is not actually the case with sex and race differences; it is only the stereotypes that make it appear so. In so constructing the argument, he not only institutes an ontology of disability as a difference inherent to the individual, but diminishes the role that stereotypes have played in marginalizing people with disabilities and preventing them from attending regular schools. Some have argued, from the perspective of a social model of disability, that the stereotypes have become so institutionally entrenched in the case of disability that their application goes entirely unnoticed; the Supreme Court ruling in this instance may well be a good example of such entrenchment. The Court of Appeal ruling was an institutional acknowledgement that discrimination on the basis of disability is rooted in the assumptions of pedagogical theory, statutory law and social constructs of disability. The result of the Supreme Court ruling may act to continue the long-standing denial that such is the case: disability really is a difference that may require exclusion in the name of a person's best interests. As the tribunal argued, and as the Supreme Court allowed:

- Emily was not benefiting by being in the regular class;
- she was effectively isolated (or educated) in that setting;
- the experience of integration was actually harmful to her;
- it is in her best interests to be in a special class.

These are precisely the arguments that the backlasher uses. In other words, Emily got caught in the fight against equality. While the decision has a significant impact on disability equality, particularly for access to education for children with disabilities, the case was not all bad (see Endicott 1977 for an interpretation of the case). In holding against Emily in that particular case, it provided guidance in terms of inclusive education. The *Eaton* decision holds that the norm for deciding on the placement of children with disabilities is integration, thereby placing the responsibility on a school board to justify its action in excluding a child from the regular classroom. (See Lepofsky (1997) for a discussion of the court's distinction between a norm of integration and a presumption in favour of integration and for his analysis of the impact of the *Eaton* decision generally.)

Importantly, it also provides guidance on the meaning of equality. The test for discrimination for Section 15(1) of the Charter remains: that if, based on disability, you are treated in legislation or by the practice of governmental agency in a manner that disadvantages you relative to persons who do not have a disability, then your equality rights are violated. It further held that:

> Exclusion from the mainstream of society results from the construction of a society based solely on mainstream attributes to which the disabled will never be able to gain access. It is the failure to make reasonable accommodation, to fine-tune society so that its structures and assumptions do not prevent the disabled from participation, which results in discrimination against the disabled.
>
> (Eaton, para: 69)

That equality incorporates the notion of reasonable accommodation and affirmative action is important for ensuring disability equality rights. So there are gains and there are losses as equality rights advocates are confronted by those who oppose them.

Significantly, on the international scene, one month after that court decision in Canada, the Supreme Court of Costa Rica (the Fourth Room), ruled that all students with disabilities must not only be included but must be allowed to graduate with their peers.

The human spirit

Despite disturbing trends and backlash, the human spirit overcomes many things. We can find examples throughout the world where human rights and disabilities have been linked and opportunities created to ensure inclusion in schools, in communities, in movements and in making changes to social and economic policies. It is in these cases where the myopia and opposition of the backlashers gets defeated.

For example, in April 1996, in Nicaragua, veterans who had a disability, some of whom were former Contras and some of whom were former Sandinistas, came together because they realized they might have something in common. They recognized that what kept them from exercising their citizenship rights was the same thing that blocked other persons with disabilities from achieving equality. So they decided that not only did they have to work together – the disabled Sandinistas and Contras – but they had to work with all people who had a disability and other equality-seeking groups. And they concluded that inclusion of all marginalized groups is a prerequisite to peace, which is their goal.

Another example was found in a university course run by the University of Guyana in Surinam. The course, in social development, is based on a human rights approach to understanding disability, and each student is required to do a community development project as part of their requirements. SCCOPE, which stands for Services and Communities Creating Opportunities for People with Disabilities through Equality, is a Social Development Certificate Programme designed to provide the students with a human rights approach to understanding disability. It was developed jointly by Mount Royal College, CAMRODD and the Roeher Institute between 1994 and 1995. To date, it has been given by the University of Guyana in Guyana and Surinam and the University of West Indies in Trinidad, Barbados and Curacão. Several years ago a student from Surinam, who runs an SOS village (communities for children who have been abandoned by their families), recognized that the SOS communities had never included children with disabilities and as his community development project for the course, he set out to ensure that some children with disabilities became part of the village. He spent months convincing the board and the community to do this as a matter of human rights. He was successful in integrating several children in the village, only to realize that the school they were attending was unable to provide a real education for them. He went back to the drawing boards – to have inclusion in the community meant having a school with the ability to teach all children, including those who had intellectual disabilities. The village has now incorporated Montessori methods into its classrooms. He could not achieve his goal by simply including the children; it required, as we well know, that there be systemic change, change that benefited all the children.

A mother in Barbados, having taken a course in leadership development in human rights and disability, went back home and went to the principal of the school in her neighbourhood and explained that from now on both of her children would be attending the school – the one who had always been there and the one with a disability who had never been allowed in. She argued that race could not keep her out and neither would disability. The child has been there for nearly six years and has become an insider.

Canadian courts and the Canadian public have come down on all sides of the inclusive education issue. While disability, either mental or physical, is clearly a prohibited ground of discrimination in human rights law and a ground for equal entitlement and equal benefit both before and under the law within the Constitution, this has not necessarily resulted in children being in their neighbourhood schools. Children with disabilities are expected to prove that they can benefit from the educational system, as it is structured, if they are to be included in the system. Non-disabled children are not similarly asked to prove they will succeed before being given the opportunity to try. And it is this inherent contradiction which faces every student with a disability as he or she enters the regular classroom. If these students fail, it simply reinforces the belief that they would do better in a segregated setting – a special class or a designated school with an alternate curriculum. And the teacher, the school board and indeed the government do not agree that they have an obligation to ensure that these children succeed. In this way education can become a private responsibility for children with disabilities and their families.

However, the public education system (the state system of schools) has developed and changed in many significant ways in the past 50 years. Starting with an era when children with disabilities were considered ineducable or not worthy of education, Canada moved in the 1950s and 1960s to a system of special schools and classes, run by families and charities at first, then funded by governments as part of the education expenditures. Despite its advantages over the social isolation, it still meant that students with disabilities were not attending school along with their non-disabled peers. In the 1970s, there was a shift towards the philosophy of integrated education – or at least education in the least restrictive environment, a model which promoted the rights of all children to an education to reach their full potential, full public financing for all students and the integration of students for as long as possible. The inclusion movement emerged in the mid-1980s. It proposed a single, holistic system of education, based on the premise that all children, not just those with disabilities, have different learning needs which can and should be accommodated. It mandated flexibility, innovation and adequate resources in classrooms and schools to enable the teachers and students to receive the support and assistance needed to teach and learn effectively.

Every province and territory in Canada has an Education Act or Schools Act that governs the provision of education at the primary and secondary levels. These Acts differ in their definition of disability in an educational context, and they are subject, as has been shown in this chapter, to the interpretation of the courts. Most of this legislation is permissive, meaning that it allows, but does not require, school districts and school boards to include students with disabilities in the regular classrooms. This ambiguity has led to legal, social and practical confusion about how educators and school districts interpret their responsibilities. This is further influenced by the political and economic issues, which drive the education agenda.

There are components of inclusive education which have an agreed currency in the Canadian experience. Inclusive education is the situation where students attend regular classes with similarly aged non-disabled peers in their neighbourhood school or a school of the family's choosing; the classroom teacher is responsible for students' education; curriculum is appropriately adapted to suit the student but the student follows a curriculum and instructional programme similar to the other students; diverse instructional methods are applied; there is widespread collaboration among teachers and other professionals within the classroom; and the student is included in the social life of the school (see Roeher Institute 1996b).

Inclusion in Canada now extends beyond the primary and secondary levels and incorporates education at the post-secondary level (see Roeher Institute 1996a) and into inclusive literacy (see Roeher Institute 1989). Recent thinking has evolved to suggest that an appropriate definition of literacy is 'literacy as communication', which theorizes that inclusion has to extend to the way communication is designed. Literacy in this interpretation goes beyond reading and writing and even the broader definition of critical literacy. It includes the concept that literacy is about having the status in society to have one's particular forms of communication acknowledged (see Roeher Institute 1999).

All of these are positive moves. Recently, a major Canadian university collapsed its special education programme into its regular teacher training degree, on the argument that every teacher had to be a special education teacher. It is those moves that create the optimism, as do the many students with disabilities who are included in the regular classes in their neighbourhood schools with the support they need to follow the curriculum and to be involved in the social life of the school.

Inclusive education, like other issues related to disability, is a barometer. It reflects the degree to which there has been fundamental movement towards a recognition of human rights. The backlash we feel is not just the backlash towards inclusive education but a statement of the level of resistance to equality more generally. We should call this claim for what it is: a position that would withhold from some the social, economic and political citizenship rights that bind schools, other communities, nations and communities of nations together. It is also a refusal to acknowledge that achieving equality need not be a zero-sum game. Only with such an acknowledgement can we, as Justice Arbour so well puts it, learn that we can live together.

Fortunately, there are people throughout the world who are willing, as there have been in other civil rights and human rights struggles, to stand up and demand the equal access to the political, civil, economic and social rights of citizenship to which they are entitled. The pressure that disability brings to complacent systems forces changes that radically transform the underlying framework within which societies have so comfortably operated. It raises inescapable dilemmas, which cannot be ignored, but which need not lead to false antagonisms that are the bread and butter of the backlashers. The dilemmas can be resolved if we accept that greater equality and well-being will come only with a respectful dialogue about our differences, real and perceived; and an acknowledgement that when it comes to citizenship rights we are fundamentally the same.

Throughout New Brunswick, Canada, where every child is integrated by law into neighbourhood schools, and in many progressive schools in other parts of the country, non-disabled students and their families have become the greatest advocates for inclusion. They recognize that through inclusion they learn what children should be learning in schools – that people are no less equal because they are different – and kids with disabilities are just kids.

Questions

1 Questions about the inclusion of children with disabilities have raised issues in law, ethics and policy in Canada about how this will impact on non-disabled children. If a society like Canada maintains that every child is entitled to learn, then what evidence would sustain an argument that this particular group of children can be kept out of their neighbourhood schools without trampling on their human right?
2 Are the arguments for keeping children with disabilities out of their neighbourhood schools anything more than an admission that pedagogical theory is a failed methodology, in that educators simply do not know how to individualize their teaching?
3 How important are the international economic agendas of globalization and international competitiveness to the local issue of children with disabilities getting into neighbourhood schools with their peers or being given opportunities to learn? Is the increasing emphasis on the economic contribution of individuals and the measurement of individuals in economic terms acting as a deterrent to inclusive education?

Acknowledgement

I would like to thank Michael Bach for his helpful comments on this chapter.

References

Endicott, O. (1997) *Emily Eaton's Case in the Supreme Court of Canada: a Critical Commentary*. Unpublished.

Lepofsky, M. D. (1997) A report card on the Charter's guarantee of equality to persons with disabilities after 10 years. What progress? What prospects?, *National Journal of Constitutional Law*, 7(3): 263.

Lipset, S. M. and Rabb, E. (1970) *The Politics of Unreason: Right-wing Extremism in America, 1790–1970*. New York: Harper & Row.

Mahoney, K. (1996) Is there a backlash to human rights?, in T. A. Cromwell *et al.* (eds) *Human Rights in the 21st Century: Prospects, Institutions and Processes*. Ottawa: Canadian Institute for the Administration of Justice.

Porter, G. L. and Richler, D. (eds) (1991) *Changing Canadian Schools: Perspectives on Disability and Inclusion*. North York, Ontario: Roeher Institute.

Rioux, M. H. (1996) Overcoming the social construction of inequality as a prerequisite to quality of life, in R. Renwick, I. Brown and M. Nagler (eds) *Quality of Life in Health Promotion and Rehabilitation: Conceptual Approaches, Issues, and Applications*. Thousand Oaks, CA: Sage.

Roeher Institute (1989) *Literacy and Labels: a Look at Literacy Policy and People with Mental Handicaps*. North York, Ontario: Roeher Institute.

Roeher Institute (1996a) *Building Bridges: Inclusive Post-secondary Education for People with Intellectual Disabilities*. North York, Ontario: Roeher Institute.

Roeher Institute (1996b) *Disability, Community and Society: Exploring the Links*. North York, Ontario: Roeher Institute.

Roeher Institute (1999) *Connecting the Points: Literacy, Communication and Inclusion*. North York, Ontario: Roeher Institute.

Sachs, A. L. (1996) Human rights in the twenty first century: real dichotomies, false antagonisms, in T. A. Cromwell *et al.* (eds) *Human Rights in the 21st Century: Prospects, Institutions and Processes.* Ottawa: Canadian Institute for the Administration of Justice.

Staples, B. (1997) Special education is not a scandal, *New York Times* magazine, September 21.

 **7**

Disability, human rights and education: the United States

Alan Gartner and Dorothy Kerzner Lipsky

Overview

In the United States, provision of education to students with disabilities encompasses issues of: educational services to children and youth; federal–state relationships; the rights of parents of children with disabilities; pedagogy; ways of conceptualizing disability; and civil and human rights. It is our belief that the order of listing represents the priorities that have been given to these issues over the past several decades. In keeping with the unique perspective of this book, this chapter will give particular attention to the last two factors, the ways of conceptualizing disability and civil and human rights. It will do so, of necessity, in the context of paying attention to the other factors as well. Analysis of the newly reauthorized Individuals with Disabilities Education Act (IDEA) (PL 105-17) will provide a vehicle for addressing these issues.

Introduction

While free public education for all is often thought of as a hallmark of American society, in fact across the course of United States history female children, children of the poor, children of the 'wrong' religion, children of immigrant parents, and children of colour were excluded from the public schools of one or another state.[1] While over the course of time the exclusion of each of these groups was ended, for children with disabilities it was only in the third quarter of the twentieth century that their exclusion came to an end. Illustratively, Gilhool (1997) cites the following provisions of the Pennsylvania School Code.

> Temporary or permanent exclusion from the public schools of children who are found to be uneducable and untrainable in the public schools . . .

When a child is thus certified the public schools shall be relieved of the delegation of providing education or training for such child.

A board of school directors may refuse to accept or retain beginners who have not attained a mental age of five years. Exceptions for compulsory attendance: Any child who . . . has been found to be unable to profit from further school attendance and who has been reported to the board of school directors and excused.

These provisions were overturned in 1972, in *Pennsylvania Association for Retarded Children (PARC)* v. *Commonwealth of Pennsylvania*, in which Gilhool was counsel for the plaintiffs.

The attitudes that led to such policies gained momentum in the first decades of the twentieth century. For example, using the newly developed Binet IQ test, on behalf of the United States Public Health Service, H. H. Goddard tested those arriving at Ellis Island. He found in 1913 that 79 per cent of the Italians were feeble-minded, as were 80 per cent of the Hungarians, 83 per cent of the Jews and 87 per cent of the Russians (cited in Gilhool 1997: 268). In the same era, Jim Crow laws were established across the south, and 'negroes and immigrants were lumped together as inassimilable aliens' (Stampp, cited in Gilhool 1997: 268).

Nearly half a century later, John W. Davis, counsel for the defendant South Carolina school district in *Brown* v. *Board of Education*, again linked race and disability:

if the appellants' construction of the Fourteenth Amendment should prevail here, there is no doubt in my mind that it would catch the Indian within its grasp just as much as the Negro. If it should prevail, I am unable to see why a state would have the right to segregate . . . on the ground of sex or on the ground of age or on the ground of mental capacity.

With the passage in 1975 of PL 94-142, The Education for All Handicapped Children Act, Davis's fear was realized, as concerns students with disabilities. That law, as its title states, required states[2] to assure that all handicapped children receive a 'free appropriate public education'.

Lisa Walker (1987: 98–102), a key Congressional staff person in the writing of PL 94-142, identified the following nine basic principles of the law:

1 Establishes the right of access to public education programmes.
2 Requires the individualization of services to alter automatic assumptions about disability.
3 Establishes the principle that disabled children need not be removed from regular classes.
4 Broadens the scope of services provided by schools.
5 Establishes a process for determining the scope of services.
6 Establishes general guidelines for the identification of disability.
7 Establishes principles for primary state and local responsibility.
8 Clarifies lines of authority for educational services.
9 Moves beyond staffing and training of personnel.

With a somewhat different emphasis, Gilhool (1997: 270–1) identifies the following five crucial requirements of PL 94-142:

1 Parental direction of their child's education.
2 The integration imperative.
3 The requirement that schools know and adopt 'effective' and 'promising' practices.
4 Effective early education.
5 A 'zero-reject' system.

Although Karst (1977: 6) was not addressing PL 94-142 (he was writing about the 1976 term of the Supreme Court), he identified the human rights issues that concern us here. He wrote:

> The principle of equal citizenship presumptively insists that the organised society treat each individual as a person, one who is worthy of respect, one who 'belongs.' Stated negatively, the principle presumptively forbids the organised society to treat an individual either as a member of an inferior or dependent caste or as a non-participant.

In the quarter of a century since the passage of PL 94-142, access to a free appropriate public education has been achieved for (nearly) all students with disabilities; less so has been the achievement of beneficial outcomes and full participation. A part of the law since its inception, the emphasis on standards and what increasingly is termed as 'inclusive education'[3] has come to the fore with the reauthorization of the Individuals with Disabilities Education Act (IDEA) in 1997.[4] Before addressing the new law, we turn to consideration of ways of understanding disability.

Ways of thinking about disability

The lives of persons with impairments, especially children, are not set in fixed and immutable arcs but are open to a range of opportunities, limited less by the impairments than by societal attitudes. The determination of these attitudes is a consequence of the way people view others, including those with disabilities. Is it as deficit, implicit in the medical model and traditional special education? Or as difference? Or as alternative? Or in a socio-political context? Or in a civil or human rights formulation? Goffman (1963: 2) captured this point, stating, 'Society establishes the means of categorising persons and the complement of attributes felt to be ordinary and natural for members of each of these categories.' Responses to disability are not 'natural'; rather, they are invented, different at one time or another, from one culture or another, from the perspective of one discipline or another.

Disability as deficit

The most common formulation of disability incorporates a medical definition. 'From a medical vantage point, the problems of a disability arise almost exclusively from pathological impairments, or a physical or mental inability to perform so-called normal tasks' (Hahn 1997: 317).[5] This emphasis on science replaced a religious or moral interpretation of disability as either a curse or a legitimate object of charity.

Gleidman and Roth's (1980) critique of Erik Erikson's typology of human development makes clear the consequence of this formulation. 'If we are to apply this typology to people with disabilities', they point out, then we must 'approach disability by means of a deviance analysis, looking at the problems of the handicapped by identifying specific areas of potential deviance for each stage.' This requires, however, that we 'prejudge precisely those developmental questions about handicap which, above all others, require painstaking investigation' (p. 106). For example, they point to Erikson's formulation that the child's mastery of body functions, which is central to resolving issues of autonomy versus shame and doubt, remains an open issue for the adult with a disability who either lacks bladder control or is dependent on an attendant (or family member). Thus, quoting Erikson, 'There is an "infantile" quality to the way he [the adult with a disability] must assert mastery over his body. Like the young child who must call his mother for help, the physically handicapped person must sometimes relate to his own body by means of another (able-bodied) person' (Gleidman and Roth 1980: 107). Gleidman and Roth assert that one cannot approach the development of a child with disabilities 'on terms spelled out in advance by personality theories developed for able-bodied children and adults' (p. 113). Such an approach would be akin to studying the development of stages of people's moral growth with data drawn solely from males. The point is that before assuming 'facts' and drawing conclusions about a group, one must examine the reality of the group members' lives. Without disregarding the reality of an individual's impairment(s), increasingly the deficit model is under challenge.

Disability from an academic discipline perspective

Traditional academic disciplines provide differing lenses in examining disability:

> Psychological analyses tend to regard it [disability] as an individual experience, with an eye to understanding how physical and mental limitations interact with personality development.
>
> Economic analyses treat disability as a social position with its own income stream, much like a job, and seek to explain the extent to which individual choice determines the assumption of the disabled role.
>
> Sociological analyses focus on the institutions that treat, house, and manage disabled people, including families, schools, hospitals, and rehabilitation clinics, and above all, they examine disability as a stigmatised social status exploring the means by which stigma is created, maintained, and resisted.
>
> [A] political approach . . . explore[s] the meaning of disability for the state, the formal institutions of government, and the intellectual justifi-

cations that give coherence to their activities ... Why does the state create a category of disability in the first place, and how does it design a workable administrative definition?

(Stone 1984: 3–4)

The sociologist's concept of disability is based on a social construct, without which, Liachowitz (1988) argues, an examination of legislation is incomplete.

What is not accounted for is the fact that laws that deal with handicapped people reflect not only the political problems posed by conflicting interest groups, but also the views that biological deficiency confers social deficiency and that handicapped people deserve (perhaps desire) a place outside of the mainstream of society. Furthermore, useful legislative evaluations need to take into account the processes by which people who deviate from accepted physical norms are devalued and segregated and, as a result, disabled.

No one of these lenses is better than another; nor should one assume that these lenses, derived from Western academic disciplines, necessarily apply cross-culturally.

Disability as a human condition

The phrase 'impairment as a human constant' is both the title of a useful survey article (Scheer and Groce 1988) and the expression of reality. What varies is how over the course of history 'societies have defined what did and did not constitute a disability or a handicap' (Scheer and Groce 1988: 23). They note, for example, that while among the Incas persons with disabilities were sent outside the city on fiesta days, in Samoa persons with physical disabilities were included in ceremonial dancing.[6]

Contrasting the broader American society's views of various impairments with the Black community's attitude to sickle cell anaemia, Asch (1988: 87) comments on a position statement of the National Association for Sickle Cell Disease.

> Striking about the position statement is its matter-of-fact treatment of the topic. Its message; part of being black is knowing that a small percentage of individuals carry the gene for the trait and a smaller percentage have the disabling condition. The discussion neither exaggerates nor minimises the consequences of the condition. [S]uppose Down syndrome, cystic fibrosis, or spina bifida were depicted not as an incalculable, irreparable tragedy but as a fact of being human.

For example, on Martha's Vineyard, Massachusetts, which from the seventeenth century to the early part of the twentieth century was the home of the largest concentration of people who were deaf, disability was part of the normal context of society.

> Most Vineyarders remembered that those who were deaf regarded their inability to hear as a nuisance rather than an overwhelming problem.

Most, when pressed on the point, believed that local people, hearing or deaf, preferred to have hearing children, but the birth of a deaf child was regarded as a minor problem rather than a major misfortune.

(Groce 1985: 53)

This attitude was a function of the community's inclusion of persons with deafness, particularly through all persons learning sign language, thus addressing the impairment (absence of hearing) and not allowing it to become a handicap. Groce (1985: 4) reinforces the point.

> Although we can characterize the deaf Vineyarders as disabled, they certainly were not considered to be handicapped. They participated freely in all aspects of life in this Yankee community. They grew up, married, raised their families, and earned their living in just the same manner as did their hearing relatives, friends, and neighbours.

Disability as difference

Addressing disability in the context of American law, Minow (1990) views disability as difference. The 'dilemma of difference' occurs, she states, when

> programs . . . presume the status quo to be natural, good, or immutable, where the status quo assigns the label of difference and its burdens to some and refuses to make room for a range of human conditions. Reframing social experience to transcend the difference dilemma means challenging the presumption that one either is the same or one is different, either one is normal or one is not.

(Minow 1990: 95)

It is in the concept of social experience that the consequence of the difference formulation is expressed. Rather than treating difference as inherent in the 'different' individual, a social relations approach moves the focus from the individual to the social construction of differences. This new approach

> has its roots in a dramatic shift of attention during the twentieth century – across the sciences, social sciences, and humanities – toward relationships rather than to discrete items under observation. For many, this shift has brought a new focus on relationships between people within which individuals develop a sense of autonomy and identity. For others, the shift turns to the relationship between the knower and the known . . . Another topic of attention is the relationship between the parts and the wholes, and still another is the mutual dependency of theory and context. From work in relativity theory and the indeterminacy principle in physics to deconstructive strategies in literary interpretation, these relational concerns are occupying scholars in challenges to the assumptions of their fields.

(Minow 1990: 379–80)

The shift of focus from the individual to the social context can be seen in reviewing the options considered in providing services for Amy Rowley

(*Board of Education* v. *Rowley*, 102 S.Ct. 3034 (1982); see also Smith 1996), a student who is deaf. The school system 'assumed that the problem was Amy's; because she was different from other students, the solution must focus on her' (Minow 1990: 82). Implicit here was a conceptualization of teaching and learning that posited a one-to-one relationship between teacher and student: the teacher teaches and the student learns. Rather, one can conceptualize the class as a learning community and Amy as a collaborative worker with her classmates. This shifts the focus from Amy and the problem to the remedy, and involves all the students.

> After all, if Amy cannot communicate with her classmates, they cannot communicate with her, and all lost the benefit of exchange. Moreover, conducting the class in both spoken and sign language would engage all the students in the difficult and instructive experience of communicating across traditional lines of difference. All the students could learn to struggle with problems of translation and learn to empathise by experiencing first hand discomfort with an unfamiliar mode of expression. It would be educational for all of them to discover that all languages are arrangements of signs and to use group action to improve the situation of an individual.
>
> (Minow 1990: 84)

Recognizing the social nature of the problem and 'involving classmates in the solution affords a different stance toward the dilemma of difference: it no longer makes the trait of hearing impairment signify stigma or isolation but responds to that trait as an issue for the entire community' (Minow 1990: 84). The consequence not only involves the person with disabilities but also has consequences for the learning and perspectives of students without disabilities.

> When students in the majority avoid the experience of not being understood, or not understanding what others say, they fail to learn about the limits of their own knowledge. They miss a chance to discover the importance of learning another language. By their very comfort in the situation, they neglect the perspective of any student they consider different from themselves.
>
> (Minow 1990: 29)

Disability as alternative

Concepts concerning 'multiple intelligences' and individuals' 'jagged profiles' (i.e. 'intelligent' in some areas, not so in others) (Gardner 1983) have been blended with ideas about the unique characteristics of people with disabilities (Sacks 1995). Difference is then viewed not as deficit but as strength. Sacks described the views of a biologist, Temple Grandin, who has autism:

> She thinks that there has been too much emphasis on the negative aspects of autism and insufficient attention, or respect, paid to the

positive ones. She believes that, if some parts of the brain are faulty or defective, others are very highly developed – spectacularly so in those who have savant syndromes, but to some degree, in different ways, in all individuals with autism . . .

[M]oved by her own perception of what she possesses so abundantly and lacks so conspicuously, Temple inclines to a modular view of the brain, the sense that it has a multiplicity of separate autonomous powers or 'intelligences' – much as the psychologist Howard Gardner proposes in his book *Frames of Mind*. He feels that while the visual and musical and logical intelligences, for instance, may be highly developed in autism, the 'personal intelligences,' as he calls them – the ability to perceive one's own and others' state of mind – lag grossly behind.

(Sacks 1995: 290)

The balance of loss and enhancement among other groups of people with disabilities has been described by Sacks (1995: 140):

It has been well established that in congenitally deaf people (especially if they are native signers) some of the auditory parts of the brain are reallocated for visual use. It has also been well established that in blind people who read Braille the reading finger has an exceptionally large representation in the tactile parts of the cerebral cortex . . . it seems likely that such . . . differentiation of cerebral development would follow the early loss of a sense and the compensatory enhancement of other senses.

The concept of enhancement is of particular importance to education. According to A. R. Luria (cited in Sacks 1995: xvii),

A handicapped child represents a qualitatively different, unique type of development . . . If a blind or deaf child achieves the same level of development as a normal [*sic*] child, then the child with a defect [*sic*] achieves this *in another way, by another course, by other means* [emphasis in the original]; and, for the pedagogue, it is particularly important to know the uniqueness of the course along which he must lead the child. This uniqueness transforms the minus of the handicap into the plus of compensation.

There is a parallel between the views of Sacks (1995: xvi), who found that 'defects, disorders, diseases . . . can play a paradoxical role, by bringing out latent powers, developments, evolutions, forms of life, that might never have been, or even be imaginable, in their absence', and thus have their own 'creative' potential, and those of Longmore (1995: 6), who saw accommodations such as architectural modifications, adaptive devices and services as merely 'different modes of functioning'. Longmore saw these differing modes as 'not inherently inferior', and Sacks (1995: xx), writing in much the same vein, contended that the different states of being 'are no less human for being different'.

Disability in a socio-political context

The socio-political approach views disability as a consequence of the interaction between individuals and the environment. Thus, disability is no longer seen as a personal deficit or deficiency; instead, it is primarily the product of a disabling environment. The emerging field of disability studies,[7] based on the experiences of people with disabilities, contributes a significant dimension to understanding disability and developing a pedagogy appropriate to the learning of students with disabilities. The field borrows from a minority group paradigm, and civil rights work in the 1960s, thereby linking the experience of persons with disabilities with that of other minorities, e.g. African-Americans and Latinos, language and religious minorities, gays and lesbians. As with those groups, there is the inequality faced by persons with disabilities,[8] which can be traced to public attitudes (Hahn 1996). Hahn further argues that as all aspects of the environment are fundamentally shaped by public policy, changes in the life condition of people with disabilities are a function of such policies. For example, it is the decision not to have ramps or kerb cuts that denies accessibility.

This perspective argues for 'the need to alter the educational environment rather than to pursue continuous efforts to modify the functional characteristics of disabled students' (Hahn 1994: 9). Echoing the language of race relations, he further stated: 'Since separation on the basis of disability is apt to leave an enduring imprint on the hearts and minds of disabled young people, desegregation or inclusion is a fundamental component of this process' (*ibid.*). Morris (1990: 53) similarly contended that

> People's expectations of us are informed by their previous experience of disabled people. If disabled people are segregated, are treated as alien, as different in a fundamental way, then we will never be accepted as full members of society. This is the strongest argument against special schools and against separate provision.

With some whimsy (and tartness), Hahn (1997: 321) applies what he calls the principle of 'equal environmental adaptations' to the matter of chairs in the classroom.

> Chairs are an accommodation to the needs of [physically] nondisabled students; but they are of no value to many disabled persons, such as myself, who are considerate enough to bring our own chairs. Without chairs, nondisabled students would undoubtedly become fatigued from standing or sitting on the floor, they would probably be discouraged from attending classes, and their performance on tests and other evaluation might be adversely affected.

Disability as a rights issue

In Canada, Section 15 of the Charter of Rights and Freedoms, adopted in 1982, attempts to provide a balance between equality and attention to difference. It states,

1 Every individual is equal before and under the law and has the right to equal protection and equal benefit of the law without discrimination and, in particular, without discrimination based on race, national or ethnic origin, colour, religion, sex, age, or mental or physical disability.
2 Subsection (1) does not preclude any law, program, or activity that has as its object the amelioration of conditions of disadvantaged individuals or groups including those that are disadvantaged because of race, national or ethnic origin, colour, religion, sex, age, or mental or physical disability.

Addressing the balance of equity in the context of disability, Funk (1987: 24), a founder of the Disability Rights Education and Defence Fund (DREDF), wrote:

> The concepts of equal opportunity and integration must be based on the reality of the differing needs and potential of people who are disabled. Thus equal opportunity must be defined as providing each individual with the chance to achieve, to develop [his or her] abilities and potential to the fullest.

The Salamanca Statement and Framework for Action on Special Needs Education

This statement (UNESCO 1994), adopted by representatives of 92 governments and 25 international organizations, addresses the topic of rights in the context of societal goals for all children. Noting that 'every child has a fundamental right to education', and that 'every child has unique characteristics, interests, abilities, and learning needs', the statement says, 'Those with special needs must have access to regular schools which accommodate them within a child-centred pedagogy capable of meeting these needs' (UNESCO 1994 vii–ix).

The statement then turns from goals to educational practice:

> Experience in many countries demonstrates that the integration of children and youth with special needs is best achieved within inclusive schools that serve all children within a community. It is within this context that those with special needs can achieve the fullest educational progress and social integration.
>
> *(ibid.*: 11)

The statement asserts that, as a result of a restructured educational system,

> Regular schools with this inclusive orientation are the most effective means of combating discriminatory attitudes, creating welcoming communities, building an inclusive society and achieving education for all; moreover they provide an effective education to the majority of children and improve the efficiency and ultimately the cost-effectiveness of the entire educational system.
>
> *(ibid.*: ix)

Significantly, the statement places educational policy in a broader framework:

> The trend in social policy during the past two decades has been to pro-
> mote integration and participation and to combat exclusion. Inclusion
> and participation are essential to human dignity and to the enjoyment
> and exercise of human rights. Within the field of education, this is
> reflected in the development of strategies that seek to bring about a gen-
> uine equalisation of opportunity.

> *(ibid.*: 11)

The seven ways to understand disability, presented above, are analytic
schemes. While discrete for the purpose of conceptualization, in the world of
law and schooling the categories are not so separable. Indeed, the federal law
concerning the education of students with disabilities utilizes components of
each of these conceptualizations.

IDEA 1997

The fundamental principles incorporated in the 1997 reauthorization of The
Individuals with Disabilities Education Act (PL 105-17) have been present in
the federal law since its inception in 1975, as The Education for All Handicapped Children Act (PL 94-142). The central feature of the law is a rights
formulation; namely that all children with handicapping conditions are
entitled to a 'free appropriate public education'. This is the so-called 'zero-
reject' principle. This was disputed by special education professionals in the
debates prior to enactment of PL 94-142, and then contested by school districts after the law was passed, but the courts have held to the absolute standard that no child with a disability was to be excluded from the law's scope.[9]

Other key principles include the entitlement of parents to participate in the
decisions affecting their child(ren), also a rights matter; the requirement that
a programme be crafted to meet the child's individual needs; and the requirement that to the maximum extent possible students with disabilities be educated in the general education environment, with the necessary supplemental
aids and support services.[10]

In the two decades since the passage of PL 94-142, school districts across
the country have been successful in providing access to children and youth
with disabilities. Less successful have been the outcomes for these students[11]
and their education with same-age non-disabled peers.[12] Longitudinal
studies and research findings confirmed the experience of students, parents
and teachers that the design of separate general and special education systems was flawed and unequal. This has led many to champion a new model,
building on several principles: that students are more alike than different;
that with effective educational practices schools can educate well and
together a wider range of students with better outcomes for all; and that
separation is costly, a civil rights violation and itself a cause of limited outcomes for students.

Similar beliefs motivated the administration and the Congress in delibera-
tions concerning the reauthorization of the law. Culminating a two year
process, IDEA (PL 105-17) emphasizes two major principles:

1 That the education of students with disabilities should produce outcomes
   akin to those expected for students in general education.
2 That they should be educated with their non-disabled peers. These features
   are expressed in the law's 'findings' section, its implementation provisions
   and the funding provisions.

Findings[13]

The Congress asserted that the education of students with disabilities would
be made more effective by 'having high expectations for students and ensuring their success in the general curriculum'; '[ensuring] that special education
can become a service for such children rather than a place where they are
sent'; and 'providing incentives for whole school approaches'. The House and
Senate reports that accompany the law highlight the primary purpose of the
new Act as going beyond access to the schools, to secure for every child an
education that yields successful results.

Implementation

Here, there are two sets of requirements that will have direct consequences
for students: those concerned with student evaluation and those involving
instruction and its assessment. In considering whether a student is to be classified as having a disability and requiring special education services, schools will
be required to consider whether there are factors other than disability affecting a child's performance. Specifically, the law states that a child may not be
identified as a child with a disability if the determining factor for such labelling
is the inadequacy of instruction in reading or mathematics. In other words, if
the failure is in the school's services, then the remedy is not labelling the child
but fixing the school's programme. Additionally, referral is not to be made if
based on the student's limited proficiency in English.

IDEA consistently reinforces the expectation that the child with a disability
will be educated in the general education environment. If the student is, or
may be, participating in the general education programme, the team which
determines the child's programme must include a general education teacher.
The rationale for the participation of the general education teacher is to bring
to the process someone familiar with the general education curriculum,
which is to be the basis of the student's programme.

Should the school district propose that the child with a disability not participate with non-disabled students in academic, extracurricular or non-
academic activities, such non-participation must be specifically justified.
Supplemental aids and support services in the general education environment
and in the general education curriculum are to be considered the norm;

exclusion in any of these areas must be explained and justified. Only then may other placements be considered.

Performance goals drawn from what is expected of students in general education in the state must be developed for all students with disabilities. Performance indicators to assess achievement of these goals must be developed, with necessary adaptations and modifications. The results of the performance of students with disabilities must be incorporated in the school's and district's public reports. This is a requirement for all schools and covers all students.

Funding

While the federal law is governing, funding for special education is largely a matter of state and local resources.[14] Historically, the formulae used by states to provide funds to local school districts have favoured placing students in more (rather than less) restrictive environments (Parrish 1997). IDEA 1997 requires that states change their funding formulae to remove incentives for placing students in more restrictive settings. This will require changes in all but a handful of states. The previous provision that IDEA funds may not be used to benefit non-disabled students has been rescinded. Given that general education teachers will have a major role in providing services to students with disabilities, IDEA personnel preparation funds may be used to train them. In language accompanying the appropriations bills, the Congress has emphasized that the substantial new funds allocated are to be used for such activities.

Implementing inclusive education programmes

The provisions of IDEA 1997 take effect in school year 1998–9. Inclusive education programmes, however, have been implemented for nearly a decade and that experience provides a basis for looking to the future.

A national study of the implementation of inclusive education programmes was conducted by the National Center on Educational Restructuring and Inclusion (NCERI 1994, 1995). From one year to the next (1994 to 1995), the number of districts reporting inclusive education programmes tripled, to nearly a thousand. Data in the *National Study* (1994, 1995) and a growing body of research (see Lipsky and Gartner 1997, especially Chapter 14, for a summary of these reports) indicate that well implemented inclusive education programmes benefit both disabled and non-disabled students, academically, behaviourally and socially. While districts vary as to the number and disability category of students who are in the 'inclusive education' programmes, data in the *National Study* (1994, 1995) indicate that school districts can effectively include students with each of IDEA's 13 categories of disability, at all levels of severity. While there are more inclusive education programmes at the elementary level, there are an increasing number of successful inclusive education programmes at the middle and high school levels involving older children.

Analysis of reports from school districts implementing inclusive education programmes indicate that there are seven factors which account for successful programmes.[15] They are:

1 *Visionary leadership.* This leadership can come from many sources, including school superintendents, building administrators, teachers, parents, school board members, disability advocates and universities. Regardless of the initial source of leadership, for inclusive education programmes to be successful all stakeholders must take responsibility for the outcome.

2 *Collaboration.* In the process of inclusive education, the collaboration is of three types: (a) between general and special educators; (b) between classroom practitioners and related services providers; (c) between those involved in student evaluation and programme development and classroom practitioners. Time for collaboration is an important variable.

3 *Refocused use of assessment.* The traditional screening for separate special education programmes must be replaced by assessment that is more authentic, addresses student strengths as well as their difficulties and provides useful guidance for classroom practitioners. Adapted methods to assess student knowledge must be developed and utilized. Called into question is the use of traditional measures of potential (such as IQ tests), rather than curriculum-based assessment. When screening is no longer used to determine a separate 'place' for the special education student to be educated, but rather to determine the supplemental services to be provided in the general education classroom, curricular approaches are more often used.

4 *Supports for staff and students.* Essential factors are time for school staff to collaborate and the provision of effective professional development programmes. Staff development must be sensitive to the needs of adult learners and involve ongoing classroom based experiences. Supports for students should include the full panoply of supplemental aids and support services that the law mandates, e.g. curricular modifications, alternative instructional strategies, adapted assessment measures and procedures, use of technology, roles for para-professionals and other support personnel.

5 *Appropriate funding levels and formulae.* School districts report that after initial start-up costs for planning and professional development, a unitary system is not more expensive than operating separate special education programmes. If funds follow students with special needs into the general education classroom, these resources provide preventive services for students and enhanced learning opportunities for others, thereby making inclusive education cost-effective for all students. If, however, districts continue to operate an extensive dual system, this will be more costly.

6 *Parental involvement.* Since parental involvement is essential, schools report creative approaches to encourage them to become an integral part of the school community. This goes well beyond the procedural due process requirements of the law.

7 *Use of effective programme models, curricula adaptations and instructional strategies.* There is no single model of inclusion. Most common is the pairing of

a general education and special education teacher to work together, with general and special education students. At the middle school, a special education teacher often becomes a part of the grade team. In some schools, a special education teacher serves as a 'consultant' to several general education teachers, in whose classes students with disabilities are included. Increasingly districts are seeking teachers who are dual licensed, and can themselves teach an inclusive classroom.

Often, special education teachers report their lack of knowledge of the general education curriculum, while general education teachers report their lack of knowledge as to individualizing instruction. However, after a year of collaboration, both report greater knowledge and comfort in these areas. Not surprisingly, they use many of the same instructional strategies in the inclusive classroom that are effective for students in general classrooms. These include cooperative learning, 'hands on' learning, use of peer and cross-age tutoring and support models, recognition of students' multiple intelligences and adapting instruction to tap into them, use of technology integrated into the classroom and use of para-professionals and classroom assistants (not 'velcroed' to the individual child but serving the whole class).

Conclusion

The two essential principles expressed in the 1975 law, PL 94-142, are that:

- children with disabilities were to be treated as individuals worthy of respect (i.e. capable of benefiting from education);
- they were to be a part of the larger society (i.e. they were not to be segregated from their nondisabled peers).

The honouring of the first of these principles was at the root of the major debate as Congress deliberated. In the face of extensive testimony from special education professionals as to which students could (or could not) benefit from education, the Congress, more as a matter of belief than from a research base, declared and asserted in the law's title that 'all handicapped children' could benefit from an education. Thus, the guarantee was extended to all.

In keeping with the principle of treatment of each as an individual, the law provided that:

- each child was to be individually assessed as to whether he or she was handicapped and in need of special education services;
- an individually designed programme was to be developed for each child, which was to be documented in an individual education plan (IEP).

The principle that each belongs was expressed in the law's requirement that to the maximum extent students with disabilities were to be educated with their non-disabled peers, and that they were to be removed from regular classes only when they could not be educated in this setting with supplemental aids and support services.

The expression of human rights in the education of students with disabilities is seen in the honouring of the principles of respect and belonging. And in keeping with the understanding that disability must be seen in a social context, the implementation of these principles requires not simply individual adaptations but overall school restructuring.

Questions

1 What are the consequences of understanding disability in a human rights framework?
2 What is the nature of the tension between higher standards for all students and students with special needs being fully integrated into regular programmes?
3 Based upon the US experience, what are the pitfalls to avoid and successful strategies to be utilized in addressing issues of disability, human rights and education?

Notes

1 Public education is a state responsibility in the United States.
2 In light of the principle that education is a state responsibility, the law was constructed such that states had the option of participating. Within several years of the law's passage, all 50 states opted in.
3 The term 'inclusive education' appears neither in PL 94-142 nor in the reauthorized IDEA. Nor does the term 'mainstreaming' or 'integration'. What Gilhool (1997) calls the 'integration imperative' is expressed in the law's least restrictive environment (LRE) principle. We have defined 'inclusive education' as, 'Providing to all students, including those with significant disabilities, equitable opportunities to receive effective educational services, in age-appropriate classes in their neighborhood schools, in order to prepare students for productive lives as full members of society' (Lipsky and Gartner, 1995: 36).
4 In 1982, as part of the reauthorization of the law, it was renamed The Individuals with Disabilities Education Act.
5 The strength of this formulation is to be found throughout the field of services for persons with disabilities, both children and adults. Indeed, the medicalization of disability is at the root of the conceptual basis of the International Classification of Impairments, Disabilities, and Handicaps (ICIDH), published and used by the World Health Organization (Pfeiffer 1998).
6 For a fuller discussion of the responses of different cultural groups, see Gartner *et al.* (1992), especially Chapter 2.
7 The Society for Disability Studies, established in 1983 by the late Irving Kenneth Zola, is the field's 'professional' organization.
8 Hahn (1997) cites extraordinarily high rates of poverty, welfare dependency and

unemployment among persons with disability, as well as obstacles faced in transportation, communications, housing and public accommodation.

9 Contested, however, has been the extent of services to which students with disabilities were entitled, i.e. the nature and extent of a 'free appropriate public education'. See especially Smith (1996).

10 The term 'least restrictive environment' has been used to express this principle. Neither that term, nor the other similar terms (e.g. mainstreaming, integration or inclusion), appears in the law.

11 The failure in outcomes is reflected in student learning, graduation rates, dropout rates, continuation in post-secondary education and training, and community living. For a fuller discussion of these issues, see Lipsky and Gartner (1997), especially Chapter 2.

12 The most recent data from the US Department of Education reports that 55 per cent of children with disabilities, aged from six to 21, are served in other than regular classes. (US Department of Education 1997: Table AB1), despite the fact that greater than 71 per cent of the five million students with disabilities, aged from six to 21, served per IDEA in the 1995–6 school year, had the least severe impairments: learning disabilities (51 per cent) and speech or language impairments (20 per cent) (*ibid.*: Table II-6).

13 In major pieces of legislation, there is a 'findings' section, which presents the basis upon which the Congress is acting and offers a perspective on its overall philosophy.

14 PL 94-142 provided that the federal government would fund 40 per cent of the excess costs of special education services. In fact, the federal support has never exceeded 12 per cent; it came to little more than 8 per cent in the most recent fiscal year (US Department of Education 1997: Table I-2).

15 These are congruent with the findings of a Working Forum on Inclusive Schools convened by ten national organizations. (Council for Exceptional Children 1995).

References

Artilles, A. J. and Larsen, L. A. (eds) (1998) Special issue: International perspectives on special education reform, in *European Journal of Special Needs Education*, 13(1): 5–133.

Asch, A. (1988) Reproductive technology and disability, in S. Cohen and N. Taub (eds) *Reproductive Laws for the 1990s*. Clifton, NJ: Humana Press.

Council for Exceptional Children (1995) *Creating Schools for All Our Students: What Twelve Schools Have to Say*. Reston, VA: Council for Exceptional Children.

Funk, R. (1987) Disability rights: from caste to class in the context of civil rights, in A. Gartner and T. Joe (eds) *Images of the Disabled, Disabling Images*, New York: Praeger.

Gardner, H. (1983) *Frames of Mind: the Theory of Multiple Intelligences*. New York: Basic Books.

Garner, P. and Daniels, H. (eds) (1999) *The Worldbook of Education, 1999, Inclusive Education*. London: Kogan Page.

Gartner, A., Lipsky, D. K. and Turnbull, A. P. (1991) *Supporting Families with a Child with a Disability: an International Outlook*. Baltimore: Paul H. Brookes Publishing.

Gilhool, T. K. (1989) The right to an effective education: from *Brown* to PL 94-142 and beyond, in D. K. Lipsky and A. Gartner (eds) *Beyond Separate Education: Quality Education for All*. Baltimore: Paul H. Brookes Publishing.

Gilhool, T. K. (1997) The events, forces, and issues that triggered enactment of the

Education for All Handicapped Children Act of 1975, in D. K. Lipsky and A. Gartner (eds) *Inclusion and School Reform: Transforming America's Classrooms*. Baltimore: Paul H. Brookes Publishing.

Gliedman, J. and Roth, W. (1980) *The Unexpected Minority: Handicapped Children in America*. New York: Harcourt Brace Jovanovich.

Goffman, E. (1963) *Stigma: Notes on the Management of Spoiled Identity*. Englewood Cliffs, NJ: Prentice Hall.

Groce, N. (1985) *Everyone Here Spoke Sign Language: Hereditary Deafness on Martha's Vineyard*. Cambridge, MA: Harvard University Press.

Hahn, H. (1994) New trends in disability studies: implications for educational policy. Paper presented at the National Center on Educational Restructuring and Inclusion invitational conference on inclusive education, Racine, WI, 28 May.

Hahn, H. (1996) Anti-discrimination laws and social research on disability: the minority group perspective, *Behavioural Sciences and the Law*, 14: 41–59.

Hahn, H. (1997) New trends in disability studies: implications for educational policy, in D. K. Lipsky and A. Gartner (eds) *Inclusion and School Reform: Transforming America's Classrooms*. Baltimore: Paul H. Brookes Publishing.

Karst, K. (1977) The Supreme Court, 1976 term forward: Equal citizenship under the Fourteenth Amendment, *Harvard Law Review*, 91: 1–6.

Liachowitz, C. H. (1988) *Disability as a Social Construct: Legislative Roots*. Philadelphia: University of Pennsylvania Press.

Lipsky, D. K. and Gartner, A. (eds) (1989) *Beyond Separate Education: Quality Education for All*. Baltimore: Paul H. Brookes Publishing.

Lipsky, D. K. and Gartner, A. (1995) Common questions about inclusion: what does the research say?, *Exceptional Parent*, September.

Lipsky, D. K. and Gartner, A. (1996) Inclusion, school restructuring, and the remaking of American society, *Harvard Educational Review*, 66(4): 762–96.

Lipsky, D. K. and Gartner, A. (1997) *Inclusion and School Reform: Transforming America's Classrooms*. Baltimore: Paul H. Brookes Publishing Co.

Longmore, P. K. (1995) The second phase: from disability rights to disability culture, *Disability Rag and Resource*, September/October: 4–11.

Minow, M. (1990) *Making All the Difference: Inclusion, Exclusion, and American Law*. Ithaca, NY: Cornell University Press.

Morris, J. (1990) Progress with humanity? The experience of a disabled lecturer, in R. Reiser and M. Mason (eds) *Disability, Equality in the Classroom: A Human Rights Issue*. London: ILEA.

NCERI (1994) *National Study of Inclusive Education*. New York: National Center on Educational Restructuring and Inclusion, Graduate School and University Center, City University of New York.

NCERI (1995) *National Study of Inclusive Education*. New York: National Center on Educational Restructuring and Inclusion, Graduate School and University Center, City University of New York.

Parrish, T. B. (1997) Fiscal issues relating to special education inclusion, in D. K. Lipsky and A. Gartner (eds) *Inclusion and School Reform: Transforming America's Classrooms*. Baltimore: Paul H. Brookes Publishing.

Pfeiffer, D. (1998) The ICIDH and the need for its revision, *Disability and Society*, 13(4): 503–23.

Sacks, O. (1995) *An Anthropologist from Mars*. New York: Alfred A. Knopf.

Scheer, J. and Groce, N. (1988) Impairment as a human constant: cross-cultural and historical perspectives on variation, *Journal of Social Issues*, 44(1): 23–37.

Smith, R. C. (1996) *A Case about Amy*. Philadelphia: Temple University Press.

Stone, D. A. (1984) *The Disabled State*. New York: Russell Sage Foundation.

UNESCO (1994) *The Salamanca Statement and Framework for Action on Special Needs Education. World Conference on Special Needs Education: Access and Equality*. New York: UNESCO.

US Department of Education (1997) *Nineteenth Annual Report to Congress on the Implementation of The Individuals with Disabilities Education Act*. Washington, DC: US Department of Education.

Walker, L. (1987) Procedural rights in the wrong system: special education is not enough, in A. Gartner and T. Joe (eds) *Images of the Disabled, Disabling Images*. New York: Praeger.

⊖ 8

Special education and human rights in Australia: how do we know about disablement, and what does it mean for educators?

Roger Slee

Overview

Many educators fail to see educational disablement as an issue of human rights. For them, the education of the so-called 'special educational needs' student is a technical issue to be played out through a highly bureaucratized medical model of diagnosis and treatment which is described and pursued through a redistribution of resources and 'expert' personnel. That this is so is not surprising. Our understanding of disability has been shaped by an ensemble of powerful knowledge that establishes impairment as individual defect and disabled people as objects for treatment and research by professional experts. Knowing disability and disablement (Oliver, 1990) in education has not been responsive to the growing body of disability studies led by disabled researchers. For this reason understanding disablement in schools and other educational sites remains incomplete. Most importantly the knowledge, for too many educators, is not undergirded by an established principle of political struggle for 'rights of passage'.

Introduction

Prior to the formal announcement of the 3 October 1998 federal election in Australia, the political psyche seemed fixed on issues of 'race'. The confluence of a number of factors contributed to this disposition:

- The successes of the *Mabo and Ors* v. *The State of Queensland* (1992) and Wik High Court ruling (1996) that native title could coexist with pastoral rights and pastoral leases, which, in turn, led to subsequent state and federal native title legislation (Native Title Act 1993).

- The inevitable vitriolic backlash to such advances by the mining and pastoral industries and their conservative allies.
- The electoral success of Pauline Hanson and the One Nation Party, which stood on a platform of opposition to Asian immigration and Aboriginal land rights.
- The growing recognition of indigenous culture and the embracing of the Aboriginal political struggle by mainstream and youth popular culture (e.g. Archie Roach, Midnight Oil, Paul Kelly and Tiddas).
- The publication of the Report of the Royal Commission of Inquiry into Aboriginal Deaths in Custody and the Stolen Generation Report (HREOC 1997).

Since the declaration of the October election by Prime Minister John Howard, the polity has had its attention irresistibly redirected to questions of a goods and services tax (GST) and economic management.

It is worth returning to the ongoing process of reconciliation between the invading European Australians and the indigenous Aboriginal and Torres Strait Islander populations to consider the state of human rights for disabled Australians. Acknowledging his own European complicity, then Prime Minister Paul Keating (1992) declared that, 'We took the children from their mothers', and 'We had failed to ask – how would I feel if this were done to me?' (Beresford and Omaji 1998: 11). As part of the National Reconciliation, *sorry books* were installed around the country where citizens could sign up to a national apology and record their own thoughts about the residual impact of the European invasion and the dispossession of the Aboriginal people. The Lord Mayor of Brisbane, Cr Jim Sorely, hosted a Sorry Day celebration, where King George Square was the forum for a series of speeches and the official offering of an apology on behalf of the people of the City of Brisbane. The federal Liberal government has steadfastly refused to apologize lest it imply legal culpability, leading to litigation against the state. Although the polity has divided on this issue, questions of Aboriginal rights are being debated, and there has been a growing movement in support of indigenous people. Nevertheless, all the economic and social indicators, such as rates of incarceration, alcohol and substance abuse, infant mortality, health, housing, educational outcomes, unemployment and so on, depict a long way to go in making good our apology.

My point is a very simple one and it is not meant to diminish the centrality of questions of justice for Aboriginal people to, and the profound implications of native title for, Australia's human rights record. Nothing is gained from the creation of an artificial rivalry over who is the most oppressed. Gains accrue from alliances to advance human rights across a range of forms of disadvantage. It would seem that the very significant advances that have been hard fought for and won by indigenous people in Australia have not even registered on the Richter scale of public consciousness with respect to the rights of disabled people in Australia. Simply put, the struggles of marginalized and excluded groups of people, such as disabled people and Aborigines, may be recognized as a common struggle against abuses of power and the denial of human rights. Getting the Australian community to recognize this requires new disability knowledge.

There are some striking similarities between these marginalized people. Like Aboriginal Australians, disabled people (it is important to note that I use *disabled* as a verb) have a history of separation from their families (Morris 1997). Sometimes they are forcibly removed, sometimes separated out of fear of the stigma attracted by a disabled family member, and at other times because of the absence of support, but mostly on the basis of people being told what is 'in their best interest' by well meaning professionals (Potts and Fido 1991). Just as people of colour are essentialized and come to be 'known' according to pseudo-scientific knowledge of 'race', disabled people are the objects of the professional gaze (Foucault 1973; Rose 1989; Oliver 1996). Discourses have produced discrete and competing forms of knowledge of the 'disabled' (Fulcher 1989; Oliver 1996; Allen 1999). 'Science' claimed a *cure* for Aboriginality through miscegenation (Rowley 1972). The eugenics movement (Lewis 1993) and the pervasive politics of IQ rehearsed most recently by Herrnstein and Murray (1994) and robustly critiqued as 'measured lies' (Kincheloe *et al.* 1996), and now the medical world, hold out the hope of a cure for a disabled identity (Shapiro 1994). Ironically, medical progress has directly increased the numbers of disabled people (Shapiro 1994). Historically subjected to prejudice and loathing (Barnes 1996), disabled people are the object of ridicule, pity, charity and forced incarceration (Bogdan 1988; Gilman 1988; Hevey 1992). Unemployment rates for disabled people are disproportionately high (Australian Bureau of Statistics 1993), even when the doubtful existing measures are used (Gleeson 1998). This also applies to the UK (Barnes 1992) and the USA (Gans 1995). Disabled people have been exploited in sheltered workshops where they have been paid slave wages in return for the 'privilege of work'. It has been argued, in a debate conducted in the pages of the Australian Disability Review, that unfair wages are compensated for by giving disabled people meaning, by giving them something to do (Stern 1992, 1993). There is a history of forced sterilization, of segregated education, of restricted movement and differential status before the law. Generations have been stolen, imprisonment is disproportionately high, there are deaths in custody and community care is too frequently a euphemism for homelessness, starvation and death.

This must not be read as a competitive bid for sympathy. The point is simple. Disablement is just not recognized by middle Australia as a set of human rights questions. People do not acknowledge a 'politics of disablement' (Oliver 1990). Hence, it fails to make significant inroads into the Australian political agenda. What, then, are the roadblocks? How have they been constructed? Can they be dissembled and removed? How might this task be accomplished?

This chapter takes up these questions in relation to education, where human rights are routinely denied, albeit through a veil of ignorance and/or 'benevolent humanitarianism' (Tomlinson 1982). In the following section I will briefly explore the epistemological foundations of these human rights transgressions in education as a prelude to considering the maintenance of disabling forms of education. One cannot confront the task of theorizing disablement and its implications for education without addressing questions of voice, the non-disabled researcher and political activism. The final section takes up this challenge, suggesting that the quest for reconciliation extends beyond its present configuration.

Knowing the disabled: the politics of common and professional knowledge

Writing about the memorial service for disabled civil rights activist Timothy Cook, Joseph Shapiro (1994: 3) concluded that 'Nondisabled Americans do not understand disabled ones.' His conclusion was derived from the heartfelt tributes of Cook's non-disabled friends. ' "He never seemed disabled to me", said one. "He was the least disabled person I ever met", pronounced another.' Shapiro's analysis of this discourse is worth repeating.

> It was the highest praise these nondisabled friends could think to give a disabled attorney who, at thirty-eight years old, had won landmark disability cases, including one to force public transit systems to equip their buses with wheelchair lifts. But more than a few heads in the crowded chapel bowed with uneasy embarrassment at the supposed compliment. It was as if someone had tried to compliment a black man by saying, 'You're the least black person I ever met', as false as telling a Jew, 'I never think of you as Jewish', as clumsy as seeking to flatter a woman with, 'You don't act like a woman'.
>
> Here in this memorial chapel was a small clash between the reality of disabled people and the understanding of their lives by others. It was the type of collision that disabled people experience daily. Yet any discordancy went unnoticed even to the well-meaning friends of a disability rights fighter like Cook . . . taking pride in his disability was for Cook a celebration of the differences among people and gave him a respectful understanding that all share the same basic desires to be full participants in society.
>
> (Shapiro 1994: 3–4)

Shapiro's observation is certainly not new. Parents have related dozens of teachers' faux pas to me. While sometimes they laugh at the clumsy 'social stupidity', to coin Jules Henry's (1968) term, of 'educated' people who simply do not understand their children and the set of complex relationships that constitute impairment and social disablement, their pain is thinly veiled. I remember a teacher, and she was also the mother of a disabled child, in one of my policy classes expressing her private dismay to discover the 'teachers of my daughter' in the discourse of her class peers when they debated inclusive education. It was then that she told me that her daughter's teacher allowed her to prepare a costume for the child to take part in the school play. The teacher allowed the child to rehearse with all the other children, allowed the child to become excited about the prospect of her performance and then, on the evening of the performance, kept the child backstage while the other children presented the play. There was an explanation for the devastated parents: 'I didn't want her to feel bad about looking different.'

A school principal explained to a panel of inquiry, of which I was a member, that although he wanted an inclusive school, he could not admit a child in a wheelchair. Why? If he were to do so, in the event of evacuation if a bomb were planted in his school, the normal (not my word) kids would be stuck in the corridor behind the disabled child. I hasten to add that this was a school in rural Australia not well known as a target for international terrorism. A class of teachers once asked an advocate for inclusive education, 'What happens when we have classes of 20 kids who need to be toileted?' I'm not a student of probability, but such a scenario anywhere other than in a special school for the 'bladder impaired' would seem as unlikely as the explosion in the previous school.

A school in Queensland invoked the duty of care provisions of the Education Act to exclude a child with Down's syndrome because he was looking after himself after school. His mother, a sole supporting parent, was working when school was dismissed and arrived home later than her son. The Disability Discrimination Act was enlisted to establish the injustice of the school's stance. Rebecca Walsh (1993) describes the folly of a school counsellor assessing her IQ to determine whether she was going to be able to cope with integration in the class that she had been a member of since starting primary school some years earlier. It was thought that because her vision had seriously deteriorated and because she was now officially disabled the issue of integration presented itself as an option. The test applied to her was sight based! As she reflects with searing irony, she was indeed disabled by many of the supports provided 'in her best interest'. Her curriculum was narrowed, her social contacts were restricted and she was thrust into an unfamiliar environment. These were major impediments for her to overcome to enter and complete a tertiary education. Jenny Corbett (1993) has previously reflected upon the lowered expectations of special schooling as an educational suppressant.

So where do teachers, and others, get their ideas about disability? Typically they get them at a distance. Typically they get them from non-disabled people, from experts, from specialists. This is hardly surprising given that we have been subjected to an ignorance-inducing form of educational organization that pretends the sameness of the favoured student cohort and relegates 'others' to a segregated provision. Segregation is not always a question of physical location.

My own biography produces shameful memories. I recollect the way that my friends and I would break into a run as we passed Mullaratarong (many special centres were given Aboriginal names, but not I think as a sign of solidarity). It was necessary to run in order to avoid ending up like the kids inside. The mythology, an epistemic etching, exerted such power over us. Parents disabused us of the fear of contagion and adjusted our emotions to an attitude of pity. Thinking back, it now occurs to me that I never saw any of the kids inside behind their purpose-built high fences. The point was, we didn't need to, we had knowledge about them revolving around loose conceptions of illness, deformity and above all else 'abnormality'. As with all things, the issues were complicated by the range of dispositions on offer. Our fourth grade teacher was reading us the story of Douglas Bader at the time. This helped to establish the image of the heroic disabled person who overcame the tragedy of their disability and was not to be pitied. Mike Oliver (1996: 14–17) reflects upon the deleterious impact of such portrayals and cites alternative 'heroes' who suggest critical understandings of oppressive social relations.

Years later I received new intelligence, a new set of discourses on disability. Discursive practices have constructed the category, official knowledge and treatment (Foucault 1973) of the special educational needs student. This discourse continues to inform policy blueprints for inclusive education. I use 'discursive practices' following Foucault (1997) to reflect the complexity, discontinuities, contradictions and fragmentary nature of 'powerful knowledge' (Usher 1998) deployed in the regulation of, and thereby becoming the governmentality for, a fragmented population (Rose 1989). Again, turning to Foucault (1997: 11):

> Discursive practices are characterised by the demarcation of a field of objects, by the definition of a legitimate perspective for a subject of knowledge, by the setting of norms for elaborating concepts and theories. Hence each of them presupposes a play of prescriptions that govern exclusions and selections.

The field of special education has drawn heavily from medicine and psychology first to establish, and later to modernize, discourses of the 'backward child' (Burt 1937) or 'slow child' (Schonell 1942) as a subject for diagnosis and segregated educational treatment (Tomlinson 1982; Lewis 1993; Skidmore 1996). 'More often, it happens that a discursive practice brings together various disciplines or sciences, or it passes through a number of them and gathers several of their areas into a sometimes inconspicuous cluster' (Foucault 1997: 11). The power of traditional formulations of disability as defective individual pathology separated from political, cultural and historical specificity is ubiquitous.

> Discursive practices are not purely and simply modes of manufacture of discourse. They take shape in technical ensembles, in institutions, in behavioural schemes, in types of transmission and dissemination, in pedagogical forms that both impose and maintain them.
>
> (Foucault 1997: 12)

Fulcher (1989) and Skrtic (1991) observe the co-implication of the professional interests of the special education industry, teachers and administrators in regular schools, and machine bureaucracies. Embracing psycho-medical discourses for purposes of diagnosis and remediation, education workers also took on a bureaucratic discourse that fixed the 'special educational needs student' as a policy problem requiring a policy solution (Branson and Miller 1989). I have described elsewhere (Slee 1996) the resilience of special educators and psychologists in maintaining their traditional diagnostic and treatment job descriptions, albeit in regular educational settings and described within a fashionably inclusive discourse. Alongside of them are an expanding group of bureaucrats who apply professional 'ascertainment' of degree of impairment and disability to formulate the necessary resource allocations to ensure the inclusion, or is it assimilation, of the special needs student. There has been a comfortable fit between the discursive practices of special educators and psychologists and the bureaucratic discourse which defers to this form of knowledge about impairment and disablement to maintain the institutional equilibrium of schools (Slee 1998). This new calculus of distributive justice (Rawls 1972) fails to confront disablement as an issue of cultural politics (Young 1990; Yeatman 1994).

These discursive alliances remain largely untouched by the contribution of disabled researchers, and their non-disabled supporters, to critical sociological analyses of special education (Tomlinson 1982; Oliver 1985, 1987; Barton 1987). In a relatively recent analysis of theory in special education, Clark *et al.* (1995) suggest that 'imported theories', both psychological and sociological, are reductionist. Both, they contend, ignore educational complexities that impede theoretical foreclosure. Moreover, a psychological perspective fails to explicate its epistemological foundations, and sociology attenuates teaching in special education. Of course there is a difficulty, of which I have indeed been guilty, and that is the failure to avoid collapsing disciplines into particular genres or theorists therein.

This chapter maintains the importance of critical sociology for the advance of a human rights research agenda. Contrary to Clark and her colleague's criticism that sociological theorizing eschews the practical improvement of life in schools and classrooms, I argue the reverse. Added to this is the more reflexive disposition of sociological researchers (Gitlin 1995), and the subsequent embrace of respectful approaches to the people under the researcher's gaze. The importance of voice has been established in feminist (Weiner 1995) and anti-racist (Troyna 1993) research, but is something that continues to be suppressed in the special needs research agenda, as pointed out by Oliver (1992) and Clough and Barton (1995).

The point of commencement for disabled researchers' interrogations of education for disabled students is with the fundamental question of power and whether there is an abuse of it.

> When I moved from being a lecturer on disability to one on special education I was amazed at how similar the issues were and how similar were the experiences of users of special education to the users of other welfare services. All such services were, and still are, dominated by professionals who produce them, were patronising and failed to offer disabled people choice or control in their lives . . . the education system has failed disabled children in that it has neither equipped them to exercise their rights

as citizens nor to accept their responsibilities . . . the special education system has functioned to exclude disabled people not just from the education process but from mainstream social life.

(Oliver 1996: 79)

The routine denial of human rights through educational disablement is a structural feature of educational provision articulated through pedagogy, curriculum and the institutional arrangements of schooling. Education policy pivots on the pathologizing of failure as 'personal troubles' for defective students; the culpability of schooling in the 'social issue' (Wright Mills 1959) of educational failure is denied by dominant special educational discursive practices.

Just as overcoming the damaging impact of patriarchal schooling was not seized as an opportunity to make girls more masculine, anti-racist education is not to be confused with liberal expressions of multicultural education. bell hooks (1994: 31) proclaims this as 'the stuff of colonizing fantasy, a perversion of the progressive vision of cultural diversity', and cites an interview with Peter McLaren to further reject assimilationist imperatives:

> Diversity that somehow constitutes itself as a harmonious ensemble of benign cultural spheres is a conservative and liberal model of multiculturalism that, in my mind, deserves to be jettisoned because, when we try to make culture an undisturbed space of harmony and agreement where social relations exist within cultural forms of uninterrupted accords we subscribe to a form of social amnesia in which we forget that all knowledge is forged in histories that are played out in the field of social antagonisms.

So too for inclusive or enabling education. Supporting human rights for disabled people in education invites a politics of recognition and eschews oppressive forms of special educational knowledge. Parading a naive claim of being rational, apolitical and committed to educational progress, Jenkinson (1997: 218) fails to acknowledge a theoretical position that defers to experts and professionals and fails to provide space for disabled research voices. New ways of knowing disablement and impairment have emerged from disabled researchers which acknowledge the historical, cultural and material specificity of impairment (Abberley 1987), the personal experience of impairment (Morris 1992) and disablement (Oliver 1990). New forms of disability knowledge support the reconstruction of schooling which takes all comers (Biklen 1985) and supports pride in difference.

Different educational projects and the rights of passage

Supporting human rights in education is a large and ongoing political project. It speaks to all students and, in doing so, to disabled students. However, new forms of knowing and thinking about the structure and expression of power in education and, in turn, about educational disablement are required. In essence this is an educational task – a call for imagination and reconstruction. Ira Shor talks of this work with his college students:

> Critical thinking needs imagination where students and teachers practice anticipating a new social reality. Imagination can be exercised as a resource to expel dominant ideology and to open up some space in consciousness for transcending thinking. I've asked students to be imaginative generally in courses I teach. Our social inquiries regularly include a moment called 'reconstruction', where I ask students to imagine alternatives to the social problem they have investigated, as a model of future solutions.
>
> (Friere and Shor 1987: 185)

In his consideration of the state of educational studies, Stephen Ball (1995) examines the moral technologies or discursive practices of educational management theories and school effectiveness research and, although using different theoretical implements from Foucault's 'toolbox', like Shor presses us to 'think otherwise'. Concerned about the grip of 'unmediated knowledgability', he suggests 'we have too much knowledge and not enough understanding' (Ball 1998: 78). In the case of disability research, we have too much professional knowledge about special educational needs, which is itself part of the process of disablement.

Earlier in this discussion I referred to the way in which discursive practices form an alliance that pursues an assimilationist agenda described in a language of 'inclusion'. In other words, residual professional interests of those working in the field of special education have necessitated resilience over changing political imperatives. Predominantly unchanged practices are described in new terms. Inclusion is practised, in traditional ways, by those who presided over exclusion. The aim is to have 'othered' children fit the schools we provide with a minimum of fuss and without disrupting the institutional equilibrium. This is assimilation. Inclusive education ought to suggest a process of cultural reconstruction.

The first educational project must be the reconstruction of knowledge about education and difference with regard to disability. This project depends upon the will to host new expressions of knowledge across educational settings. In other words, do we continue to draw our advice and education about disability and disablement from the traditional sources of professional expertise? The argument of this chapter is that the uncritical reception of this intellectual and professional tradition stands between disabled people and their shaping as 'subjects' to defend their 'freedom of power' (Tourraine 1995: 264).

We do not have to commence from scratch with this project. Disabled researchers provide the imagination, leadership and experience of impairment and disablement through subjection to powerful professional knowledge and interventions to be at the vanguard of an educational and social reconstruction. Such calls for the 'deconstruction' and 'reconstruction' of special and regular education have been dismissed as ideological by writers such as Jenkinson (1997), who, like many of her special educational colleagues, fails to acknowledge that her own position is intensely political. Tom Shakespeare (1996: 191) reflects upon the politics of researching disability:

> There is quite an industry producing work around the issue of sexuality and disability, but it is an industry controlled by professionals from medical and psychological and sexological backgrounds. The voice and experience of disabled people is absent in almost every case. As in other areas, disabled people are displaced as subjects, and fetishised as objects. A medical tragedy model predominates, whereby disabled people are defined by deficit, and sexuality is either not a problem, because it is not an issue, or is an issue, because it is seen as a problem.

Of course, reconstruction involves partisan research (Troyna 1993: 105–6). It is ideological. Given that disablement (Oliver 1990) proceeds from an abuse of knowledge/power, a new politics of knowledge is required. The new politics must address the issue of who speaks for whom. I remember Allan Luke saying in a conference address that the most important lesson for educators to learn pursuant to inclusive education is knowing when to keep quiet, knowing when to listen.

This chapter has no conclusion, the agenda it foreshadows is considerable and it speaks to all sites of education policy making and teaching and learning. Disabled children are vulnerable in the face of present education policy discourses, such as school improvement and school effectiveness (Slee 1998). The current political disposition towards the education market place does not value the currency with which some children have to trade (Gewirtz *et al.* 1995). Performance league tables, the stepping up of testing schedules and the narrowing conception of curriculum and pedagogy place limitations on a range of students, including disabled children. A 'benchmark' of progress towards the achievement of human rights in education for disabled children is the degree to which there is an acknowledgement that 'sorry books' and the need for reconciliation adheres to this political project.

While there is no conclusion to this chapter, for there is much 'unfinished business', perhaps we can depart from this discussion with some central questions. This chapter has argued that like other struggles of marginalized people, schools are a site of political struggle for disabled students. However, this has not been recognized. Very powerful forms of knowledge and professional practice have coalesced to suggest that the nature of the problem is medical, psychological or technical. The problem, according to these discourses, can be resolved through the relocation of the student in the 'most appropriate educational setting' or the 'least restrictive environment', or through the provision of technical, material or human resources to ease the disabled student into the 'normal' educational setting. This approach is rejected. The reader may want to use the following questions as a way of approaching the project of supporting the rights of disabled students in education.

Questions

1 What are the meanings of the common descriptors used to categorize our children in schools (special educational needs student, disabled student, normal student, exceptional learner etc.) and where does this knowledge come from?
2 Who benefits from the application of such descriptions?
3 What are disabled researchers telling us about the experience of disability and education?
4 What is the status of this research in the field of special educational research and in the development of special needs policy?
5 How might we reconceptualize schooling so as to acknowledge the politics of representation?

References

Abberley, P. (1987) The concept of oppression and the development of a social theory of disability, *Disability, Handicap and Society*, 2(1): 5–20.
Allen, J. (1999) *Actively Seeking Inclusion*. London: Falmer Press.
Australian Bureau of Statistics (1993) *Disability, Ageing and Carers Australia, 1993: Summary of Findings*. Canberra: Australian Government Printing Service.
Ball, S. J. (1995) Intellectuals or technicians? The urgent role of theory in educational studies, *British Journal of Educational Studies*, 43(3): 255–71.
Ball, S. J. (1998) Educational studies, policy entrepreneurship and social theory, in R. Slee, G. Weiner and S. Tomlinson (eds) *School Effectiveness for Whom?* London: Falmer Press.
Barnes, C. (1992) Disability and employment, *Personnel Review*, 21(6): 55–73.
Barnes, C. (1996) Theories of disability and the origins of the oppression of disabled people in western society, in L. Barton (ed.) *Disability and Society: Emerging Issues and Insights*. Harlow: Addison Wesley Longman.
Barton, L. (ed.) (1987) *The Politics of Special Educational Needs*. Lewes: Falmer Press.
Beresford, Q. and Omaji, P. (1998) *Our State of Mind. Racial Planning and the Stolen Generations*. South Fremantle: Fremantle Arts Centre Press.
Biklen, D. (1985) *Achieving the Complete School*. New York: Teachers' College Press.
Blau, J. (1992) *The Visible Poor*. New York: Oxford University Press.
Bogdan, R. (1988) *Freak Show: Presenting Human Oddities for Amusement and Profit*. Chicago: University of Chicago Press.
Branson, J. and Miller, D. (1989) Beyond integration policy – the deconstruction of disability, in L. Barton (ed.) *Integration: Myth or Reality?* Lewes: Falmer Press.
Burt, C. (1937) *The Backward Child*. London: Hodder and Stoughton.
Clark, C., Dyson, A., Millward, A. and Skidmore, D. (1995) Theorising special education. Paper presented at International Special Education Congress, Birmingham, 12 April.
Clough, P. and Barton, L. (eds) (1995) *Making Difficulties. Research and the Construction of SEN*. London: Paul Chapman Publishing.
Corbett, J. (1993) Hanging on by a thread: integration in further education in Britain, in R. Slee (ed.) *Is There a Desk with My Name on It? The Politics of Integration*. London: Falmer Press.

Foucault, M. (1973) *The Birth of the Clinic: an Archaeology of Medical Perception.* New York: Vintage Books.

Foucault, M. (1997) The will to knowledge, in P. Rabinow (ed.) *Michel Foucault. Ethics. The Essential Works 1.* London: The Penguin Press.

Friere, P. and Shor, I. (1987) *A Pedagogy for Liberation. Dialogues on Transforming Education.* Basingstoke: Macmillan.

Fulcher, G. (1989) *Disabling Policies?* Lewes: Falmer Press.

Gans, H. J. (1995) *The War Against the Poor.* New York: Basic Books.

Gewirtz, S., Ball, S. J. and Bowe, R. (1995) *Markets, Choice and Equity in Education.* Buckingham: Open University Press.

Gilman, S. L. (1988) *Disease and Representation: Images of Illness from Madness to AIDS.* Ithaca, NY: Cornell University Press.

Gitlin, A. (ed.) (1995) *Power and Method. Political Activism and Educational Research.* New York: Routledge.

Gleeson, B. (1998) Disability and poverty, in R. Fincher and J. Nieuwenhuysen (eds) *Australian Poverty Then and Now.* Carlton South: Melbourne University Press.

Henry, J. (1968) Education for stupidity, in *Reason and Change in Elementary Education.* Washington, DC: United States Office of Education.

Herrnstein, R. J. and Murray, C. (1994) *The Bell Curve. Intelligence and Class Structure in American Life.* New York: The Free Press.

Hevey, D. (1992) *The Creatures Time Forgot.* London: Routledge.

hooks, b. (1994) *Teaching to Transgress. Education as the Practice of Freedom.* New York: Routledge.

Human Rights and Equal Opportunities Commission (1997) *National Inquiry into the Separation of Aboriginal Children and Torres Strait Islander Children from Their Families.* Sydney: HREOC.

Jenkinson, J. C. (1997) *Mainstream or Special? Educating Students with Disabilities.* London: Routledge.

Kincheloe, J. L., Steinberg, S. R. and Gresson, A. D. (eds) (1996) *Measured Lies. The Bell Curve Examined.* New York: St Martin's Press.

Lewis, J. (1993) Integration in Victorian schools: radical social policy or old wine?, in R. Slee (ed.) *Is There a Desk with My Name on It? The Politics of Integration.* London: Falmer Press.

Morris, J. (1992) Personal and political: a feminist perspective in researching physical disability, *Disability, Handicap and Society,* 7(2): 157–66.

Morris, J. (1995) *Gone Missing? A Research and Policy Review of Disabled Children Living Away from Their Families.* London: The Who Cares Trust.

Morris, J. (1997) Gone missing? Disabled children living away from home, *Disability and Society,* 12(2): 241–58.

Oliver, M. (1985) The integration–segregation debate: some sociological considerations, *British Journal of Sociology of Education,* 6 (1): 75–92.

Oliver, M. (1987) The political context of educational decision-making: the case of special needs, in L. Barton (ed.) *The Politics of Special Educational Needs.* Lewes: Falmer Press.

Oliver, M. (1990) *The Politics of Disablement.* London: Macmillan.

Oliver, M. (1992) Changing the social relations of research production? *Disability, Handicap and Society,* 7(2): 101–13.

Oliver, M. (1996) *Understanding Disability. From Theory to Practice.* London: Macmillan.

Potts, M. and Fido, R. (1991) *A Fit Person to be Removed: Personal Accounts of Life in a Mental Deficiency Institution.* Plymouth: Northcote House Publishers.

Rawls, J. (1972) *A Theory of Justice.* Oxford: Oxford University Press.

Rose, N. (1989) *Governing the Soul: The Shaping of the Private Self.* London: Routledge.

Rowley, C. D. (1972) *The Destruction of Aboriginal Society.* London: Penguin Books.

Schonell, F. C. (1942) *Backwardness in the Basic Subjects.* Edinburgh: Oliver and Boyd.

Shakespeare, T. (1996) Power and prejudice: issues of gender, sexuality and disability, in L. Barton (ed.) *Disability and Society.* London: Longman.

Shapiro, J. P. (1994) *No Pity. People with Disabilities Forging a New Civil Rights Movement.* New York: Times Books.

Skidmore, D. (1996) Towards an integrated theoretical framework for research into special educational needs, *European Journal of Special Needs Education,* 11(1): 33–47.

Skrtic, T. (1991) *Behind Special Education.* Denver, CO: Love Publications.

Slee, R. (1996) Inclusive education in Australia? Not yet! *Cambridge Journal of Education,* 26(1): 19–32.

Slee, R. (1998) High reliability organisations and liability students – the politics of recognition, in R. Slee, G. Weiner and S. Tomlinson (eds) *School Effectiveness for Whom?* London: Falmer Press.

Stern, W. (1992) A plea for rationality, *Australian Disability Review,* 4: 3–10.

Stern, W. (1993) A further plea for rationality, *Australian Disability Review,* 1: 14–21.

Tomlinson, S. (1982) *A Sociology of Special Education.* London: Routledge and Kegan Paul.

Touraine, A. (1995) *Critique of Modernity.* Oxford: Basil Blackwell.

Troyna, B. (1993) *Racism and Education.* Buckingham: Open University Press.

Usher, R. (1998) Seductive texts: competence, power and knowledge in postmodernity, in R. Barnett and A. Griffin (eds) *The End of Knowledge in Higher Education.* London: Cassell.

Walsh, R. (1993) How disabling any handicap is depends on the attitudes and actions of others: a student's perspective, in R. Slee (ed.) *Is There a Desk with My Name on It? The Politics of Integration.* London: Falmer Press.

Weiner, G. (1995) *Feminisms in Education.* Buckingham: Open University Press.

Wright Mills, C. (1959) *The Sociological Imagination.* New York: Oxford University Press.

Yeatman, A. (1994) *Postmodern Revisionings of the Political.* New York: Routledge.

Young, I. M. (1990) *Justice and the Politics of Difference.* Princeton, NJ: Princeton University Press.

 **9**

Educational opportunities and polysemic notions of equality in France

Nathalie Bélanger and Nicolas Garant

Overview

This chapter examines different meanings attached to the notion of 'equality', in a theoretical way as well as in the specific context of France. It suggests ways in which this notion, which is at the heart of the struggle for human rights, is articulated in relation to special education in France. Special education, as a specific social institution, is analysed in terms of policy making and the roles of professionals in creating and perpetuating categories. More particularly, the educational psychology project, which emerged in France after the Second World War, is discussed in order to show how educational psychologists have become pivotal in the development of special education. Paradoxically, this situation can be explained in terms of a specific conception of equality, which constantly adjusts education provisions to the 'special needs' of children.

Introduction

> Ce n'est pas dans la déclaration des droits qu'on doit trouver la liste de tous les biens qu'une bonne constitution peut procurer aux peuples. Il suffit ici de dire que les citoyens ont droit à tout ce que l'Etat peut faire en leur faveur.[1]
>
> (Sieyès)
>
> Les sujets faiblement atteints peuvent être sauvés par une éducation rationnelle et scientifique; les sujets plus sérieusement atteints sont susceptibles d'amélioration.[2]
>
> (Premier congrès international d'éducation et de protection de l'enfant dans la famille, Bruxelles 1905)

In many countries, various policies have led to the creation of educational settings for 'people moderately or seriously impaired'. As Meijer *et al.* (1997: 1) remark, experts, educators and administrators have put 'a great deal of effort into the development of a thorough and widely accepted system of special schools.' However, these settings have not prevented processes of segregation and exclusion. This outcome of special education is ascribed not as much to a deliberate or malevolent intention as to the paradoxical effect of 'caring' attitudes to children, expressed successively in terms of pity, social duty, social justice and medical intervention. In response to the experience of exclusion, some disability movements, particularly in the UK, have argued for legislation emphasizing 'rights' rather than individual 'needs', focusing on the 'disabling society' and giving voices to disabled people themselves (Barton 1996, 1997). They demand a 'comprehensive legislative programme which establishes a suitable framework for the enforcement of policies which ensure the integration of disabled people into the mainstream economic and social life of the community, and provides public confirmation that discrimination against disabled people, for whatever reason, is no longer acceptable' (Barnes and Oliver 1995: 114). In France, similar debates are under way, but in terms of equity and 'social participation'. Some disability organizations, as Plaisance (1998) notes, wish to move away from the medical model, which locates difficulty within the individual.

This chapter is divided into three main parts. First, we discuss different meanings attached to the notion of 'equality', which is at the heart of the struggle for human rights, and then attempt to understand the ways in which this notion is articulated in relation to special education in France as a specific social institution. We examine special education in relation to the educational psychology project since 1945, in order to show how educational psychologists – who have become pivotal in the development of special education – have taken into consideration the rights of children, especially the right to education for *all* children. We do not look at the educational psychology project as an entity in itself, but as a vehicle through which the broad system of special education in France can be understood.

Human rights, equality: two lovebirds

The human rights approach advocated by some disability organizations in order to legitimate their claims and support their action involves a reflection on equality. This notion is challenged by the barriers in society which prevent disabled people exercising, and benefiting from, their rights. A further conceptual difficulty arises from the different meanings given to the notion of equality in the modern applications of the law, which determines who will benefit (and how) from the rationalization and democratization of societies. Equality is a polysemic notion or, according to Rousseau, a 'theoretical chimera'.[3] Consequently, a reflection on the evolution of this idea means a reflection on the practices involved in the application of its interpretations, and notably, on the way in which the law is conceived and operated.

The struggle by disabled people to gain effective rights, while focusing on the singularity of their condition, takes place within a broader historical debate. It is part of a long process arising from struggles against the arbitrariness of the law and, specifically, the patrimonial conception of society based on a differential system of justice. We shall schematize and divide the evolution of this process into three conceptual stages, linked to three general approaches to equality: equality *in the eyes of* the law, equality *in* the law, equality *by* the law.

Unequal equality: towards a differentiation of the law

'Equality *in the eyes of the law*' (or *before* the law) found a notable endorsement with the outbreak of the French Revolution and the *Déclaration des droits de l'homme et du citoyen* of 1789 (26 August). The first article of the Déclaration argues that 'tous les hommes naissent et demeurent libres et égaux en droits'.[4] The egalitarian impulse of the Revolution was largely directed against the privileges of the nobility and the arbitrary application of justice. As article 6 says: 'la loi doit être la même pour tous, soit qu'elle protège, soit qu'elle punisse. Tous les citoyens sont égaux à ses yeux.'[5] The main consequence of this conception of equality is to introduce regularity in the administration of the law, and more precisely, to suppress the aristocratic, municipal and ecclesiastical conceptions of justice opposed to the uniform action of the law. For the same reason, this conception of equality is quite indifferent to the content of the law, and the legislation enforced by Parliament. Historically, it has been possible to discriminate against and segregate some particular groups of persons (black people, women etc.) without contradicting this particular conception of equality. Of course, it was also a conception quite indifferent to its consequences, to the effectiveness and, particularly, to the equity of its action.

It is with the democratization process and the emerging of a new sensibility that equality, i.e. '*equality in law*', becomes a norm that can be imposed on the content of the law (Proulx 1988). This conception is associated with a progressive attempt (or concern) to extend rights to all citizens, including women and ethnic minorities. To the procedural and uniform action of '*equality in the eyes of* the law', this new conception of equality adds a jurisprudence which allows interpretation sensitive to particular situations. It is an attempt to change the generality of the law, by which similar treatment of different cases results in unfairness. In relation to a 'real equality' – as is suggested in the examination of several French policies later in this chapter – this conception of equality entails an adaptation of rules in order to fit with reality. 'Is treating in the same way people whose situations are very different respecting principles of equality in anything but name only? In order to respect equality in a real sense, policy makers and judges differentiate laws and procedures according to the particular situations to which they refer. In adopting such discriminatory practices, policy makers and judges do not think they are contravening principles of equality but, on the contrary, think they are upholding them (Rivero 1965: 35).[6]

The different ways of applying the law, between equality *in* the law – obviously connected with the development of a welfare state and social democracy – and equality *in the eyes of* the law (also known as the 'rule of law') underlie two conceptions of liberty. Taking for granted that everyone has the same opportunity in society to enjoy individual freedom and liberty and to achieve individual goals, equality in the eyes of the law or the 'rule of law' seeks to keep rules as general as possible in order to allow people to adapt to those rules more easily. The 'rule of law' – meaning that rules have to be limited, precise, general, universal, predictable and fixed – has been considered as an ideal to pursue in order to establish a regime in which rules would not be exposed to a discretionary and despotic application. Hayek, particularly, has defended the importance of those criteria characterizing the 'rule of law', and has dramatized the alternative to the generality of the law as a pathway leading inevitably to a tyrannical or totalitarian regime, as, indeed, the 'road to serfdom':

> Nothing distinguishes more clearly conditions in a free country from those in a country under arbitrary government than the observance in the former of the great principles known as the Rule of Law . . . this means that government in all its actions is bound by rules fixed and announced beforehand – rules which make it possible to foresee with fair certainty . . . Within the known rules of the game the individual is free to pursue his personal ends and desires, certain that the powers of government will not be used deliberately to frustrate his efforts.
>
> (Hayek 1976: 54)

The opposition between this formal conception of justice and equality *in* law (or substantive equality) is, again, very well expressed by Hayek:

> A necessary, and only apparently paradoxical, result of this is that formal equality before the law is in conflict, and in fact incompatible, with any activity of the government deliberately aiming at material or substantive equality of different people, and that any policy aiming at a substantive ideal of distributive justice must lead to the destruction of the Rule of Law. To produce the same result for different people it is necessary to treat them differently. To give different people the same objective opportunities is not to give them the same subjective chance.
>
> (*ibid.*: 59)

It is precisely against this very 'restrictive flexibility' of the 'rule of law' and its 'ideological refusal' to adjust the content of the law to particular conditions that several criticisms emerge. Considering that a right is not a right if we do not facilitate its concretization or its affirmation, multiple references and differentiations in the proceedings of the law have been increasing. In order to realize a concrete equality (and liberty), and not only an *a priori* one, the application of the law abandons its abstract vision of the human being (which implies a universalistic approach) and considers the person as located in specific economic, social and cultural contexts. Application of justice and regulation drop the general orientation of the 'rule of law' and open the way to various statutes and differential treatments. In this context, as Goyard (1977) points out, the interventionist state legislator particularizes prescriptions, and boundaries, among individuals and groups, and imposes many kinds of categories and sub-categories, even superimposes distinctions between them.

This differentiation in the administration of the law, the 'equality *in* law' approach, takes another turn when differentiation is no longer seen as the expression of equity, but merely as a means of achieving equality of conditions and allowing effective equality for all citizens in full possession of their rights. This equality approach, also known as 'positive discrimination' or *'equality by the law'*, renounces an individualistic approach to human rights, but supports affirmation of people in accordance with their 'peer reference group' (*groupe social d'appartenance*). This new differentiation, opponents hold, entails, for example, an increase in bureaucracy in order to respond to differentiation in the administration proceedings, and an inflation of the discretionary power given to administrators who have to handle differential treatments of justice. However, for those who defend this approach, the importance of such differentiation is to counteract inequalities sustained by an institutional equality and cumulated by an 'equality *in the eyes of* the law'.

'General will' versus pluralism: a historical tension

Although this rapid summary of the evolution of the equality notion does not deal directly with the issue of disability, it enables us to identify different meanings inscribed in the law, and their consequences for the fulfilment of human rights, which concern disabled people as much as any other citizen. This discussion raises two questions concerning the issue of disabled people in France in terms of 'social participation' and 'equity'.

First, as for any country, it is clear that the goal of 'social participation' cannot be achieved in France without a differentiation of rules; and that would mean an opposition to the liberal prerequisites of the 'rule of law'. However, it would be surprising to see 'equality *in* law' evolve towards 'equality *by* the law' and positive discrimination based on particular social categories. It would be in opposition to the 'French republican tradition [which is] readily distrustful with regard to pluralism because of its attachment to a sovereign law that is supposed to express the general will' (Bouretz 1992: 992). On this matter, the United States can be seen as acting contrary to this French consensual stance, which considers that groups attempting to promote some particular interests (religious, racial, economic etc.) undermine the common good and citizenship values. The long American tradition of pluralistic approaches, and the effectiveness within these of pressure groups and lobbies – promoted by such writers as Madison, Bentley, Truman and Dewey – is important in understanding the emergence of 'positive discrimination' activities in this society.

Second, embodied in the proclamation of national sovereignty and the expression of a common will, the Declaration of Human Rights of 1789 evokes a positive conception of liberty through which the state is not seen as an entity against which rights can be used, but rather as a means, a *passage obligé*, to the realization of human rights, liberty and citizenship. This general disposition seems to fit with the fact that a 'needs approach', as we will see in the next section, has become progressively a dominant stance of special education in France.

The right to education and the development of special education

If we examine the major French policies relating to special education[7] since the beginning of the twentieth century, it is clear that they progressively articulate a substantive idea of equality ('equality *in* the law'), as seen in the first part of this chapter, although some of these are considered today to be highly discriminatory and clumsy. Historically, these policies have created the institutional segregation of many schools, classrooms and structures designed for children who experience difficulties at school. In drawing a framework of these main policies, we must consider different ways in which disabilities are understood, categorized and labelled within those policies, and also analyse the meanings and terminologies used by different groups of professionals. In this sense, 'it is difficult . . . to talk about special education as if it were a unified system' (Armstrong 1996: 300). This is especially the case in France, where there is not one system of special education, but many systems controlled by different government departments and voluntary bodies. Given the limitation of space in this chapter, we focus on policies adopted by the Ministère de l'Éducation nationale (in the past called Ministère de l'Instruction Publique) for the primary school. A study of such early policy making provides insights into recent and ongoing policy making, which embodies some ideas inherited from the past.

The complex and contradictory nature of policy making

Participating in the Premier congrès international d'éducation et de protection de l'enfant dans la famille, held in Liège (Belgium) in 1905, famous experts such Alfred Binet and Ovide Decroly addressed the question of 'abnormal' or 'irregular' children, who were roughly classified into five categories: 'undisciplined' children; deaf, dumb and blind children; epileptic children; infirm, illegitimate and abandoned children; and children with language troubles. Decroly thought that the question of classification was fundamental. He argued, 'without classification, it is difficult to know what we have to do.' He wished to develop more and more research into 'abnormality' in order 'to study, to label, to care for each case and, also, to prevent other cases.' He added, 'there are, at the moment, only two criteria: (1) the child has difficulties in his family; (2) the child has difficulties at school. The child is perceived as "irregular" because of individual difficulties or because of his or her social background.'[8]

Examining debates from this congress, we can find a *leitmotif* in relation to the idea of social duty and justice: 'At the beginning, people who were in charge of abnormal children were motivated by a feeling of pity; subsequently, we noted that it is more than just a question of sentimentality, there is a social duty to fulfil. Today, it is a concern with justice which preoccupies instructors of "irregular" children in the fulfilment of their task' (p. 275).[9]

This international congress had an important impact on policy making in France at the beginning of the twentieth century. In 1909, the French government adopted a policy to create new classrooms, called 'classes de perfectionnement'[10] designed for 'special' pupils who were considered 'educable'. The purpose of this policy was to extend the realization of the Education Act of 1882, which made education compulsory. It is, as it were, the 'founding moment' of special education in France. Placed within a historical context, special education systems were developed, in part, to extend educational opportunities and to go from an equality *in the eyes of* the law to an equality *in* the law.

Challenging the view that, with the advent of mass compulsory education after 1882, teachers would have been 'bewildered' in front of the increased number of children who experienced difficulties at school (Muel-Dreyfus 1975), Vial (1979, 1990) argues that a large majority of children, even before the adoption of the compulsory act, already attended school. As Weber (1986) and Bourdieu (1986) have argued, 'fact precedes the law'. And, as Richardson (1992: 221) argues, 'debates over the educability of special groups conferred legitimacy on mass education.' Examining debates held before the adoption of the '1909 policy', which entailed the institutionalization of special education in France, Vial paradoxically shows that teachers at the beginning of the twentieth century did not ask for the creation of special educational settings. In fact, the adoption of the '1909 policy' owed much more to the progressive development of medico-psychological knowledge experts like Binet than to teachers' opposition to the presence of children with difficulties in ordinary classes. Vial recalls the fact that when Binet asked teachers to say which of their pupils were presenting particular difficulties, most teachers did not seem able to identify them. They probably did not understand the medical and psychological categories referred to by Binet. Teachers at this time were much more interested in questions of discipline. As Claparède argues, there was some hostility to the work of Binet; many even made fun of his intelligence scale (quoted in Wolf 1971).

Although the legislative apparatus of special education, which effectively licensed the 'field of special education', was in place, its work did not really get under way before the Second World War. It is only with policies adopted under the Vichy government and, then, renewed under the Fourth Republic that special education began its incredible expansion (Chauvière 1980). For example, Prost (1990) points out that in the French primary school age group in 1958 there were 56,400 pupils in special educational settings and by 1973 this number had grown to 189,500 pupils.

During the years following the end of the Second World War, Henri Wallon and René Zazzo, two principal sponsors of French educational psychology, declared their aim to be to help all children to maximize their chances of success at school, and not merely children who were experiencing difficulties at school. The aim of educational psychology was humanistic[11] and represented a part of the Langevin–Wallon Plan of 1947, which aimed, in accordance with the principles of social justice and equality of opportunity, to enlarge educational opportunities to include all children. Successive reforms have been inspired by this important plan (Prost 1986; Dubet 1996; Dubet and Martuccelli 1996). The aim of educational psychology might have been achieved without any contribution to the construction of the field of special education, but many unexpected circumstances, as we shall show, have brought about the creation of an educational psychology linked to special education.

The role of professionals in creating and perpetuating categories

In keeping with Vial's study, we wish to raise questions concerning the commonly accepted and rarely challenged notion that educational psychology was 'necessary' to enable the transformation of the school system in which education had become compulsory for all and where the number of children identified as experiencing difficulties in learning had progressively increased. This assumption arises from a functionalist conception of society and was criticized during the 1960s, particularly in relation to the question of exclusion. Educational psychologists recruited in France since 1945 to deal with the 'problem' of pupils who present difficulties met some resistance from teachers who did not share this perception. Some teachers considered educational psychologists, who had initially been teachers, to be 'false brothers' or as another form of inspector. Thus, it is relevant to interrogate educational psychology as an organization which has constantly tried to define its foundations and status.

In particular, when educational psychologists defined their position during the 'Berthoin reform' of 1959–60, they contributed significantly to the development of special education. The Berthoin reform proposed the extension of compulsory education up to 16 years of age. The policy of 22 April 1958, which created the 'commissions médico-pédagogiques', and the following unofficial decree of Lebettre adopted in November 1960 (without publication in the 'Journal Officiel'[12]), which underlines the role of educational psychologists in the 'commission médico-pédagogique', involved increasing the specifications of the field of special education. These commissions determined 'which pupils cannot be admitted or supported in mainstream classrooms and, among them, those who can be placed in a special school or classroom.'[13] The purpose of this policy is still to provide adequate educational settings for all children. In the policy of 1958 and more particularly in the following document written by Lebettre in 1960, educational psychologists were seen essentially as partners in the process of assessment. It is probably during this period that the role of educational psychologists becomes strongly associated, or linked, by 'circumstantial decision', with the field of special education, where their actions 'were the most understandable or obvious', as one pioneer educational psychologist remarked when interviewed (Bélanger 1997). These policies both define the professional footing of educational psychologists – which was quite precarious at the beginning of the 1950s – and extend and consolidate the field of special education until 1967–8. The powerful debates which emerged in the period surrounding May 1968 threw up questions about many kinds of exclusions, among them the consequences of special educational settings. These questions open up important discussions about the prevention of educational difficulties and integration in mainstream educational settings.

In June 1975, the 'Loi d'orientation en faveur des personnes handicapées' (the Law of Orientation in Support of Handicapped People) was adopted as an apparent rejection of the medical model based on the diagnosis of individual defects. The new legislation sought to promote the integration of pupils 'with learning difficulties' into mainstream educational settings.[14] In the statutes of 1975, as Plaisance (1996) points out, there is a deliberate omission of any definition of the term 'handicap' in order to avoid providing any future categorizations or grounds which might be used as a basis for exclusions. 'Commissions d'éducation spéciale' (Commissions for Special Education) were created on 22 April 1976 with the purpose of providing, where necessary, financial allowances based on case-by-case consideration of those who might be considered disabled. In reality, it appears that, in many cases, when these commissions examine a case, they tend to ratify the request for exclusion from mainstream educational settings according to the availability of special provision in each geographical department, thus matching 'needs' to 'resources' and consequently applying the brake to the policy of integration (Godet-Montalescot 1995). While the 'law of orientation' endorses practices of integration, Ravaud (1995) argues that it is only a message of encouragement to integrate ('pious wishes') rather than a firm commitment. Morever, as Armstrong (1996: 77) notes, this policy 'did not take any steps towards dismantling the complex system of different schools and institutions for children and young people with disabilities and difficulties in learning.' One possible explanation for this situation may lie in the fact that formal policy making emerges from many years of oppositions and controversies prior to its adoption (Chauvière 1995). Thus, it is only in the context of subsequent policies (especially those of 1982 and 1983) that a real preoccupation with integrative practices is discernible (Ravaud 1995; Plaisance 1996). One declared aim of the statute of 1982 was 'to struggle against social inequalities' by instituting a complex system of integration in which 'special' institutions would not appear to be segregative. It argues: 'special institutions and their staff must be directly involved in this development [integration] and can, furthermore, provide technical support to integration.'[15] Integration is advocated 'when it is possible'. The 1983 document determines who is affected by integration:

children and teenagers who experience difficulties because of disability, disease or personality and behavioural disorders, and who 'can be inserted into a mainstream educational setting'. In the same text, a distinction is also made between 'individual' and 'collective' integration.[16] The first of these suggests full- or part-time integration into an ordinary classroom, while the second refers to schooling in a specific special unit alongside pupils having, in principle, the 'same characteristics'.

Although the 'complex system of different schools and institutions' has not been fully dismantled, there are, at least, many projects established with the purpose of preventing difficulties or minimizing their effects. Among these attempts, there are the 'groupes d'aide psycho-pédagogique' (GAPP) (groups for psycho-pedagogical help) made up of educational psychologists and 'rééducateurs' (special teachers), whose role is to bring educational help to children, rather than involving medical or therapeutic intervention from outside agencies. However, this project has been progressively abandoned for several reasons: (a) the objective of providing all departments in France with a GAPP structure was considered too difficult to realize in the context of economic recession; (b) the definition and purpose of these groups were considered too 'woolly' or vague; and (c) their psycho-pathological conception of school failure was perhaps entailed by an approach firmly rooted in medical and psychological models. These groups were abolished in 1990 when the 'Réseaux d'aides spécialisées aux élèves en difficulté' (specialized help networks) were set up in their place. Despite formal integration policies and the adoption of the 'Jospin law' in 1989,[17] which emphasized the importance of direct government contribution in matters of education in relation to equality of opportunity (including disabled people who must be 'favoured' and for whom disabilities must be 'detected'), during the 1980s and the 1990s many new categorizations and even new exclusions have emerged. For instance, the policies of 1989 allow 'responses' to particular 'needs' by adapting technical educational conditions in relation to different disabilities.[18] However, at the same time, these policies open the door to new segregations by allowing special institutions ('médico-éducatives') to apply charges laid down by the state, thus encouraging a sort of 'consumerism' (Godet-Montalescot 1995; Plaisance 1996). Consequently, this situation has firmly reinforced and extended the sector of special education. Among the policies of 1988–9, we find information about institutions for children who have auditory or visual impairments, 'motor deficiency', 'intellectual deficiency' or 'polydisability' recognized by a 'commission for special education' (Ravaud 1995: 121). It is important to make clear that these conditions have been established under the auspices of the law on integration, which still recommends that special institutions should be seen not as segregative ones but as participating in the broad purpose of integration: 'the channelling of children or teenagers towards special institutions represents an adapted response to their educational and therapeutical special needs . . . and must not be perceived as unjustly segregative.'[19] These conditions have been created with the purpose of achieving an effective 'equality' or 'equality *in* law'.

In addition, several further policies have been implemented which purport to favour integration into mainstream schools. We will outline two. First, the creation of the 'classes d'intégration scolaire'[20] (CLIS) (classes for educational integration) is a product of the '1989 Jospin law', which abolished the 'classe de perfectionnement' (instituted in 1909). In theory, these classes are intended for children for whom a disability has been recognized by 'commissions for special education'. Four 'categories of children', i.e. pupils who have 'mental, auditory, visual or motor disability', are considered. The CLIS are seen as a step towards integration. However, despite this policy, some teachers who work in these classes continue to call them 'classes de perfectionnement'!

Second, 'specialized help networks', already mentioned, have been thought of as a piece of the broad system of integration.[21] They consist of teachers, 'rééducateurs' and educational psychologists,[22] and are attached to a group of schools. In general, these specialists work on a withdrawal basis with individual children who are experiencing difficulties in the mainstream classroom. Armstrong (1995) notes that such 'networks' also work with children who are disruptive, experience difficulties with spelling and reading or, more controversially, have 'speech problems'. For example, Armstrong discovered, during a visit to a school, that a child called Mohammed was bilingual and that his teacher found it difficult to communicate with him. Armstrong points out that 'the difficulties experienced by children and young people are categorized either as difficulties in learning or as emotional-psychological problems and the different "solutions" which are presented derive from this categorisation' (*ibid.*: 83). Such distinctions can, argues Apple (1998), result in a 'tragical distinction' between cognitive, emotional and affective dimensions of a person. In short, and as the authors of a recent report show, too much priority is given, by these 'networks', to the psychological and therapeutical treatments rather than to educational approaches, even if, in general, the work they do seems to be helpful; for example, in supporting annual academic progress (Inspection générale de l'Éducation nationale 1997).

Conclusion

Notions of human rights and equality are closely linked. The notion of human rights is surrounded by polysemic definitions of equality, which can be summarized as equality *in the eyes of* the law, equality *in* law and equality *by* the law. Equality *in* law, which is associated with the development of the welfare state, emerges in opposition to the generality of the 'rule of law' (or 'equality *in the eyes of* the law') and its incapacity to take into account diverse contexts and specific situations of people. The third equality, i.e. equality *by* the law, relates to the positive discrimination approach that renounces an individualistic conception of human rights but supports affirmation of people in accordance with their 'peer reference group'.

It has been argued, in the second part of this chapter, that the creation of special educational settings in France is paradoxically associated with equality *in* the law. This conception of equality seeks to adjust education provisions to specific 'needs' of children in order to allow them to benefit from their rights: for example, their right to be educated. In brief, this conception seeks to address many unfair situations but also opens the door to unexpected consequences (Boudon 1977), such as an increased number of children labelled or designated as 'special children'.

It should be remembered that the question of the right to education for all was raised by Wallon and Zazzo in 1945 and gave an impetus to the subsequent reforms. However, these reforms have, progressively, abandoned the principle of 'rights' in favour of 'special education', as well as 'integration' approaches based on the notion of 'needs'. As a result, increasing numbers of children have been identified through complex policies and the creation of new categories in response to the 'special needs of children'. However, the recognition of rights in education, argue Barton and Smith (1989), involves: (a) thinking in terms of 'rights' rather than in terms of 'needs'; (b) reducing inequalities and eroding sources of discrimination; (c) ensuring adequate educational experiences and access to mainstream education for all children and young people; and (d) giving opportunities to children to choose what is 'good' for them.

Moreover, some interpretations and applications of policies of 'integration', as we examined in this chapter, might have contributed to the social construction of 'difference' and the perpetuation of an approach that divides and separates 'us' and 'them'. Hendriks (1995: 43) argues:

'Disability' and 'ability' as well as 'difference' and 'sameness' are all relational concepts. Without comparison these terms make little if any sense. Therefore we should realise that (dis)abilities and differences are nothing but social constructions. No one is 'different' without a counter-part having some other traits and nobody is disabled as long as there is no person to compare with who is differently abled. Whereas it is a truism that able-bodied and disabled persons are, at least to some extent, different from each other . . . Each person is unique, but what we share is that we are all human beings. Differentiating between people may therefore be a highly delicate issue that may easily result in stigmatisation. Differentiating commonly becomes problematic as a result of the typical human inclination to divide humanity into 'us' and 'them'. People tend to distinguish themselves from others, who are perceived to be 'different', or – in a more pejorative sense – 'abnormal'. Following the relational nature of these terms, we should realise that our definition of 'sameness' or 'difference' very much depends on our point of comparison.

This construction of difference recalls a part of the study of Goffman (1968: 139):

The problems associated with militancy are well known. When the ultimate political objective is to remove stigma from the differentness, the individual may find that his very efforts can politicise his own life, rendering it even more different from the normal life initially denied him – even though the next generation of his fellows may greatly profit from his efforts by being more accepted. Further, in drawing attention to the situation of his own kind he is in some respects consolidating a public image of his differentness as a real thing and of his fellow-stigmatised as constituting a real group. On the other hand, if he seeks some kind of separateness, not assimilation, he may find that he is necessarily presenting his militant efforts in the language and style of his enemies. Moreover, the pleas he presents, the plight he reviews, the strategies he advocates, are all part of an idiom of expression and feeling that belongs to the whole society. His disdain for a society that rejects him can be understood only in terms of that society's conception of pride, dignity and independence. In short, unless there is some alien culture on which to fall back, the more he separates himself structurally from the normals, the more like them he may become culturally.

Considering the broader French context, it appears that the evolution of 'integration' educational policies, based on 'needs', is in accordance with the French republican tradition, which considers the fulfilment of citizenship and rights as a duty and an overriding priority of the state (Bouretz 1992). French people, argues Arendt (1990: 109), have a particular understanding of human rights: 'these rights were not understood as pre-political rights that no government and no political power has the right to touch and to violate, but as the very content as well as the ultimate end of government and power.'[23]

Like many other countries, France can be associated, generally speaking, with a process of differentiation of law and institutional rules. This evolution, unlike general application of equality *in the eyes of* the law, can be seen as the result of the process of democratization and institutional inclusion, in accordance with the endeavour to increase opportunities to those who are deprived of the exercise of their rights. Unlike in other countries, especially the United States, the process of differentiation in France does not seem to allow the emergence of a pluralism through which claims of particular groups can be articulated. According to the French republican tradition, the rights of disabled people seem to be a central concern of the state.

Questions

1 Considering the so-called scheme of 'integration' education, which does not avoid labelling processes, how can researchers, analysts and activists think in terms of inclusive education?

2 How may a nation state like France, which looks for a 'consensus' (Walzer 1998), allow a place for the claims of specific groups in order to realize an equitable approach? If specific pressure groups are considered, how will

rights be understood, and who – considering the large number of associations and coalitions of disabled people, who do not always have the same point of view[24] – will define them? The legitimization of state policies, through the participation of disabled people in policy making, does not necessarily put an end to the difficulty of arriving at a consensus.

3 Considering that differentiation of people raises complex questions about who is 'disabled',[25] how can we avoid a differentiation between able-bodied and disabled persons, and an approach in terms of 'us' and 'them'? This concern is well expressed by the Nobel novelist Toni Morrison, when she says 'Would I be authorized, at last, to write about black people without having to say that they are black, as do white people when they are writing about white people.'[26]

Acknowledgements

We thank Peter Clough and Felicity Armstrong for their advice in the translation of this text.

Notes

1 Quoted in Bouretz (1992). Our translation: 'It is not in the declaration of rights that we find the list of all goods that a great constitution can bring to people. It suffices to say here that all citizens have the right to all the state can do in their interest.' This statement by the French revolutionary Sieyès foreshadows the controversial 'caring' of the state in the fulfilment of real citizenship that characterized, for example, special education history.

2 Our translation: 'Those who are slightly impaired may be saved by a rational and scientific education; those more seriously impaired may be susceptible to improvement.'

3 This equality, people argue, is a theoretical chimera that cannot exist in practice. But if the abuse is inevitable, does it follow that we ought not even to regulate it? 'It is precisely because the force of circumstances constantly tends to destroy equality that the force of legislation should always tend to maintain it' (Rousseau 1953: 55).

4 Our translation: 'All men are born and live free and with equal rights in the eyes of the law.'

5 Our translation: 'The law must be the same for all men, whether it protects, or it punishes. All citizens are equal in the eyes of the law.'

6 Our translation.

7 We define special education as a sector of social educative practices dominated by medical and psychological interventions (Plaisance 1988).

8 Our translation.

9 Our translation. The original quotation is: 'Au début, ceux qui se sont occupés de l'enfance anormale ont tablé sur le sentiment de pitié; mais bientôt, on a constaté qu'il y a là plus qu'une question de sentimentalité; il y a là un devoir social à

remplir. Aujourd'hui, c'est le sentiment de justice qui guide les éducateurs des enfants irréguliers dans l'accomplissement de leur tâche.'

10 Armstrong (1995) translates this expression as 'improvers class' or 'remedial class'.

11 Wallon had a great belief in the anticipation of 'l'homme de demain' ('the human of tomorrow') and in the development of the 'aptitudes' of each person. He was committed to a view of human action as praxis. His humanistic values and his Marxist inclination surround this stance.

12 The official journal where legislation is published.

13 Our translation.

14 Even if this text was quite new at the time, it should be noted that in 1959 a policy was adopted to promote the education of children who have 'motor difficulties'. Circulaire of 5 January 1959: 'Scolarité des enfants atteints d'infirmités de la motricité'.

15 Our translation. Policy of 29 January 1982.

16 Policy of 29 January 1983.

17 'Loi d'orientation sur l'éducation'. Policy of 10 July 1989.

18 Especially in the annexes XXIV of 1956, reworked in 1988 and 1989, which specify how education staff can provide for children who experience specific disability.

19 Policy 91-302 of 18 November 1991. Our translation.

20 Policy 91-304 of 18 November 1991.

21 Policy 90-082 of 9 April 1990.

22 For whom a policy (90-083 of 10 April 1990) has been defined in order to specify the role of the educational psychologist in the 'specialized help network' (RASED). Within this text, educational psychologists must help teachers in order to prevent educational difficulties, to set up a school project, to conceive, set up and evaluate individual and collective help brought to children who are experiencing difficulties and to integrate disabled children.

23 'Pre-political rights' means natural or intrinsic to people.

24 For example, the following associations: Association nationale des parents d'enfants déficients auditifs, Association d'entraide des polios et handicapés, Association pour le logement des grands infirmes, Ligue pour l'adaptation du diminué physique au travail, Union nationale des polios de France, Union des papillons blancs, Association vivre debout, Association française des hémophiles, Association française de lutte contre la mucoviscidose.

25 See, for instance, the *Guardian* article 'Black Friday for disability. We need a new definition' (14 March 1998: 22). Moreover, it does not seem evident, at least sociologically, how 'to understand the real nature of disability' (Oliver, 1992: 20).

26 Toni Morrison interviewed by Josyane Savigneau in *Le monde des livres* (29 May 1998: 1). The original quotation is: 'Serai-je autorisée, enfin, à écrire sur des Noirs sans avoir à dire qu'ils sont noirs, comme les Blancs écrivent sur les Blancs?'

References

Apple, M. (1998) Between standards and markets: education the 'right way'. Lecture given to the University of Sheffield, 5 January.

Arendt, H. (1990) *On Revolution*. London: Penguin.

Ariès, P. (1960) *L'Enfant et la vie familiale sous l'Ancien Régime*. Paris: Le Seuil.

Armstrong, F. (1995) 'Appellation contrôlée': mixing and sorting in the French education system, in P. Potts, F. Armstrong and M. Masterton (eds) *Equality and Diversity in Education. National and International Contexts,* London: Open University and Routledge.

Armstrong, F. (1996) Special education in France, in A. Corbett and B. Moon (eds) *Education in France. Continuity and Change in the Mitterand Years, 1981–1995.* London and New York: Routledge.

Barnes, C. and Oliver, M. (1995) Disability rights: rhetoric and reality in the UK, *Disability and Society,* 10(1): 111–16.

Barton, L. (1996) Citizenship and disabled people: a cause for concern, in J. Demaine and H. Entwistle (eds) *Beyond Communitarianism: Citizenship, Politics and Education.* Basingstoke: Macmillan.

Barton, L. (1997) Inclusive education and human rights. Lecture given to NUT members in Birmingham, 26 November.

Barton, L. and Smith, M. (1989) Equality, rights and primary education, in C. Roaf and H. Bines (eds) *Needs, Rights and Opportunities.* London: Falmer Press.

Bélanger, N. (1997) *La psychologie à l'école et l'enfance 'inadaptée'. Le cas de la psychologie scolaire en France après la Deuxième Guerre mondiale.* Université Paris V: thèse de doctorat.

Boudon, R. (1977) *Effets pervers et ordre social,* Paris: PUF.

Bourdieu, P. (1986) La force du droit . . . Éléments pour une sociologie du champ juridique, *Actes de la recherche en sciences sociales,* 64: 3–19.

Bouretz, P. (1992) Droits de l'homme, Pluralisme and Souveraineté, in O. Duhamel and Y. Mény (eds) *Dictionnaire constitutionnel.* Paris: PUF.

Campbell, J. and Oliver, M. (1996) *Disability Policies.* London: Routledge.

Chauvière, M. (1980) *L'enfance inadaptée, l'héritage de Vichy.* Paris: Éditions Ouvrières.

Chauvière, M. (1995) Critiques oubliées. Les réactions contrastées à la loi de 1975. Lecture given at the symposium 'Les associations et l'État dans la construction sociale du handicap au XXe siècle', 14 January, Marly-le-Roi, France.

Depaepe, M. (1990) Soziale abnormität und moralische debilität bei kindern. Ein diskussionsthema auf internationalen wissenschaftlichen zusammenkünften am anfang dieses jahrhunderts, *Paedagogica historica,* 26(2): 185–209.

Dubet, F. (1996) L'exclusion scolaire: quelles solutions?, in S. Paugam (ed.) *L'exclusion, l'état des savoirs.* Paris: La découverte.

Dubet, F. and Martuccelli, D. (1996) *À l'école. Sociologie de l'expérience scolaire.* Paris: Seuil.

Godet-Montalescot, S. (1995) La politique d'intégration des handicapés, les Commissions départementales d'éducation spéciale (CDES), interface du milieu ordinaire et du secteur spécialisé, *Revue française des Affaires Sociales,* 49(2/3): 207–33.

Goffman, E. (1968) *Stigma. Notes on the Management of Spoiled Identity.* London: Pelican.

Goyard, P. (1977) Les diverses prérogatives juridiques et les notions d'égalité et de discrimination, in *L'égalité,* tome V. Brussels: Bruylant.

Hayek, F. (1976) *The Road to Serfdom.* London: Routledge and Kegan Paul.

Hendriks, A. (1995) The significance of equality and non-discrimination for the protection of the rights and dignity of disabled persons, in T. Degener and Y. Koster-Dreese (eds) *Human Rights and Disabled Persons.* Dordrecht, Boston and London: Martinus Nijhoff.

Higgins, R. (1996) Human rights, in A. Kuper and J. Kuper (eds) *The Social Science Encyclopedia.* London and New York: Routledge.

Inspection générale de l'Éducation nationale (1997) *Les réseaux d'aides spécialisées aux élèves en difficulté. Examens de quelques situations départementales.* Paris: Centre national de documentation pédagogique.

Luc, J. L. (1997) *L'invention du jeune enfant au XIXe siècle. De la salle d'asile à l'école maternelle.* Paris: Belin.

Meijer, C. J. W., Pijl, S. J. and Hegarty, S. (1997) Introduction, in S. J. Pijl, C. J. W. Meijer and S. Hegarty (eds) *Inclusive Education: A Global Agenda*. London: Routledge.

Muel-Dreyfus, F. (1975) L'école obligatoire et l'invention de l'enfance anormale, *Actes de la recherche en sciences sociales*, 1: 60–74.

Nicholls, D. (1974) *Three Varieties of Pluralism*. London: Macmillan.

Oliver, M. (1992). Intellectual masturbation: a rejoinder to Söder and Booth, *European Journal of Special Needs Education*, 7(1): 20–8.

Plaisance, E. (1988) Éducation spéciale, *L'Année sociologique*, 38: 449–57.

Plaisance, E. (1996) Les enfants handicapés à l'école, in S. Paugam (ed.) *L'exclusion, l'état des savoirs*. Paris: La découverte.

Plaisance, E. (1998) Introduction to the symposium, L'éducation scolaire contre l'éducation spécialisée. Lecture given at the Biennale de l'éducation, la Sorbonne, Paris, 17 April.

Premier congrès international d'éducation et de protection de l'enfance dans la famille (1905) *Compte rendu des réunions générales*. Brussels: A. Lesigne.

Prost, A. (1986) *L'Enseignement s'est-il democratisé?* Paris: PUF.

Prost, A. (1990) Préface, in M. Vial, *Les enfants anormaux à l'école*. Paris: Armand Colin.

Proulx, D. (1988) Vues canadiennes et européennes des droits et libertés in G. Beaudoin (ed.) *Actes des journées Strasbourgeoises*. Québec: Yvon Blais.

Ravaud, J. F. (1995) La scolarisation des personnes handicapées, in A. Triomphe (ed.) *Les personnes handicapées en France. Données sociales 1995*. Paris: INSERM-CTNERHI.

Richardson, J. G. (1992) Historical expansion of special education, in B. Fuller and R. Rubinson (eds) *The Political Construction of Education: the State, School Expansion and Economic Change*. New York: Praeger Publishers.

Rivero, J. (1965) Les notions d'égalité et de discrimination en droit public français, in *Travaux de l'Association Henri-Capitant*, tome XIV. Paris: Dalloz.

Rousseau, J. J. (1953) *Political Writings*. Edinburgh: Nelson.

Triomphe, A. (ed.) (1995) *Les personnes handicapées en France: données sociales*. Paris: CTNERHI-INSERM.

Vial, M. (1979) Les débuts de l'enseignement spécial en France: les revendications qui ont conduit à la loi du 15 avril 1909 créant les classes de perfectionnement, *Cahiers de la section de recherche de l'éducation spécialisée et de l'adaptation scolaire* (SRESAS-INRP), 18: 7–161.

Vial, M. (1990) *Les enfants anormaux à l'école. Aux origines de l'Éducation spécialisée 1882–1909*. Paris: Armand Colin.

Walzer, M. (1998) *Traité sur la tolérance*. Paris: Gallimard.

Weber, M. (1986) *Sociologie du droit*. Paris: PUF.

Wolf, T. H. (1971) *Alfred Binet*. Chicago: University of Chicago Press.

 **10**

Experience-near perspectives on disabled people's rights in Sweden

Anders Gustavsson

Overview

In a study of the everyday life of intellectually disabled people who have grown up in the Swedish welfare state of the 1970s and 1980s, two different perspectives on disabled people's rights were identified: one a rights-disability perspective, where special rights presuppose a certain helplessness in the form of a lack of competence and autonomy; the other a rights-ability perspective, where competence and autonomy are seen as possible to achieve by means of the special rights. Educational programmes and public services are likely to be influenced by the presuppositions of the current perspective. In order to empower disabled people it seems important to support the second perspective. However, the question is raised whether such a shift in perspectives could also mean reduced public support for the whole idea of rights to special services.

Experience-near understandings of human rights

During recent decades human rights have been discussed more and more often in the field of disability research, sometimes in association with evaluations of integration and inclusion. According to academic traditions, most researchers have defined and discussed such rights in terms of scientific concepts relating them to existing theories and frames of reference. A frequently used such theoretical framework is T. H. Marshall's (1965) theory of citizenship, in which he analyses citizenship in terms of three dimensions: civil rights, political rights and social rights.

However, concepts and understandings of disabled people themselves are surprisingly seldom discussed. The American anthropologist Clifford Geertz (1983) makes a distinction between *experience-near* and *experience-distant* concepts. He argues that experience-near concepts are especially important to study for researchers who try to understand people with unusual experiences, as they often capture the perspectives of the people who are the focus of the study in the best possible way.

The formulations have been various: 'inside' versus 'outside', or 'first person' versus 'third person' descriptions; 'phenomenological' versus 'objectivist', or 'cognitive' versus 'behavioural' theories; perhaps most commonly 'emic' versus 'etic' analyses, this last deriving from the distinction in linguistics between phonemics and phonetics, phonemics classifying sounds according to their internal function in language, phonetics classifying them according to their acoustic properties as such. But perhaps the simplest and most directly appreciable way to put the matter is in terms of a distinction also formulated, for his own purposes, by the psychoanalyst Heintz Kohut, between what he calls 'experience-near' and 'experience-distant' concepts.

An experience-near concept is, roughly, one that someone – a patient, a subject, in our case an informant – might naturally and effortlessly use to define what he, she or fellows see, feel, think, imagine and so on. An experience-distant concept is one that a specialist of one sort or another – an analyst, an experimenter, an ethnographer, even a priest or an ideologist – employs to forward scientific, philosophical or practical aims. Clearly, the matter is one of degree, not opposition – 'fear' is experience-nearer than 'phobia' and 'phobia' experience-nearer than 'ego dyssyntonic' (Geertz 1983: 57).

An experience-near perspective on disabled people's rights

In a study (Gustavsson 1998) of ten people (with intellectual disabilities) belonging to what I have called 'the first integration generation', i.e. people who grew up during the 1970s and 1980s, when integration was the official political goal in Sweden, I found an interesting experience-near perspective on disabled people's rights. In fact, an important characteristic of the discovered perspective was that it was maintained first of all by people with extensive personal experience of what life with an intellectual disability can be like. And this perspective also stood more or less in open opposition to a perspective maintained by people who lacked such experience.

The experience-near perspective seemed to be embedded in a more comprehensive understanding of their abilities and disabilities. The identification of the experience-near perspective on disabled people's rights came as a result of an analysis of another finding, namely that the people interviewed in the study manifested a surprising faith in their own ability to maintain a job, live on their own, be a good parent etc. Drawing on Heider's (1958) classic analysis of common-sense understanding of ability, I identified two alternative understandings of ability, one based on Heider's common-sense model and one illustrating the understanding of the people studied. According to Heider, most people in everyday life think of ability as a product of, on the one hand, the difficulties of a specific task and, on the other hand, a person's particular skills and dispositions (see Figure 10.1). The people who were the focus of the study, however, seemed to add a third dimension to their understanding of their (and others') abilities, namely the special support which they took for granted as an entitlement because of their disabilities. This is illustrated in Figure 10.2.

The context of the Swedish welfare state

Exploring this taken-for-granted idea of a right to support and services through group members' ways of expressing themselves and through their actions and behaviour in everyday life, I found explicit and implicit references to ideas of the Swedish welfare state, like the idea of being weak and therefore entitled to the support.

This indicated that current perspectives on disabled people's rights in Sweden should be understood in the historical context of the welfare state and its ideology. The basic idea of human and civil rights to equal living conditions in Sweden has for a long time been associated with a welfare state

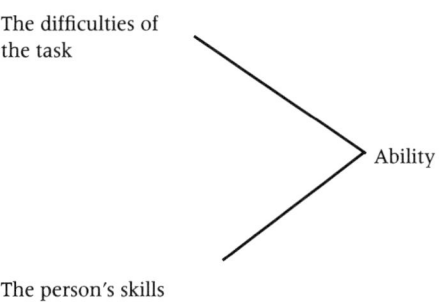

The difficulties of
the task

Ability

The person's skills
and dispositions

Figure 10.1 Common-sense understanding of ability (inspired by Heider 1958)

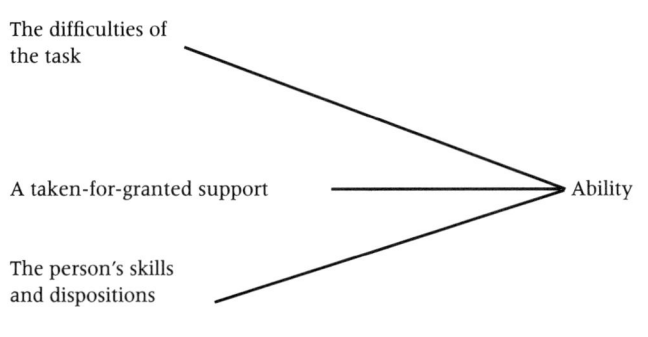

The difficulties of
the task

A taken-for-granted support — Ability

The person's skills
and dispositions

Figure 10.2 The alternative understanding of ability

concept of 'weak groups' and their special rights to support and services (see Hansson 1928). When, for instance, the term 'handicap' (*handikapp*) was introduced in Sweden in the late 1960s as the first modern, generic term for disability, it became associated with the idea of special rights for people who were disabled in the sense of weak. *Utvecklingsstörning* (here translated by 'intellectual disability') is in fact defined in relation to special rights. In Sweden, the categorization of people as intellectually disabled is based on the fact that they receive special services (for people with such disabilities) and support in their daily living, in school or at work. In Britain, these people, among others, would be labelled 'learning disabled'.

Thus, what it means to be intellectually disabled in Sweden is to an important extent linked to how special needs and rights are understood. One of my points is that these understandings may play important roles as hidden perspectives in educational as well as other supportive settings.

The idea of support to 'weak groups'

At first, I simply identified the experience-near perspective on disabled people's rights as an expression of the well known welfare state idea of *weak groups* and support for weak groups. My conclusion was that the people whom I had learnt to know in the study had taken this idea seriously and come to take it for granted.

This idea of the weak seems to have its roots in the first phase of the welfare state, often referred to as *Folkhemmet* (the people's home), and described in the following way by the leader of the Social Democratic party, Per Albin Hansson, in a famous speech to the Second Chamber of the Swedish Parliament in 1928.

> The basis of the home [Folkhemmet] is community and the feeling of togetherness. The good home does not know of any privileged or disadvantaged people, no favourites and no stepchildren. There, one does not look down on the other, there nobody seeks advantages at the expense of others. The strong does not oppress and exploit the weak. In the good home, there is equality, care, collaboration, support.
>
> (Hansson 1928)

However, it was not until the late 1960s that the term 'weak' got its well known social meaning as a characteristic entitling people to support and compensation. In the 1960s, the welfare state in Sweden was exposed to heavy critique for having 'forgotten' certain groups that had not been able to defend their place in the welfare state (from the 1940s and onwards often referred to as 'the strong society'). Among others, sick and disabled people (at the time often referred to as 'the handicapped') were identified as weak groups entitled to special support. Since then, the concept of weak groups has played an important role in the Swedish social policy rhetoric, especially in the defence of special services and rights.

I found a recent illustration of this in the debate on the economic recession and dismantling of the welfare state systems of the 1990s. In this debate, the weak groups have been asked to take their share, but the fact that a person or a group is considered to be weak has also been used as an argument against cutting down on services. In a newspaper article from 1997, a father of a disabled child defended his child's and his own family's right to be recognized as weak. He started with a general explication of how the term is used and then developed his argument for continued right to respite care and other special services to his own family.

> One of the most frequent expressions in the political rhetoric is 'the weak groups'. Weak groups must be protected, weak groups must take their share. These are familiar strains to all of us but we perhaps seldom think more closely of what they mean. However, the use of the concept 'weak' can be confusing. Politicians can describe unemployed and handicapped people as weak groups. Not having a job apparently is placed in the same category as, for instance, being tied to one's wheelchair or being blind . . . I cannot imagine any group which is much weaker than we are in society. We can compare ourselves with the so called 'grassroot' Therese Rajaniemi, who has initiated demonstrations and rebellion. Rajaniemi has four healthy children and is not badly off economically in the field of unemployment, in so far as it would be possible for her to go to the Canaries if she stopped smoking. To me, she is quite enviable . . . The consequences of the fact that the Social Democratic politicians do not understand that the handicapped are weak in a completely different way from healthy, unemployed people is reflected in the current policy. In the governmental Bill 1996/97: 124 it is proposed that the respite service from now on will be an optional service for municipalities. Municipalities are free to offer respite care, but if they do not, there is no way for the individual person to appeal. In our case this could mean that our economically pressed municipality could decide not to let Martin [the disabled son] keep his place at the group home where his respite care is given. To us, this would be a catastrophe.
>
> (*DN* 24 June 1997; my translation)

As this father of a disabled child has indicated, there has always been some confusion concerning who weak groups actually are. Poor, unemployed, sick and disabled people are, however, often regarded as weak groups. Disabled people, Söder (1990) argues, are viewed as the most typical of all the weak groups.

A rights-ability perspective and a rights-disability perspective

A young couple, in my study of the first integration generation, brought my attention to the fact that today there seem to exist two different interpretations of the welfare state idea of special support to weak groups in Sweden. Behind the strong, existing consensus on disabled people's special rights, two different rights perspectives seem to have emerged: a *rights-disability* perspective, first of all maintained by persons giving support, where rights are associated with permanent special need; and a *rights-ability* perspective, maintained by disabled persons themselves, who receive the support. To them, rights are associated with opportunities to achieve conditions of everyday life equal to those of other citizens.

The difference between the two rights perspectives seems to become especially visible in relation to autonomy. In the above mentioned couple's own understanding of their taken-for-granted right to support, they understood their intellectual disabilities as a disadvantage that they should and could be compensated for. Thus, their autonomy was not necessarily reduced.

Most non-disabled people in their environment, however, understood intellectual disability first of all as special needs. From this perspective, the right to support was founded on a permanent lack of competence and therefore also a permanent reduction of personal autonomy. The issue illustrating most clearly the two perspectives and their implicit understanding of the notion of autonomy was that of whether the couple could or could not decide for themselves whether they could manage the responsibility of being good parents. Most distinctly, the rights-disability perspective was presented by the responsible persons employed in the social services of the municipality where the couple lived. They questioned the young couple's abilities to take good care of a child and to decide whether they should be parents or not with reference to their special need for assistance. From this perspective, special need for assistance meant permanent lack of parental competence. The couple themselves, however, tended to understand the assistance – which they knew that they needed and took for granted that they would get – as a way to manage. From their perspective, the special needs were a disadvantage that they could be compensated for and, consequently, they did not see any real opposition between needs and competence.

Thus, what we have found seems to be two quite different perspectives on disabled persons' rights, one linking rights to ability and autonomy and the other linking rights to disability and helplessness. In my analysis of the collected data, I came to understand these perspectives as being related to the sort of experience that the person maintaining the perspective had of what life with a disability is like. The rights-disability perspective is in this sense an experience-distant perspective, and the rights-ability perspective an experience-nearer perspective. The latter was also maintained first by disabled people themselves, and by people who had a close enough relationship with a disabled person to have been able to discover how special support and ability can be understood from his or her point of view. The former perspective was maintained by people without such experiences. Their perspective seemed to be based on the logic of a link between rights and (permanent) weakness, where rights meant being entitled to help and care. The experience-near perspective, however, seemed to be based more on the idea of equality and the rights of disadvantaged citizens to be compensated in order to be able to live their life as other people do. Thus, the presuppositions of the experience-distant, rights-disability perspective seemed to be that people with special needs lack competence for autonomy, and therefore fill a client role. The experience-nearer, rights-ability perspective, on the contrary, expressed an emancipatory agenda, where disability had nothing to do with reduced autonomy. The two perspectives can be illustrated as in Figure 10.3.

The point of departure for the two perspectives is a taken-for-granted idea of a right to special support. From the experience-near perspective, this right to support means *ability* and autonomy. However, from the experience-distant perspective, the right to special support first of all is understood as special needs and *disability*, which in turn means helplessness and dependence on a client role. From the experience-distant perspective, the very existence of special needs and a certain helplessness is the rationale for the right to support. Having special needs means not being able to manage life on one's own. Thus, persons with special needs cannot be regarded as autonomous and responsible like other people.

An interesting finding in the study mentioned above was that the rights-ability perspective was also maintained by some non-disabled people, and it was obvious that the support these people offered disabled persons was important to their faith in this perspective. Thus, the rights-ability perspective is not an insiders' perspective in the sense that it cannot be adopted by non-disabled people. However, as mentioned above, a necessary condition for non-disabled people to adopt the insiders' perspective is that they have extensive experience of what life can be like with a disability. All non-disabled people who were observed to maintain this perspective in the study had such an experience of disability, often based on a close personal relationship with at least one disabled person. Thus, increased experience of disability through contacts with disabled people seems likely to contribute to the spreading of the rights-ability perspective.

The rights-ability perspective in the context of a changing welfare state

It is not difficult to see the link between the experience-distant perspective and the welfare state idea of weakness and support for weak groups. Trying to understand the experience-near perspective discovered in the study of the first integration generation, I also found interesting links to recent changes in the Swedish welfare state ideology. Thus, it is possible that the experience-near perspective is an expression not only of first-person experience, but also of a more general change in Swedish society that has supported the experience-near perspective and made it more visible. And it is also possible that the experience-near perspective maintained by intellectually disabled people in the study described is one of the first signs of this change in the welfare state ideology expressed by people with this disability. Similar perspectives have previously been expressed: for instance, by physically disabled people in the Independent Living Movement. My thesis is that the ideology of the Swedish

EXPERIENCE-NEAR

The demands/difficulties
of the task

A taken-for-granted right to
support (understood as)

The person's skills
and dispositions

Ability – AUTONOMY

HELPLESSNESS – *Disability*

EXPERIENCE-DISTANT

The demands/difficulties
of the task

A taken-for-granted right to
support (understood as)

The person's skills and
dispositions

Figure 10.3 Experience-near and experience-distant perspectives on the right to special support

welfare state includes, and probably always has included, several different understandings of the idea of the right to special support.

As indicated above, the idea of the weak group as a group of people with special needs and special rights is anchored in welfare state ideology. However, a close reading of the welfare state formulations from the late 1920s also provided an interesting clue to another, historically anchored meaning of weakness. As illustrated in the quotation about *Folkhemmet* above, a basic idea in the ideology of *Folkhemmet* was the idea that there existed *disadvantaged citizens* who had been deprived of their right to conditions of life equal to those of other people. It was against this background that the disadvantaged had a right to compensation through, for instance, *Folkhemmet's* systems of redistribution of incomes or other goods. The typical group here was poor people, who were considered to have been deprived of their belongings by an unfair, capitalist society protecting the privileges of some and neglecting others. An important object of *Folkhemmet* was to strengthen these people's citizenship, and this meant reinforcement of their rights to equal opportunities and equal conditions of life. In the quoted statement from Hansson, the terms disadvantaged and weak were, consequently, used in the context of oppression and exploitation.

Thus, my thesis is that the rights-ability perspective can be seen as a new expression of the old idea of the *disadvantaged person,* here applied to disabled people. This understanding of special rights has been rediscovered by people with personal experience of perspectives on disability, to some extent as a critique of the welfare state ideas of disabled people as weak or sick. In this new understanding, special rights are understood as rights of a disadvantaged citizen, in the same sense as a citizen who has been deprived of his or her belongings and therefore is entitled to rightful compensation.

Thus, we can identify two different meanings of disabled people's right to special services in the Swedish welfare state. There is a rights-disability meaning with roots in the late 1960s, when the forgotten groups of, for instance, disabled people first received public attention. This meaning was first developed within experience-distant perspectives, in the sense that it was formulated and maintained by people engaged in delivering services, like civil servants, politicians or non-disabled people contributing to special support by paying taxes.

This meaning was produced and spread during the golden era of social engineering of the 1960s and 1970s, when the welfare state model was based on the idea that societal and individual problems could be solved by experts and science. One could perhaps say that this phase of welfare state development was generally characterized by an experience-distant perspective on human and social difficulties. Some of the people receiving special services during this time probably also felt that they were deprived of their perspectives and the right to decide for themselves, but there seem to have been very few expressions of such experiences at the time.

During the 1980s and 1990s a new meaning of disabled persons' rights seems have emerged, with roots in the early welfare state ideology of the

1930s. Perhaps the taken-for-granted idea of special rights that had been so strongly anchored in Sweden during the policy of support to weak groups was a necessary condition for the emergence of the new meaning. This emergence was probably also supported by the crises striking the welfare state during these years. One crisis has been economic. A series of budget cuts meant that the big social engineering projects lost pace. Another crisis may be characterized as ideological. Here, disabled people and the disability movements have taken an active part. Ekensteen (1996), himself severely disabled, has, for instance, criticized the welfare state of the 1960s and 1970s for its objectification of service consumers and for forcing generalized service models on individual consumers. Third, a more general ideological reorientation of the entire welfare state has also contributed to a development away from central governing and social engineering towards decentralization and market control. These crises have severely reduced faith in the welfare state model of the 1960s and 1970s. In a review of integration research, Söder states:

> Belief in the centrally directed political welfare project is, if not destroyed, at least greatly modified. Decentralization and individualization have altered basic conditions. Opportunities for integration of people with disabilities have changed as well. Integration in practice is to a greater extent created through local units – schools and municipalities working with less direct steering from the central authorities – in what you might call 'the civil society'.
>
> (Söder 1997: 50; my translation)

Thus, the Swedish welfare state has changed significantly during the past 15 years. As demands for consumer influence and recognition of consumer perspectives increased, more space seems to have been created for disabled peoples' own perspectives. The expressions of the rights-ability perspective that we can observe today seem possible to understand in this context. This thesis is supported by the fact that disabled people in Sweden, during recent years, have explicitly rejected being regarded as weak. Söder (1990) has pointed out that there is a growing group, primarily of people with physical disabilities, who protest strongly against being identified as weak or as members of a weak group. He quotes Barbro Carlsson, who used to be the leader of DHR (the National Association for the Handicapped). She firmly stated that she did not want to be regarded as weak. On the contrary, she and many other people with disabilities claimed that they are strong and capable of shaping and managing their own lives, like other people.

Conclusions and questions

What will the development of the rights-ability perspective mean for disabled people? This question seems to concern researchers as well as policy makers and practitioners in Sweden today.

One natural conclusion seems to be that the rights-ability perspective will mean emancipation and empowerment of disabled people. Increased contact between disabled and non-disabled people during the era of integration of the 1970s and 1980s and onwards has, it is hoped, already reduced and will continue to reduce the influence of the hidden perspective of special needs, dependence and helplessness.

However, the question has also been raised as to whether the changes in the welfare state, and especially the disappearance of the idea of weakness and support to the weak, could not also make life more difficult for disabled people. The quotation from Söder above, about the changes in the welfare state, ends with the statement: 'Many people see a threat in this development' (Söder 1997: 50).

It has been argued that the Scandinavian welfare states have been replaced by 'welfare municipalities' during the 1980s and 1990s (Tøssebro *et al.* 1996). Decisions concerning services to people with disabilities are now decentralized and made in each municipality. When general regulations and service structures are abandoned, people fear that the groups considered weak will not have the strength to defend their right to a good life. This is the threat to which Söder refers.

Söder (1990) has also pointed out that the idea of the disabled person as a weak person with special needs might be important for people's motivation to solidarity with disabled people and to their willingness to contribute to special services. Here, the willingness to contribute is linked, Söder argues, to the representation of weakness and special needs as a personal tragedy. People contribute to special services for disabled people as a consequence of the compassion they feel for these tragic people and the terrifying personal sacrifices they are forced to accept.

How would the disappearance of the link between rights and weakness affect non-disabled people's willingness to contribute to special resources for people with special needs? Söder (1990) seems to argue that a reduced attention to weakness in general and the idea of the personal tragedy might reduce people's willingness to contribute. From a rights-ability perspective, the fundamental differences between non-disabled people and disabled people, in terms of weakness and strength, tend to disappear. Will non-disabled people still be willing to contribute to an enabling support and to the empowerment of disabled people, when the support is so effective that no obvious trace of weakness or personal tragedy is left?

However, there might be another possible answer to the question concerning the meaning of the changing welfare state. It is possible that the rights-ability perspective provides a new and more empowering ideological base for solidarity, which could replace the old welfare state idea of support to the weak. Perhaps the Scandinavian welfare state is in a transition, where the last traces of compassion for disabled people are replaced by an ideology of general, human rights to equally good conditions of life.

References

Ekensteen, V. (1986) *På folkhemmets bakgård. (In the Backyard of the People's Home).* Halmstad: Prisma.

Geertz, C. (1983) *Local Knowledge.* London: Fontana.

Gustavsson, A. (1998) *Inifrån utanförskapet (Insiders' Perspectives on Being an Outsider).* Stockholm: Johansson & Skyttmo förlag.

Hansson, P. A. (1928) *AK*, 3: 11.

Heider, F. (1958) *The Psychology of Interpersonal Relations.* New York: John Wiley & Sons.

Marshall, T. H. (1965) *The Rights to Welfare and Other Essays.* London: Heinemann.

Söder, M. (1990) Prejudice or ambivalence? Attitudes toward persons with disabilities, *Disability Handicap and Society,* 3(5): 227–41.

Söder, M. (1997) Integrering: Utopi, forskning, praktik (Integration: utopia, research and practice), in J. Tøssebro (ed.) *Den vanskelige integreringen* (The Difficult Integration). Oslo: Universitetsforlaget.

Tøssebro, J., Aalto, M. and Brusén, P. (1996) Changing ideologies and patterns of services, in J. Tøssebro, A. Gustavsson and G. Dyrendahl (eds) *Intellectual Disability in the Nordic Welfare States: Policies and Everyday Life.* Kristiansand: Norwegian Academic Press.

11

Equality and full participation for all? School practices and special education/integration in Greece

Anastasia Vlachou-Balafouti

Overview

This chapter is an attempt to locate the question of inclusive education within the wider context of the Greek educational system. It is based on the assumption that at the heart of the idea of inclusive education lie serious issues concerning 'human rights' and 'equal opportunities'. Thus, it attempts to present a number of serious contradictions and conflicts relating to notions of rights and equality which emerged out of the tensions created within stated policy and between stated and enacted policy. These include the institutional/ideological conditions and relations of education policy practices surrounding the process of 'integration' and the construction of 'special needs'. The insights included in this discussion are part of a much wider exploration which has been conducted by in-depth semi-structured interviews with eight teachers at an ordinary primary school in Athens.

Introduction

It has been reported that 'in modern societies education is one social context, if not *the social context*, wherein the tension, the dialogue and the politics of the self and others unfolds. The role that education plays in socialization, in citizenship formation, in making available the intellectual, cultural and recreational heritage of a society, in the provision of the resources of social imagination and creativity, and in enhancing one's vocational opportunities all point to the significance of education in shaping both the self and society' (Isaacs 1996: 38). It has been generally accepted that education is an 'enabling good' in the sense that it is required to obtain other social goods, such as income, employment and self-esteem.

Within the Greek Constitution, according to Article 16:

Education is the basic mission of the state, aiming at the moral, spiritual, professional and physical education of the Greeks . . . and their fulfilment as free and responsible citizens . . . All Greeks have the right to a free education at all levels in state school. The state shall support distinguished students and those deserving of assistance or special care, according to their abilities.

(Information Bulletin of Special Education 1994)

In addition, according to the official documents, the underlying political philosophies surrounding special education and/or integration are based on 'the principles of equality of opportunity in education, the idea of social inter-acceptance of disabled and non-disabled children and the promotion of educational and social mainstreaming practices and policies for children with special needs' (Information Bulletin of Special Education 1994).

While we cannot deny the importance of equal opportunities legislation, at the same time a number of contradictions and conflicts relating to notions of rights and equality emerge out of the tensions created between stated policy as it is found, for instance, in legislation, and policy as it is enacted and experienced by different social groups in varied social arenas (Fulcher 1989a). This is particularly true when we begin to look at the notion of 'inclusive' education in the context of policy and practice. As Armstrong *et al.* (1999: 2) state:

The extent to which the rights, privileges and responsibilities of citizenship are extended to all members of a society is a topic of increasing national and international importance. Ironically at the very moment when there is a growing interest in the issue of inclusion, there is mounting evidence of exclusionary practices across many societies . . . The apparently high profile which has been given to 'equal opportunities' in many European countries, both at the level of government policy and at the level of institutions over the past 15–20 years, has masked the real inequalities which exist between different groups in terms of access to experience, opportunity and power.

The political economy of schooling in terms of access and equity, and the way resources are allocated to challenge the practices underpinning exclusion, need a close and critical analysis if we really want at least to reduce dehumanizing situations of rejection and marginalization. This includes the necessity of exploring the intrinsic values and principles which structure the prevailing discourse of 'special education' and which guide its associated practices, as well as the ways in which the conflicting values and norms which govern life in school are negotiated and established (Rizvi and Lingard 1996: 25). In addition, what teachers think about such factors and how they perceive their role in a context where contradictory pressures are taking place are important topics of educational research. Teacher expectations, sensitivities, priorities and values contribute to the quality of all pupils' learning experiences and consequently teachers will influence what is taught how it is taught, and the assessment of what has been taught (Harnett and Naish 1993; Vlachou and Barton 1994).

In the light of the above this chapter locates the question of inclusive education within the wider educational context. The insights derived are part of a much wider exploration of Greek teacher attitudes towards the integration of the so-called 'children with special needs' in ordinary schools. The discussion that follows unfolds around an analysis of the extensive semi-structured interviews that I had with eight teachers at a Greek primary school in Athens. The interview material is part of a wider endeavour to understand: (a) the nature and intensity of the struggles experienced by teachers in their effort to promote more inclusive school practices; and (b) the inevitable difficulties in promoting inclusive educational practices within a system that functions via exclusive mechanisms. The chapter is based on the assumption that every discussion concerning inclusion demands first and foremost a different approach to 'special needs' and to the functioning of the ordinary school system.

An alternative approach to 'special needs'

Some historians and social theorists see it as inevitable that schools create difficulties. Schools, as institutions, are designed to fit children into a limited number of life slots and, as universal education spread, it did not respond to children's individual situations. All children of the same age were assumed to be the same for purposes of instruction, despite the fact that they are not (see Hegarty and Pocklington 1981). Those children who did not fit should have highlighted the inadequacy of the system. Instead of that, the children who did not fit into the categories that the educational system had so painstakingly allocated for them became a threat by revealing the system's inadequacies. To cover such inadequacies a variety of mechanisms were developed, according to which the children who did not fit were perceived not as the 'social products' of an insufficient system but as children with special needs; in other words, unmet needs were characterized as 'special needs'. The term 'special needs' as currently understood has become a category, gathering together widely different groups who are then assumed to be defective in some way. As Collins (1994: 173) has shown, 'needs are deficit-based within an inbuilt tendency to slip back towards individuals and their problems.' This individualistic-deficit approach to needs is fundamental to the philosophy of segregation, which separates young children from each other on the basis of their perceived 'inadequacies'. While the option of segregating some students remains, the fundamental structure of education will remain intact without challenging traditional approaches to curriculum, instruction and the existing culture and economy of schooling. As Fragou maintains, 'The history of children with "special needs" does not indicate their inability to adjust to the educational system, it rather indicates the rigidity of the educational system and its inability to adjust to their differences' (Fragou 1989: 63; my translation from Greek).

The following extract from interviews with a Greek primary school teacher is indicative of the way school practices construct 'special needs':

> Sometimes I seek the advice of other teachers. And what they tell me, and what I often see, is: 'Go according to the abilities and the needs of the average pupil.' And it can't be otherwise. You have to go at the pace of the average pupil – you bring your top one down a little and you try to bring up the most difficult one. But some [pupils] will come out the losers from this practice of promoting homogeneity. And this is where the so-called special needs come in. Can these children be educated in an ordinary class? I've read that this is the trend. I don't think that you have the time to concern yourself with them – you don't have time for something like that. And I feel guilty about it. The children who are experiencing difficulties are left aside by the teacher. I feel that I exclude them. In my class I have a little girl with difficulties, and the parents don't help and without support I don't feel that I help her either . . . and then there's this young Albanian boy who is very clever but he has difficulties in understanding the language and again I can't help.
>
> (My translation from Greek)

In order to understand the above extract there is a need to place the discriminatory practices in the particular social and historical context within which they have been developed. Thus, it is important to mention that Greece, for historical and social reasons, has traditionally been a country that exports human labour. However, recently it has had to face the new challenge of becoming a host society to refugees and immigrants from various developing countries. If the novelty of the phenomenon is taken into consideration, the presence of immigrant populations finds Greek schools totally unprepared to deal with children from other cultures who speak other languages. Teachers are not prepared and do not know how to handle the new situation. At the same time, most of the immigrant pupils, even if they are characterized by their teachers as being 'very clever' (see above extract), spend part of the time in support and/or special classes, where they are taught mainly Greek. A direct consequence of such practices is that most immigrant students have been defined as children with special needs. The vague term 'special needs' indicates a transference of features of the school environment into something that the child possesses. This is a highly political practice, as it ignores and/or obscures questions related to structural inequalities based on ethnicity and cognitive ability.

Further, such educational practices remind us of Procrousti's bed (from Greek mythology), where the legs of various people were either stretched or cut off to fit in the same bed. In the context of the Procroustian bed, those whose legs did not happen to be the same as the length of the bed were the ones who bore the burden of the problem and its consequences. In the same way, children's needs that do not fit into the predefined National Curriculum become a personal matter. Because it is extremely difficult to normalize and to change the system, the overriding effort is on normalizing pupils. The current language of integration and special education has emerged out of these 'normalization' initiatives. This deficit/individualistic approach – rooted within the medical, charity, lay and even legislative concepts of 'disability' and 'special needs' – is central to the way welfare states and educational practices respond to an increasing proportion of citizens (see Fulcher 1989b). Claiming this, I do not want to imply that there are not individual and/or within-child difficulties that impinge upon the process of learning. However, 'by emphasising the pupil's failure the fundamental issue of the system's failure to meet needs of all pupils is masked' (Barton and Oliver 1992: 14).

The special needs of the education system

It has been estimated that, from the total population of children in Greece, approximately 180,000–200,000 children will be defined at some point of their school life as having 'special educational needs'. In 1994 the Directorate of Special Education informed us that 12,383 of these children were educated in special schools or in special classes within ordinary schools. Thus, the vast majority of children that will face difficulties of any kind are currently educated within ordinary schools. One way of dealing with these children could be to create more special schools or special classes, in this way allowing the ordinary school to scrape along with its inefficiencies.

As Zoniou-Sideri (1993: 21) maintains, 'the existing educational policy aims at the establishment and the extension of special/segregated schools' (my translation from Greek). However, regardless of the expansion of special schools, there will always be children who will show up the insufficiencies of the ordinary school system.

On the other hand, the fact that the vast majority of the so-called children with special educational needs are educated within Greek ordinary schools cannot be considered as integration – indeed, in some cases I would not be exaggerating if I said that it can be considered as 'total rejection'. To illustrate this, I give below an excerpt from the interviews I had with Greek primary school teachers:

> I had Year 1 with 27 children, one of which was a child with behavioural difficulties and the other of which was mongoloid [*sic*]. I went crazy that year. I was going in that direction. I would be standing up and say to myself that I'd be lucky if I didn't faint. Let me tell you how that class evolved. Twenty-seven children with two difficult cases, and in a small classroom! It was enough to drive you crazy. They went up to Year 2. Worse still. They went up to Year 3. The development in this class was even worse. They reached Year 4 . . . nothing. I gave up and I didn't even want to see or hear of this class. I am not at all happy with the way we treated these children, with the way we responded to the problem of the progress of the class. This class was left to take its own chances . . . We allow a class to go on like this and God helps them – the problem is perpetuated.

(My translation from Greek)

This type of political and practical inertia has caused the perpetuation of the problems that the teacher faces in responding to all children in her class, and has created unbearable situations which have affected both the job of the teacher and the life of the pupils. In this case the integration argument suggests that on the grounds of educational rights everyone should have access to regular schools and classrooms. But mere access to the physical environment of schools or classrooms within schools confers no specific or necessarily appropriate opportunity to learn (Gerber 1996: 157). To place children in regular classrooms without fundamentally restructuring the current system will simply perpetuate their disadvantage.

Given that educational structures have not been changed in the direction of promoting integration, the emerging practice is to marginalize those children who obstruct the smooth functioning of the class, thus creating the 'classic scapegoats'. According to another teacher, 'So one child [with special needs] in the class, or two, let's say one, has he the right to put all the other children behind? Should we sacrifice the rest of our children in the interests of the one whom we leave free, protect and try to support?'

Who is sacrificed in the end is certainly an important matter. As is shown, in the following excerpt from the same teacher – at another point in the interview – she outlines another reality:

> No matter how hard you work, you don't have the time to do everything . . . And at some point you become indifferent. In other words, you leave the child on his own. You see that he has 'gaps', you see that day by day more and more is being added and the gap becomes wider and wider . . . I could see, however, and I still see and believe that if that child [a child defined as having special needs] had the right help, if he was in the right school, he would have learned to read and write . . . Now he leaves school incomplete as far as his education is concerned, and it is the same with his socialization.
>
> (My translation from Greek)

It can be argued that schooling is itself disabling, that its lack of flexibility in accommodating a diverse range of student attributes creates disabled students or, in the words of the above teacher, 'children with gaps'. Because the manner in which schools function is taken for granted and seen as unproblematic, the source of students' difficulties is seen to reside in their 'defects' rather than the defects and limitations of schooling. The political practice of masking the role of schooling in creating the problem serves to obscure productive solutions to enduring and persistent problems (Christensen 1996: 64).

While access and equity policies enable individuals to gain entry into mainstream institutions, they often leave the institutions themselves unaltered. Thus, while many of the so-called children with special needs are allowed access, by and large the social conditions they experience have remained much the same, leading to frustration and inability to cope on the part of both themselves and their teachers. Within this context, the notion of equal opportunities for the education of the so-called children with special needs implies the necessity of finding the 'right school' in order for them to be educated. According to the above teacher the right school is considered to be the special school. The developing divisive ideology, which is often the basis for the creation of everyday educational practices, is partly the result of the fact that, although the Education Act of 1985 approached special education as part of ordinary education – a very significant step – it failed to change the basic characteristics of the general system, which is often extremely exclusive and anachronistic – both in its structure and in its nature – not only for the so-called children with special needs but also for all the other pupils (see Vlachou 1995). Teachers were aware of this and they felt that they are expected to do more and be more responsive to the changing society while their status is declining:

> We are trying to respond to the children of the twenty-first century with certain processes and with a logic which are anachronistic . . . and I, as teacher, seem to the child to be like a doll covered with cobwebs on the shelf, and he says 'They used to play with that 30 years ago.'

> What bothers me is that we don't have any training, we haven't received new things which we can hand on to the children . . . and the children inspect the teacher, they criticize him, they look to see what he is doing and what he is going to do . . . We need renewal, we need changes and further information. Whether the teacher does something different is now up to whether he feels like doing it.
>
> (My translation from Greek)

In practice, the quality of the education of all children depends mainly on the nature and degree of dedication and willingness of teachers. Both dedication and willingness are extremely precious and necessary for the quality of educational practices. But the degree of dedication shown by teachers is influenced to a large degree by the context within which they work. One of the main characteristics of this context, at least according to the eight teachers who participated in the research, is the feeling of helplessness and isolation which they experience in their attempt to meet the complex demands and often conflicting expectations that the dynamics of the social world of 2000 impose on them. They were aware that broader social trends are changing and that children are being affected by such trends. Children were seen as presenting schools with increasingly complex demands that are social, intellectual and emotional. At the same time, they felt that schools are not prepared to deal with such demands on their own, and their dilemma was how they could manage to support children when they themselves are not supported to do what they have been expected to do.

> Society places tremendous demands on teachers, but simultaneously teachers are not covered at many levels and are not supported so that they can take on the role which is demanded of them and which they deserve . . . Their role has changed and this has not been understood, the whole thing is not understood. They come [parents and children] with

tremendous expectations of their teacher. They receive a shock when they realize that things are not the way they expected them to be.

They [political discourses] are telling us now, and I believe in it, that we have to take the children further – to another level: emotionally, in terms of their personality, to inform them, to stimulate them, to enable them to search for themselves; but we must have the opportunity of being informed about all of these, we must have some support, we must be enabled as teachers. I can't solve all the problems on my own.

The needs are as many as the number of pupils that we have. From every point of view. And we cannot meet these needs. There is a very unpleasant feeling of your own weakness – on your own, whatever you try to do you do it on your own.

(My translation from Greek)

The dangers of placing the onus for change on teachers without ensuring there are adequate structures and support systems including staff development, renders schools a *risky* place for both teachers and children:

it's a lottery. If you get a good class, you're lucky. If you don't get a good class, you have to manage on your own.

The wretchedness of the teacher comes from the existing stagnation, and then you hate what you've started to do, especially if you haven't chosen it.

My child is going to the high school next year. Do you believe that even now, without having met my colleagues, I have condemned them? I don't like what I'm saying or what I'm feeling. I talk about it with other people but it is a feeling which is not unjustified. It comes because I can see that the teacher has given up.

(My translation from Greek)

The absence of supporting networks, of collaboration, of information and of basic advisory intervention is even more marked in matters concerning 'special needs':

I'll tell you my experience when I started [in grade 1] with Pericles [a pupil with tetraplegia]. I started off with good intentions and I made some terrible mistakes on the way. What I did manage was to integrate him into the group, to teach him how to fight for his own rights, to be part and to be accepted of the class-group but I didn't help him educationally. If I had had someone who knew and who could have worked with me, this child would today be totally integrated . . . I had no other person beside me and I was 'wandering in the dark'. I could see that one way wasn't working so I tried another. I spent 6–7 hours at his house every day, without being paid. We were trying to do things, from playing together, doing gym, going out to explore the neighbourhood, to learning mathematics by counting the oranges on the orange trees. That was my mistake because I was exhausted. And when Pericles went to grade 3 I said to myself 'I cannot continue like that . . .'

(My translation from Greek)

Within a context where teachers feel insecure, lack encouragement and are provided with little serious, sustained and adequately resourced staff development, calls to promote more inclusive educational priorities will be viewed as laudable rhetoric on the level of stated policy and an additional unwanted burden on the level of enacted policy. As a teacher put it, she is not willing to take on one more role: a 'therapeutic one', meaning the education of the so-called children with special needs. The 'therapeutic' dimension that teachers perceived as embedded in the education of these children is connected with the values and principles which structure the prevailing discourse of 'special education' and/or integration.

Special education and/or integration has been developed as a technical field concerned with issues of diagnosis, assessment, causes of disability and appropriate forms of treatment including the redistribution of 'special' provision and the creation of 'special' programmes. This ideological framework is not restricted to Greece. It can also be found in other Western countries. Indeed, Fulcher's (1985) and Slee's (1996) observations of the entrapment of integration within struggles over resources in Australia can be applied to characterize the dominant situation in Greek schools. Schools now required integration teachers and aids, and the support of psychologists and special educators in order to integrate students with disabilities. Paradoxically, integration in Greece was not simply a question of relocating students from segregated settings in the educational mainstream, it also prompted the identification of students with 'impairments', 'disabilities' and 'problems with schooling' already attending regular classrooms (see also Slee 1996). As Slee maintains

Integration became the mechanism for the management of students with behavioural problems . . . as well as for minimizing the impact of disability on school programmes and structures. Advanced within a discourse of social justice and equity, integration was a regulatory framework for the surveillance and management of students who presented challenges to schooling.

(Slee 1996: 102)

This ideological framework surrounding special education and/or integration depoliticizes issues of educational reform, converting many political issues into technical ones, leaving much of the power of decision making in the hands of a few 'experts' (see Troyna and Vincent 1996).

The reality described above is very different from the official political approach to the idea of integration as stated in the Information Bulletin of Special Education (1994), which was published by the Department of Special Education:

From an educational point of view, [children with special educational needs] have rights to equal educational opportunities which will be granted to them systematically and methodically by the unified/ordinary educational system . . . without derogatory labels and racial discrimination or anti-pedagogical, anti-psychological and traumatic treatments . . . The above component elements of educational policy and philosophy have been adopted by all developed societies and are expressed globally in the declarations of the international organisations.

(Information Bulletin of Special Education 1994: 10)

To assume that change in realized unequal societal structures will arise solely from political declarations, is to ignore the politics of policy, the fact that implementation of policy does not automatically follow its creation and the fact that policy is constructed at different levels (see Fulcher 1989a; Mousley *et al.* 1993).

In practice, the educational evaluation and placement of the so-called children with special needs is being done in an arbitrary way, almost without any serious planning or valid criteria, while many programmes are designed by teachers who are not supported at all, and often such programmes are incomplete, without specific educational aims and the means for being implemented (Lambropoulou 1994). In addition, integration by adopting and adapting practices borrowed from segregative education has become directly connected with 'special needs', 'special' piecemeal programmes and 'special' provisions, perpetuating and legitimizing a situation which should be condemned. Lack of clarity about the goals of integration and means to achieve them is the dominant characteristic of the current political and educational practices in Greece. The confusion and the considerable latitude of professional discretion and power are reflected in the variety of definitions of integration that are offered.

'Integration': a highly contested concept

The process of defining terms is complex but significant, because definitions serve different, although interdependent, functions; they allow for communication, thought, social interaction and control (see Meighan 1981). That is, on the one hand they order individuals' personal and social experiences by offering an ideological framework within which people make sense of cultural, social and political phenomena. On the other hand, they are devices for the transmission of these ideological frameworks, including perceptions and conceptualizations, between individuals. Thus, definitions become the means of making sense of the world around us, setting our histories and ideologies in context and providing a basis for generating action.

Approaching the process of integration as an educational practice implies that its definitions entail a number of complexities. Educational practices are theoretically, politically and morally informed (Fulcher 1989a). In other words, they involve a series of parameters with educational, political, economic, moral, theoretical and practical implications. Pedagogical principles, humanitarian ideologies, theories of normalization, socio-political and medical as well as financially informed approaches to education are being used in a conflicting way in the cultural struggle of different interest groups; these groups are all trying, within asymmetrical power relationships, to pursue different objectives and to define, according to these objectives, specific realities. As the following discussion indicates, integration as an educational practice is a highly contested term which can be used in a variety of ways to suit a variety of political interests.

Three teachers who were interviewed approached integration via a criticism of the 'ghettoization' of special schools. Connecting life in school with the wider societal structures, they seemed to be aware that segregation institutionalized a system of consequent exclusionary practices:

> I believe that the special school is the worst place to be educated, [pause] because the child moves and lives in the wider society and will have to confront this society and not the ghetto. The overruling attitude is ghettoization, but the child will not live in a ghetto, he will live in a society and society will treat him both cruelly and kindly, will both love and reject him. He will live in an ordinary world and this is his world. Whether it is a cruel world or not, whether it is a sensitive world or not, he must learn how to face it.
>
> (My translation from Greek)

At the same time, the account provided below represents the prevalent ideology among teachers, according to which what is required in an educative context is an 'ethical/moral' perspective that seeks actively to create conditions that will nurture the individual within a *limited and a limiting environment*:

> I don't know what integration means, but I do know that the priorities are to find the children's skills, to help them, to understand them and, on top of the children's skills and abilities, to give them stimulation so that they become sensitive to their abilities. We can't put all children into the same mould, it's not possible, *yet we do it*.
>
> (My translation from Greek)

Without changing traditional approaches to curriculum and instruction, when the resourcing formulae fail, then the ideology of expertism arises, as it has, for instance, with the acquisition of special teachers. Expertism relates needs to notions of personal pathology, disorder or deficit. In such cases the underlying assumption has been that children defined as having special needs belong to a different pedagogical category and thus cannot be taught by ordinary teachers. The ideology of expertism serves to relieve general education of the pressure to respond to diverse students, and consequently perpetuates and even strengthens a divisive ideology that impinges upon efforts to create more inclusive schooling environments (Troyna and Vincent 1996). In practice, as a teacher put it:

Each school must have a specially trained teacher if they want to promote integration and if they don't want to put these children into the ghetto of special schools. To meet the needs of the child. Or to work together with the class teacher, but to have [the specially trained teacher] a teaching relationship with the pupil himself or herself for some hours. Because Kostakis [a pupil defined by the teacher as having behavioural problems] is *wonderfully* included [ironical connotation meaning mere access to the physical environment of the school] in the school but he is out of the classroom.

(My translation from Greek)

Special teachers are needed to work with children who are perceived as belonging to a different pedagogical category by withdrawing them from ordinary classes and placing them in 'special' placements elsewhere, such as in separate units, or resource, support and/or parallel classes. All may be defended as part of the integration programme. In this case, integration has become a process of minimizing the difference that is to be found in a class situation, and by doing so it maintains the structural and cultural relations of schooling. The following account illustrates that the nature of the existing structural and cultural relations of schooling cultivates the distinction between 'normal' and 'more than normal' diversity:

In our school we have a mongol child [*sic*] in grade 1; a child with a certain intelligence. I mean he is able to learn how to read and write but from what I have heard and from what I see this child is being wasted here . . . I believe that there should be two types of schools – the school for the normal children and the school for all the other children depending on their impairment so that they [special teachers at the special school] can respond to their [disabled pupils'] needs.

(My translation from Greek)

The segregation versus integration debate, or in other words the dilemma as to whether children with 'special needs' are better taught in special or in ordinary schools, is a dominant one in Greece. In other countries (e.g the UK, the USA) this question has been discussed extensively, both at an academic/research level and in the area of educational policy and practice. A critical reflection on research results regarding the integration versus segregation dilemma shows how futile and problematic this particular debate has been in the research area (see Vlachou 1997).

In the context of educational practice, the debate regarding integration versus segregation processes produces dilemmas for both teachers and parents, and often leads to the perpetuation of myths, restricting even further the aims of integration. It creates the ideology that parents of disabled children have the choice between focusing on the academic development of their child by sending him or her to a special school or focusing on his or her socialization process, implying that this is the benefit of integration. Such restrictive 'choices' simplify the complex process of integration, create certain expectations at the expense of others and raise doubts about the responsibility of the school to educate *all* children. Such restrictive choices have become the emerging trend within the Greek educational system, very often coupled with confusion and lack of knowledge regarding the aims and functions of special schooling. The following account is indicative of the confusion that surrounds special education and/or integration:

> I believe it is very important for an individual or pupil who has certain needs or who is different to be integrated. First of all, rejection by children or by society is a very bad thing and the person who experiences rejection may react badly against society and create problems. These children should definitely go to a special school so that they can later be taught, so that they can assimilate, they can take from the school what they need to function, so that this integration can exist later in society.
>
> (My translation from Greek)

This opinion contains a paradox, a contradiction in itself concerning the question of how integration into society can be promoted via segregated education. Segregated education tends to imply that the children in question have been institutionally destined to live segregated lives in adulthood. After all, a 'protective' special educational environment has little in common with the challenges and the complexities of an ordinary environment, while 'the result of "special" education is that children are destined for a "special" life career in terms of employability, self-sufficiency and dependence' (Barton and Tomlinson 1984: 70). The above confusion has been created partially because the notions of 'special/segregated provisions' (1981 Act) and 'integration' (1985 Act) were introduced within the same decade, the first being influenced by the 1944 Act in Britain and the second by the British Warnock Report and the American concept of the 'least restrictive environment' (PL 94-142). Thus, while in other countries these complex notions were introduced within a period of more than a hundred years, within Greek society both notions were introduced almost simultaneously, generating a social and practical confusion as to what equality of opportunity in education means. Both Acts, but most importantly the most recent Act, while introducing a specific ideology, lacked any serious and basic specifications and programmes that would promote its implementation.

Thus, while declarations refer to basic human rights and equal opportunities, a critical analysis of the process of integration reflects tendencies, contradictions and ambiguities which justify Oliver's statement that:

> Integration as a process has taken on the language of rhetorics . . . To put the matter bluntly, children with special educational needs still get an inferior education to everyone else, and although the rhetorics of integration as a process may serve to obscure or mystify this fact the reality remains.
>
> (Oliver 1992: 23)

Conclusion

This chapter has attempted to locate the question of inclusive education within the wider context of the educational system. The insights offered in this account presented the inevitable difficulties in promoting inclusive educational practices within a system that functions via exclusive mechanisms. This necessitates an alternative approach to the notion of 'needs' and to the functioning of the integration process.

It was argued that the popular and structural way in which 'needs' have been approached has a central role in the development of divisive ideologies and practices, while at the same time obscuring and leaving unaltered the enduring and persistent problems that schools and consequently teachers have to deal with. It was also shown that integration – though a very popular notion in the current politics of education in Greece – is a highly contested term. This is because the principles that structure the prevailing discourse of 'equal opportunity' in fact maintain the existing structural and cultural relations of schooling, perpetuating in this way social and cultural oppression to particular groups of children. As Armstrong *et al.* (1999) have argued, 'where calls for "inclusive" schools and practices are limited within a framework which appeals for equal opportunities, no serious challenge is made to the conditions under which discriminatory and exclusionary social practices operate.'

Questions such as 'How do schools deal with the issues of difference?', 'In what ways does equal opportunity legislation legitimize what it sets out to criticize/challenge?' and 'Where does equality of opportunities in education rest within current educational practices?' are of great importance in the struggle for the implementation of inclusive practices.

Questions

1 In what ways can formal legislation concerning equal opportunities mask and perpetuate discriminatory practices in education?
2 What issues arise out of the adoption of a 'needs-based' approach in developing responses to difference in educational settings?
3 What connections can be made between the arguments put forward in this chapter in relation to integration in Greece and questions concerning integration and inclusion in education in your own context?

References

Armstrong, D., Armstrong, F. and Barton, L. (eds) (1999) *Inclusive Policy and Provision: Comparative Insights and Issues.*
Barton, L. and Oliver, M. (1992) Special needs: a personal trouble or public issue?, in M. Arnot and L. Barton (eds) *Voicing Concerns: Sociological Perspectives on Contemporary Education Reforms.* Oxford: Triangle Books.

Barton, L. and Tomlinson, S. (eds) (1984) *Special Education and Social Interest.* London: Croom Helm.

Christensen, C. (1996) Disabled, handicapped or disordered: 'what's in a name?', in C. Christensen and F. Rizvi (eds) *Disability and the Dilemmas of Education and Justice.* Buckingham: Open University Press.

Collins, J. (1994) The silent minority: developing talk in the primary classroom. Unpublished PhD thesis, University of Sheffield.

Fragou, A. (1989) I Isigisis tis A. Fragou, *Because Difference Is a Right,* 6/7: 62–4.

Fulcher, G. (1985) Integration locks into fight over resources, *The Age,* 8 October.

Fulcher, G. (1989a) *Disabling Policies? A Comparative Approach to Education Policy and Disability.* London: Falmer Press.

Fulcher, G. (1989b) Disability: a social construction, in G. Lupton and J. Najman (eds) *Sociology of Health and Illness.* London: Macmillan.

Gerber, M. (1996) Reforming special education: beyond 'inclusion', in C. Christensen and F. Rizvi (eds) *Disability and the Dilemmas of Education and Justice.* Buckingham: Open University Press.

Harnett, A. and Naish, M. (1993) Democracy, teachers and the struggle for education: an essay in the political economy of teacher education, *Curriculum Studies,* 1(3): 335–48.

Hegarty, S. and Pocklington, K. (1981) *Educating Pupils with Special Educational Needs in the Ordinary School.* Windsor: NFER-Nelson.

Information Bulletin of Special Education (1994) Athens: Ministry of National Education, OEDB.

Isaacs, P. (1996) Disability and the education of persons, in C. Christensen and F. Rizvi (eds) *Disability and the Dilemmas of Education and Justice.* Buckingham: Open University Press.

Lambropoulou, V. (1994) The problems of deaf people in Greece, in M. Kaila, N. Polemikos and G. Filipou (eds) *People with Special Needs, Vol. A.* Athens: Greek Letters.

Meighan, R. (1981) *A Sociology of Educating.* London: Holt, Rinehart and Winston.

Mousley, J., Rice, M. and Tregenza, K. (1993) Integration of students with disabilities into regular schools: policy in use, *Disability, Handicap and Society,* 8(1): 59–70.

Oliver, M. (1992) Changing the social relations of research production, *Disability, Handicap and Society,* 7(2): 101–14.

Rizvi, F. and Lingard, B. (1996) Disability, education and the discourse of justice, in C. Christensen and F. Rizvi (eds) *Disability and the Dilemmas of Education and Justice.* Buckingham: Open University Press.

Slee, R. (1996) Disability, class and poverty: school structures and policing identities, in C. Christensen and F. Rizvi (eds) *Disability and the Dilemmas of Education and Justice.* Buckingham: Open University Press.

Troyna, B. and Vincent, C. (1996) 'The ideology of expertism': the framing of special education and racial equality policies in the local state, in C. Christensen and F. Rizvi (eds) *Disability and the Dilemmas of Education and Justice.* Buckingham: Open University Press.

Vlachou, A. (1995) Education and disability in Greece, in F. Armstrong and L. Barton (eds) *Comparative Perspectives on Special and Inclusive Education.* Specialised Module for the Diploma/Master of Education. Sheffield: University of Sheffield.

Vlachou, A. (1997) *Struggles for Inclusive Education.* Buckingham: Open University Press.

Vlachou, A. and Barton, L. (1994) Inclusive education: teachers and the changing culture of schooling, *British Journal of Special Education,* 21(3): 105–7.

Zoniou-Sideri, A. (1993) The integration of disabled children at the pre-school and primary school level, *Educational Community,* 21: 21–5.

12

Disability, human rights and education in Cyprus

Helen Phtiaka

Overview

Education and employment for children and adults with disabilities has recently been a hot issue in Cyprus. This is partly owing to recent educational and legislative developments regarding the issue of integrated education for children with special needs. It is also owing to a fund-raising activity for children and adults with special needs which was first launched in 1990 and has recently turned into a major nationwide annual charity event called Radio-Marathon. Events such as this have raised all sorts of issues regarding disability and human rights, and it is true to say that they have increased public awareness on what used to be a taboo subject. At what cost? The charity model has become well established in people's consciousness at the expense of a human rights model. Who benefits from this, how do disabled people feel about it and what can be done in the future? The chapter that follows will attempt to answer these questions.

Introduction

Issues of disability, human rights and education have a parallel but not necessarily interlinked history in Cyprus. This is to say that although all three topics have often been debated in public, especially at times when this was expedient, such as the International Year for the Disabled (1981), the three issues very rarely appear interrelated. This is particularly true of issues of education and human rights. On the eve of the introduction of new educational legislation for children with special needs this is particularly obvious. The new legislation will come to replace the outdated existing legislation of 1979 (Ministry of Education and Culture 1996). According to existing legislation, four categories of special need are still in use for education purposes, and 'maladjusted, trainable, physically handicapped and educationally delayed children require special education which is provided in special schools and special classes' (Ministry of Education and Culture 1996: 73). In the proposed legislation for special education (Ministry of Education and Culture 1998), the law, obviously influenced by British educational philosophy and legislation of the late 1970s and early 1980s, (the Warnock Report of 1978 and the Education Act 1981) speaks only of 'children with special needs'. These are defined as 'children who have serious learning or adaptive difficulties owing to physical, mental or psychological inadequacies making special education necessary' (Ministry of Education and Culture 1998: 2).

It is apparent that the definition of educational needs is still based on a deficit model. Consequently, access to mainstream education is not perceived as a basic human right for these children, but as a necessary legislative modification which will: (a) bring the legislation up to date; (b) be in accordance with perceptions of contemporary international educational practice; and (c) cover current educational practice in Cyprus. Integration of children with special needs in mainstream classrooms has been an informal Ministry of Education practice since the late 1980s. The Ministry of Education and Culture's declared philosophy on special education further clarifies the issue, as it makes no mention of human rights:

It is generally accepted today that children with special needs must have equal educational opportunities of co-education with their peers in their neighbourhood schools. Furthermore, it is becoming increasingly acceptable that many of the learning and other problems children with special needs have can be dealt with satisfactorily inside the ordinary classroom with the use of differentiation and the appropriate equipment and organization of the learning environment.

(Ministry of Education and Culture 1996: 10)

For the time being, a combination of the use of mainstream classes, special classes in mainstream schools and special schools is in existence, depending on the child's condition and degree of disability. This arrangement naturally deprives a number of children from access to the national curriculum and therefore from access to further and higher education.

Interestingly enough, the ministry officials, quite possibly influenced by university philosophy (Phtiaka 1996a) speak of (albeit without satisfactorily defining it) an inclusive school which will 'educate all children' (Ministry of Education and Culture 1996: 10). According to their suggestion, this school 'must accept all children regardless of their physical, mental, social, emotional, linguistic or other condition.' This statement, bold as it appears to be, coming from an official document, is closer to the rhetoric than to the philosophy of inclusive schooling. This is because it is not substantiated or facilitated in any way and is furthermore a long way away from current Cypriot educational practice. It can therefore be interpreted as the enlightened vision of a small group of officials who possess neither the coherent philosophy nor the necessary power to influence educational policy to such an extent. The introduction of an inclusive school system would require – quite simply – the complete destruction of the education system as we know it in Cyprus today (Phtiaka 1996d). And this is unlikely to happen either very soon or very easily. The intense antagonism of the existing system coupled with an inflexible centralized administration and a very rigid content-oriented national curriculum make a radical change very unlikely in the near future. Nevertheless, a changing rhetoric is a good sign if it takes us in the direction of a changing philosophy.

This being the situation concerning existing and proposed legislation in special education and educational access of children with special needs in Cyprus, let us move on to broaden the scene. Given the complexity of the issues at hand, and in order to cover as wide an area as possible, the chapter follows a modular structure offering glimpses of current practice and debate in three spheres: (a) the dominant model of thinking in the area of disability and special needs (human rights?); (b) the role and the struggle of the disability movement (disability); and (c) the current debates in special education (education). The first part is necessarily the largest, as it examines the prevalent philosophy in the area and provides the context for the other two.

A note on terminology might be necessary before we start. Throughout this chapter the terms disabled and disability will refer particularly to adults and the term special needs particularly to children. Riddell's (1993) definitions of both disability and special educational needs might be helpful here, as she notes the conflicting connotations of both terms and points to the common points between them. Like her, I shall adopt Oliver's position that

> similar forces have shaped social policies towards disabled people and educational policies for children with special needs. As a result of this, theoretical understandings of disability may be applied to the field of special educational needs.
>
> (Riddell 1993: 446)

Human rights conceived

How is the human rights issue conceived in Cyprus regarding disabled people?

The Radio-Marathon

Dear sir
The advertising for this year's Radio-Marathon has already started. The TV adverts in particular are bombarding us with images of money, piggy banks, collection stalls, receipts, and generally individuals who contribute financially. We ask the organizers: are they trying to promote the idea that the special needs of these people begin and end in the financial context of monetary contributions? Is that the message they are trying to

send to everyone, including young children, tomorrow's citizens? Do they really want to change current attitudes, or just retain them for their own interest? Is this the awareness increasing exercise they are boasting about? What social integration do they achieve in this way? How much information do they really think they offer towards the right direction of the appropriate handling of these people and the finite solution of their problems? We are awaiting your answers. Thank you for the hospitality. Andros Prokopiou – a person with special questions, 22 October 1996.

This is a copy of a letter sent by the vice-president of the Cyprus Paraplegic Organization (CPO), Andros Prokopiou, to a newspaper on the eve of the big national fiesta called Radio-Marathon. Launched on 20 November 1990 by a local radio station, the Radio-Marathon has recently turned into a major nationwide annual charity event supported by the national radio and a national bank. Prokopiou appears to find the whole event misled and distressing. He is not alone in that. He speaks for a number of disabled people in Cyprus. He also speaks for a number of non-disabled people. I am not a person with immediately identifiable special needs. Yet I too find this event annoying, insulting even. I find the persistence of the organizers in money gathering aggressive, often abusive, especially for people who do not happen to share their philosophy. Yet year after year I give in. I contribute to the fundraising, having been battered for a month by advertising in the intense soundtrack of Carmina Burana, and having been bombarded for two days by sentimental radio talk about 'those children not as fortunate as us'. At the closing of the event, with an intense feeling of having absconded from a national effort to build a better future, I hesitantly join in the festivities and humbly give my contribution. I am a weird exception. Most people appear to celebrate the event and share its 'generous' philosophy. The enthusiasm of the radio presenters seems to be catching. The whole country seems to be moving for two days to the powerful sounds of Carmina Burana.

My personal position and my eventual surrender, which are in direct conflict, indicate quite clearly the overwhelming power of the charity model which is the basic philosophy underlying the whole event. Obviously, neither the hustle and bustle of the organizers nor the unquestioning enthusiasm of the people is the most worrying aspect of the event. Those of us who disagree with the principle could perhaps lock ourselves away until it is all over and refuse flatly to join in the festivities. Or we could try to question it in private and in public, even though this is no easy task. What is much more worrying is the fact that through this event the charity model is prevailing over any other philosophy regarding disability, and the Radio-Marathon seems to be establishing itself in people's consciousness as the main body in the country responsible for special needs issues: a private trust instead of the state. This seems to be wholeheartedly supported and encouraged by state officials whose job is to deal precisely with these issues. It is common practice, for instance, for parents trying to secure a class assistant for their child with special needs in the ordinary class to get the following response from Ministry of Education officials: 'We have no funds for this, but have you tried the Radio-Marathon?' What are the parents to do? They usually try the Radio-Marathon. If the child is lucky, the all-knowing governing body approves the request and this year's class assistant is secured. Next year? We start again. It is interesting to note here a question Prokopiou posed in a public speech on 29 December 1993: 'What will happen if we push this situation to its limits and if at some point people get fed up with it all and stop offering money? What will become of these people (who depend on the money)?' The short answer is that they will have to fall back on their own (and their family's) devices, having limited structures of formal state support available. However, to understand the issues involved fully we need to go back a little and take things one at a time.

This is a fairly happy era for Cyprus. Despite the fact that the political problem remains unresolved, Cypriot people have, after long years of struggle, achieved a high standard of living. They have a good life (under the circumstances), and quite a number of them have an income that allows them to help others 'less fortunate'. The amount of money collected each year by a number of charities, Radio-Marathon in particular, is astounding for the island's population of 700,000 people. To quote Prokopiou again: 'within 48 hours we can motivate the whole country and collect all this money which is disproportionate to our size.' It is perhaps not a coincidence that such an event was only launched at the beginning of the 1990s when the political situation was relatively stable and the financial situation had improved considerably.

Sixteen years before that the Turkish invasion had left the island in a state of devastation and shock numbering 200,000 refugees (in a population of 500,000) and 1619 missing persons (still missing 25 years later). The year 1974 is not a long time ago, and people, when asked to give money for children in need, may well still remember their own children or themselves as children in need. They are therefore exceptionally generous in their offer. With the assistance of the special socio-historical conditions of the island, where the state is under 40 years old, the charity model is well established in people's minds and their response is immediate. It has been argued in the literature (Tomlinson 1982; Wolfensberger 1989; Barnes 1994; Vlachou 1997) that the charity model is a very powerful tool, not least because it puts itself 'above suspicion'. Who can argue with the principle of helping the fellow (wo)man without being in danger of being considered nasty and callous? It is very difficult indeed to overcome this hurdle and start asking difficult questions, such as 'who benefits from such a model?' More so in a country where suffering is still alive in people's memories and their first reaction would be to ease each other's pain. If, however, we insisted on being nasty and callous and asked this question regarding the Radio-Marathon, we may get some very interesting answers.

Who benefits from the Radio-Marathon fiesta?

In the past two years alone, the bank involved in the fund raising has pocketed approximately two million Cypriot pounds (that is about US$4 million for international comparisons), which it has not deposited with its rival banks but has kept to itself. Naturally, by the end of the year the money is spent, but at exactly the time when the bank account is empty autumn comes and the Radio-Marathon is on the road again. Every year for the two days of the Marathon the national radio station lives on its most impressive ego trip of the year. Organizers are congratulating themselves and each other (not forgetting the people who are offering the money), no doubt feeling very virtuous. Broadcasters encourage people with special needs of any kind to come and beg on the air for anything that catches their fancy (see also Barnes 1994: 207, on how 'charity advertisers present disabled people as pitiable and pathetic in order to raise money'). And people do. In order to cover a perceived need, they often expose themselves to public pity: 'My little boy cannot walk or talk or whatever, and what would really make his days happier is a . . .' The broadcaster then asks on the air: 'Who will be generous enough to give little . . . some happiness by offering him a . . .?' It is perhaps not surprising that the vast majority of people who are highly visible during these long two days and who respond to such invitations are children with various types and degrees of learning impairment. The disability movement is strikingly absent from the event, as are most adults with special needs. Prokopiou is very helpful again when he comments in a letter of 24 October 1996:

> We ask the organizers. Why did they never respond to a suggestion by the Coordination Committee of Struggle for the Disabled made two years ago for paraplegic, blind, deaf and other disabled athletes to get involved [in the athletic fiesta for the Radio-Marathon]?

The exclusion of disabled adults from the event is overshadowed by the participation of a large number of children, mainly from special schools. Participation in the event enhances and promotes the image of special schools all over the country and it is therefore very interesting to examine the role of the professionals involved (teachers and school administrators) in encouraging and supporting participation of children attending these schools in the festival. This is arguably the best 'advertisement' segregated education receives in the course of the year. Clearly this is not an event that promotes the idea of an inclusive school, as differences between children are exacerbated, if anything, and disabled and non-disabled children who happen to be participating in it are on two very different sides of the event: the former being the recipients and the latter the donors of the charity that takes place. Interestingly enough, donations are offered by special schools too (such as the school for the deaf), presumably for those who are less fortunate than themselves. We can stop and ask here whether such acts of generosity may sow the seeds of discriminatory divisions within the disability movement later on by encouraging speculations about what kind of disability might be less disabling and therefore closer to the norm. Such divisions do not benefit anyone but the state, which, instead of being confronted with a strong united and demanding disability movement, is dealing with small powerless groups of people requiring idiosyncratic and differentiated forms of assistance.

What of the trust's governing body? As is common practice for trusts of this type and well documented in the literature (Tomlinson 1982; Copeland 1995), the governing body consists of well established figures of Cypriot society – they could easily be named pillars – who do not necessarily have any professional relationship with the field of special needs, but are well known nationally for their charity work. What they get from it all, apart from the high profile, seems to be social and political influence and power, which in a small society like ours can easily be translated (for example) into votes during election time, should they or theirs decide to stand for office. The same is true of public figures who are publicly seen to donate large sums of money or, even worse perhaps, offer personal items for auction.

It is only fair to state that the herds of volunteer workers who roast in the sun for two days collecting money may get only the moral satisfaction and the souvenir T-shirt. This is to say that it is not my point to dispute the goodwill of individuals involved in this fund-raising exercise, but rather to expose some of the hidden curricula of such an event. A final important point that needs to be mentioned is the complete lack of accountability of the governing body regarding the use and allocation of funds. It appears to be in their total discretion what they do with it, how they use it and who they allocate it to. Not surprisingly, each year a fair amount goes to special schools and institutions. Prokopiou asks in a further letter (26 October 1996):

> It appears that approximately half the money is given to institutions. We ask the organizers. Are we wrong or mistaken when we hear them declare that the main goal of the event is to increase public awareness and (consequently) to help to deinstitutionalize people with special needs?

Prokopiou is very accurate in pointing to the intense conflict between the declared goals and the actual practice of the event. This is not only the result of a confused philosophy, but also a very successful way of keeping everyone happy without in the least challenging the status quo. All those mentioned above benefit from this arrangement, as private interests are masked behind a facade of public offering. We could, however, argue that the state is the main beneficiary yet again, as it saves on funds that it would be required to spend on dependent schools and institutions. Moreover, it benefits because it sheds exclusive responsibilities of having to cater for the needs of a number of its citizens on to a private trust that is not dependent on anyone and not accountable to anyone. Yet it is well known for its activity in the area of special needs and would function as a first port of call for people seeking support. In this sense, disabled people's claims will remain reduced to private requests for help instead of taking the shape of a state challenge for rights.

As the years pass, the event – and the trust – become well founded in people's consciousness and the charity model flourishes. In the past few years, and certainly during my time in Cyprus (from 1992 onward), the Radio-Marathon has dramatically grown in size and income every year. Yet its true beneficiaries cannot by any means be said to be disabled people or even children with special needs. The bank, the national radio, the special schools and the ideas they promote, the governing body, the organizers, public figures donating apparently large sums of money and, more noticeably, the state seem to be benefiting much more from the whole affair than those whom it is said to benefit.

The only positive outcome of the fiesta (if there is such a thing) is that children with special needs are now much more visible than they have ever been before. The children themselves, it has to be said, are very happy during these days, as they consider it their festival. Many parents are too. Parents of children with special needs feel they have now acquired a commonly understood vocabulary to introduce their children to other people. This does not mean that attitudes have changed drastically. To indicate this I need only mention the account of a mother of a child with Down's syndrome (Theophilides 1995), whose son escaped her attention and started playing with the phone. He called the same number again and again and spoke to the people there. The receiver of the calls called the police, and a gentle policeman rang the boy's house. As the mother answered the phone the policeman – obviously well trained and sensitive on these issues – asked: 'Do you have an idiot in your house?' The mother, initially taken aback, drew breath and replied: 'No, but we do have a child with special needs!' The policeman must have had enough exposure to the charity fiesta to comprehend this term, but he clearly had not had enough sensitivity to use it in the first place. It was perhaps little consolation to the mother that she could use a term that could be understood and that she could employ the Radio-Marathon experience to lecture the policeman on his approach.

Disability is not conceived as a human rights issue by everyone in Cyprus. Most of the time it is not conceived as such at all, although many people who work very hard for events such as the Radio-Marathon would be very hurt if they were confronted with this statement. The charity model is still the dominant mode of thinking regarding issues of disability, and this is not accidental. Organized bodies which have a vested interest in keeping this model alive promote the charity ideal, confusing the issue with arguments that emphasize pity and dependence, and which work – very effectively, I might add – on people's guilty consciences. It is at the moment very hard openly to challenge the charity model, especially during the days of the fund-raising, when the challenge would perhaps be most effective, without being misunderstood, accused of meanness and becoming marginalized. The disability movement seems to be still baffled as to what is the best way to approach this event and pass on the right message. In the meantime, professionals in the field of special needs gratefully accept this money on disabled people's behalf. Some disabled people do too. Disabled officials make careful declarations – when asked – trying not to turn down any money offered (they need it under present circumstances) or upset the organizers (it would be unwise to make enemies of such powerful figures). Oliver's point about forced charity might also be applicable here:

many disabled people are forced into the position of passive recipients of unwanted gifts or inappropriate services, for to refuse such 'generosity' would be to confirm the 'fact' that disabled people have not come to terms with their disability and have a 'chip on their shoulder'.

(Oliver 1989: 16)

For all these reasons the charity model is still holding strong and disability is rarely considered a human rights issue in Cyprus.

Human rights understood

What do we celebrate on 3 December?

As became clear in the previous section, the dominant model dealing with disabled children and adults in Cyprus is one of protection, donation and charity. Keith (1994: 2) describes a similar situation very powerfully when she states that she has become 'someone people felt sorry for, someone who could be approached by total strangers in public places and asked intrusive questions.' Even the notion of special educational needs is new, and so novel that public attitude has not matured enough to move from allowing disabled children's participation in mainstream schools and the open society to accepting their rights in life, education and employment on equal terms with the rest of the community. For this to be true, disabled claims would have to be promoted to disabled rights, social pity to social obligation and state charity to state responsibility.

The main venue where questions of human rights are raised is perhaps the disabled organizations; that is to say, the organizations which are set up and run by disabled people as pressure groups demanding education, civil and human rights, and which in their totality represent the disability movement. These organizations seem at present to be caught between their own past, public opinion and the state. Their past reflects a history of civil and legal battles with the state. In his account Florentzos (1998), president of the Pancyprian Organization for the Blind and also president of the Cyprus Federation of Organizations of the Disabled, speaks of the domination of private initiative in the area of vocational rehabilitation of people with disabilities right up to the 1980s. It is perhaps no coincidence that 1981, when 'the legal and moral obligations of the state were officially pronounced for the first time' (Florentzos 1998: 2), was the International Year for the Disabled and disabled people were for the first time personally involved in shaping legislation which concerned them. The Cyprus Federation of Organizations of the Disabled was consequently founded in 1984, its membership being 'Organisations consisting exclusively of people with disabilities and of the Pancyprian Association of Parents of Mentally Handicapped Persons' (Florentzos 1998: 2). The main endeavour of the Federation as described by Florentzos has been:

to achieve a system of legislation and administrative measures, which would coordinate and guide the existing private initiative and extend, above all, the care and social policy of the State, independent from the uncertain and unstable private initiative.

(Florentzos 1998: 2–3)

Florentzos reports some success and a good relationship between people with disabilities and the state.

Public opinion is also increasingly sensitive but exclusively in terms of the charity model, and the state while for years responding slowly to their demands bound by international agreements (Florentzos 1998), seems to have recently relaxed as public opinion becomes more sensitive and private funds are mounting. To quote Prokopiou once more (from a greeting to the UN International Day for the Disabled in Nicosia on 3 December 1995): 'there are obvious examples that the present government denounces more and more its own social role, while encouraging charity at the expense of a welfare state.' Concern regarding the prevalence of the charity model is also expressed by Florentzos, who notes his personal dissatisfaction with this philosophy and that of the Federation thus:

In spite of the fact that the organisations of people with disabilities and our Federation itself have repeatedly demanded to participate in the organisation of that annual event [the Radio-Marathon], the organisers, who are powerful businessmen, insist on rejecting it. Of course, people with disabilities feel very bad about it all.

(Florentzos 1998: 4)

While stepping back and allowing private initiative to lead is suspected as unofficial government practice, government rhetoric differs. State officials speak of the disabled people's human rights as expressed at the 1996 United Nations Resolution on Equal Opportunities Regulations for Handicapped People. During a public speech at the celebration of 3 December (The International Day of the United Nations for Disabled People) the chair of the Office for the Care of the Disabled (Ipiresia Merimnis Anapiron) declared:

In societies all over the world there are still hurdles which preclude disabled people from exercising their rights and their freedoms and which make their full involvement in community activities difficult. It is the responsibility of the state to take appropriate measures so that these hurdles are removed. Disabled people and their organizations must have an active role in this process as partners. Equality of opportunity for disabled people is an important contribution to mobilization of human resources.

(Efrem 1997: 4)

Despite this impressive rhetoric, in a sincere self-examination of the Cypriot state's response to the UN Regulations for Equal Opportunities for the Disabled in December 1993, Efrem declared that there is more continuing effort and goodwill than actual achievement in Cyprus on a number of issues, such as information, rehabilitation, technical support, access, education, employment and welfare, while personal issues such as marriage and sexual experience are nowhere near the target level. To quote him again:

> Regulation number 9 refers to the right on family life, opportunities for sexual experiences, the possibility of the provision of counselling for marital purposes etc. In Cyprus disabled people live mostly with their families, while marriage is almost unthinkable for some categories of disability, as is the possibility of sexual experiences.
>
> (Efrem 1997: 7)

How do disabled people themselves view the situation? We need to remember here Barton's statement (1993: 239) that 'disabled people are not homogeneous', just as the rest of society is not. Some are content with their achievements so far and optimistic about the future: 'In Cyprus we have achieved a lot, in many instances much more than other Europeans . . . What we urgently need is a legal framework and mechanisms which will produce the appropriate social policy in each area' (Hapoupis 1997: 1). It is not a coincidence that the person delivering this speech is blind. Blind people have the oldest and perhaps the most successful disabled organization in Cyprus, having secured for their members education and employment privileges which are unknown to many other organizations. This is partly owing to their long history of existence (the school for the blind was the first special school to be set up in 1929), and partly owing to their powerful governing body, which has successfully lobbied the state for education (there is a special entry category for blind students at the University of Cyprus) and employment (there is priority employment for telephone operators in all state services and a number of blind lawyers at the Public Prosecutor's office, a privilege that no other disabled body has enjoyed). He is therefore quite right. As an organization the blind have achieved the most in terms of education, employment and access in Cyprus. They have by far the most university graduates and they are not in the deprived categories that Efrem previously mentioned, as many have families of their own.

Giannakis Christophorou of the Pancyprian Organization for Disabled Persons is more critical:

> Our experience so far has shown that the most important problem for people with disabilities is employment. And this is the result of [inadequate] education and culture. This is why I turn to the state . . . and suggest that it creates a comprehensive employment programme starting with education – it is well known that inadequate education creates insuperable problems for future employment.
>
> (Christophorou 1997: 2)

Despite their (justified) different views on what has been achieved so far, both speakers are particularly concerned to address the term disabled (*anapiros* in Greek) and to differentiate it from the term unable (*animboros* in Greek). They both suggest that being disabled does not mean that a person needs to be dependent for life. This is of course a point well documented in literature (Oliver 1989; Barton 1993; Riddell 1993; Barnes 1994). Adequate training and education, they suggest, make disabled people as productive as anyone else in society in areas where they can be productive – as indeed is the case with able-bodied people. Christophorou is therefore quite justified to state that:

> What we feel is lacking, is a comprehensive policy for disabled people which will recognise them not as a burden that has to be dealt with through social support and contributions, but whose inclusion is taken into account in the financial plans of the country, as an integral part of the structure and function of our society.
>
> (Christophorou 1997: 3)

Interestingly, in his greeting for the day, the Minister of Employment and Public Welfare, who is responsible for disability issues, is in absolute agreement with him, at least in theory: '3 December, apart from its symbolic and jubilant nature, functions for us as the starting point for the renewal of our efforts to materialize the principles of the United Nations Charter' (Minister of Employment and Public Welfare 1997: 3). Is this a rhetorical statement for the day, or does it have any substance? This remains to be seen, as the phenomena we are dealing with are contemporary and therefore constantly changing and developing. What needs to be made clear here is that the voice of disabled people exists but is still (with one or two exceptions) too weak to be heard outside their own forums and in the public domain. At the moment it is covered by other voices, which are meant to represent them but which do not speak the same language as disabled people do, such as the voices of professionals in the field. It is also covered by the voices of people who traditionally have also spoken for disabled people, such as the important public figures who staff the governing bodies of special schools and charity organizations. This makes disabled adults invisible and promotes on their behalf views which are not theirs. It also disempowers them politically and allows decision making on issues such as education and employment to be largely made for them and without their participation. If we want to hear their voice we need to come to their meetings and listen very carefully. What they are saying is this:

> What [Cyprus] definitely lacks is the legal and administrative basis for providing people with disabilities with all the necessary special services required for their rehabilitation, social integration and every day needs. The state has never seriously dealt with this immediate need.
>
> (Florentzos 1998: 5)

On 3 December Cyprus celebrates what has been achieved in the area of human rights for the disabled, but much more what is yet to be achieved in this area. Human rights and achievements are experienced differently by different disabled organizations, as disabilities have a diverse history in Cyprus and some seem to have been seen as less inhibiting than others regarding education and employment. Nevertheless, human rights for the disabled seem to be understood in a very similar way by different organizations, as they all state that being disabled does not mean being unable. There is universal agreement – at least in principle – that disabled people are/must be an integral part of our society, equal partners in our life and our struggle for a better future. So far we are a long way from this target.

Human rights interpreted

What are we doing about it?

It is finally pertinent to look at what is at the moment being done to help to materialize human rights for disabled people. There are at present before Parliament two White Papers that aim to legitimize disabled people's claims to their right for education and employment. Given that education precedes and prepares for employment, I shall concentrate on the 1998 White Paper on Special Education.

The 1998 White Paper is broadly based on the recommendations of the Constantinides Report published in 1992. The report is the product of work of a special committee established in 1991 to examine special education provision and to look into the educational needs of children with disabilities in Cyprus. The committee worked under the guidance of Giannakis Constantinides, a high court judge. Based on the report's recommendations, a White Paper on special education was first proposed to the government in 1995. The paper was considered too ambitious, its regulations too costly, and so it was returned for amendments. One of the main points of contention seems to have been the suggestion that the responsibility of the state to children with special needs and their parents begins at birth. The same process was repeated in 1997 with recommendations which secured a smaller cost, this time the suggestion being that the responsibility of the state to children with special needs begins at the age of three. This was also considered costly and the White Paper was turned back for further cuts. The White Paper that was presented to the house of representatives on 31 April 1998 was discussed in the education committee of the Parliament in two sittings: 9 June and 23 June 1998. It states that the responsibility of the state towards the child with special needs and his or her family begins with school, at six years of age. At the time of writing it awaits further discussion in a full sitting of Parliament.

It needs to be noted that this is a rather poor legislative interpretation of the responsibilities of the state towards the disabled child and his or her family – and, indeed, of the original suggestions of the Constantinides Report. Notwithstanding the fact that free pre-school education should be a given state responsibility for all children and their families (which it is not under present educational legislation), children with special needs are even more in need of such a commitment from the state than other children are (Diakidoy and

Phtiaka 1998). If we were to examine this from a human rights point of view, we would note that by denying them instant support at birth the state is in fact depriving these children of the opportunity to achieve their maximum potential in later development, and therefore education and employment. An educational/therapeutic decision made at the age of six is simply a decision made six years too late (Phtiaka 1998). As noted earlier in this chapter, there is no explicit link between human rights and education in the proposed legislation. If, however, we were to make this link ourselves, we would need to argue that this is perhaps one of the major human rights issues in dispute within the proposed legislation. The other is obviously the fact that disabled children and children with special needs of any kind are dealt with by a separate piece of educational legislation. This discriminates them from their non-disabled peers and makes them stand apart. As long as this continues to happen we shall never be able to reconcile the needs and the rights of disabled and non-disabled children.

What is the gain in terms of human rights? In the proposed legislation children with special needs are at last officially part of the mainstream education system, an educational right so far formally denied them, although in practice partially exercised. This recognition will secure for them, within the mainstream, provisions that were so far only available in special schools, thereby facilitating as well as legitimizing their right to be educated alongside their peers. Integration of children with special needs into the mainstream school system will at last become official policy instead of experimental practice. This has to be an advantage over a situation where integration was dependent on the parents' efforts, the school's generosity and the teachers' goodwill. A legislative framework may also help to support integration where inadequate staff preparation and training and lack of resources and equipment have for the past ten years endangered its whole philosophy. This piece of legislation, inadequate and ungenerous as it may be, comes at a crucial moment, when integration is severely tried in Cypriot primary schools and sporadic attempts are made at reintroducing special classes. It seems that our task is to improve it, to support it and to see it through Parliament. As soon as this is done we need to start working on the next piece of legislation, which will address education as a whole and will make the newly passed piece of legislation as unnecessary as this will now make all the segregatory special education legislation of the past.

Legislation to improve the human and the educational rights of disabled children is continuously proposed and improved. We have, however, a difficult task ahead if we are to realize the dream of an inclusive society. The inclusive school can be a first important step in this direction, and this we are slowly working towards. Crucial in this effort is the struggle to turn the question of special education into a human rights debate. This will help to achieve a 'public acknowledgement that discrimination does exist, that it is unacceptable and that the principle of equality (should) be given the protection of the law' (Barton 1993: 244), by embracing all children of educational age in a common piece of legislation.

Conclusion

Summarizing, we need to state that disability is not yet discussed in human rights terms in Cyprus; the disability movement – despite its achievements so far – is still largely invisible and inaudible; and inclusive education is moving ahead at a very slow rate. A lot of work has been done, mainly in the past ten to fifteen years, but much more is still lying ahead.

It seems that we can take only one step at a time. Cyprus is a young state with a long history of colonial dependence and occupation, a devastating war on its fourteenth birthday, one third of its land occupied by foreign troops, refugees, missing people and a serious unresolved political problem. The university is just seven years old, constantly battling against ignorance, prejudice and priority on defence expenses. We need to battle on, convinced that the future will be better than the present and much better than the past. We need to ensure that disabled people will soon achieve equal human rights with non-disabled people in Cyprus. We need in parallel to make sure that non-disabled people too have their human rights fully reinstated on this island of ours.

Questions

I conclude here with some questions that will extend the discussion on issues that have been raised in this chapter.

1 What would be the best way to deal with the charity model?
2 What is the role of the disability movement in the building of a better future?
3 How can we best introduce and implement educational legislation leading to inclusive schooling?

Constant worry and debate on such issues cannot but help us move ahead.

Note

All extracts and quotations of Greek writers are translated from the Greek.

References

Barnes, C. (1994) Institutional discrimination, disabled people and inter-professional care, *Journal of Inter-professional Care*, 8(2): 203–12.
Barton, L. (1993) The struggle for citizenship: the case of disabled people, *Disability, Handicap and Society*, 8(3): 235–48.
Christophorou, (1997) Greeting at the UN International Day for the Disabled, School for the Blind, Nicosia, Cyprus, 3 December.

Constantinides, I. (1992) *Report of the Special Committee for the Study of Ways of Providing Help to Children with Special Needs.* Nicosia: Ministry of Education and Culture.

Copeland, I. C. (1995) The establishment of models of education for disabled children, *British Journal of Educational Studies,* 43(2): 179–200.

Diakidoy, E.-A. and Phtiaka, H. (1998) Early years education: significance and objectives, *Educational Review,* 27: 7–30 (in Greek).

Efrem, C. (1997) The UN International Day for the Disabled: history – meaning – the message of the day. Introductory Speech at the Celebration of the UN International Day for the Disabled, School for the Blind, Nicosia, Cyprus, 3 December.

Florentzos, M. (1998) The factual and legal situation of people with disabilities in Cyprus. Unpublished paper.

Hapoupis, A. P. (1997) Greeting at the UN International Day for the Disabled, School for the Blind, Nicosia, Cyprus, 3 December.

Keith, L. (ed.) (1994) *Mustn't Grumble: Writing by Disabled Women.* London: Women's Press.

Minister of Employment and Public Welfare (1997) Greeting at the UN International Day for the Disabled, School for the Blind, Nicosia, Cyprus, 3 December.

Ministry of Education and Culture (1995) *The 1995 Education Law for the Education of Children with Special Needs.* (Ypourgeio Paideias kai Politismou, *Nomoschedio me titlo o peri agogis paidon me eidikes anages nomos 1995.*)

Ministry of Education and Culture (1996) *Information Booklet on Special Education* (Ypourgeio Paideias kai Politismou, *Deltio Plirophorion Eidikis Ekpaideysis.*)

Ministry of Education and Culture (1997) *The 1997 Education Law for the Education of Children with Special Needs.* (Ypourgeio Paideias kai Politismou, *Nomoschedio me titlo o peri agogis paidon me eidikes anages nomos 1997.*)

Ministry of Education and Culture (1998) *The 1998 Education Law for the education of Children with Special Needs.* (Ypourgeio Paideias kai Politismou, *Nomoschedio me titlo o peri agogis paidon me eidikes anages nomos 1998.*)

Oliver, M. (1989) Disability and dependency: a creation of industrial societies, in L. Barton (ed.) *Disability and Dependency.* Lewes: Falmer Press.

Phtiaka, H. (1996a) The training of today's teachers on special education issues: The challenge for the University of Cyprus. Presentation at the Second Pancyprian Educational Conference of the Independent Movement of Teachers and Nursery Teachers: the provision of special education to children with special needs and their integration to mainstream schools, University of Cyprus, Nicosia, 17 February.

Phtiaka, H. (1996b) Special education in Cyprus – future perspectives. The vision of special education and the University of Cyprus. Presentation at the Cypriot Association of Special Education Day Conference on Special Education in Cyprus: Past Experiences and Future Perspectives, University of Cyprus, Nicosia, 4 May.

Phtiaka, H. (1996c) Are we ready to meet the challenge? Integration, inclusive education and children with special educational needs. Paper presented at the British Educational Research Association Annual Conference, University of Lancaster, 12–15 September.

Phtiaka, H. (1996d) Each to 'his' own? Home school relations in Cyprus, 1996, *Forum of Education,* 50(3): 47–59.

Phtiaka, H. (1997) Inclusive school: the role of the University of Cyprus. Presentation at the Cypriot Association of Special Education Day Conference Inclusive School, Interdisciplinary Support and the University of Cyprus, 17 May.

Phtiaka, H. (1998) Comments on the White Paper for Special Education 1998. Presentation at the Education Committee Meeting of the Cypriot Parliament, 9 June.

Riddell, S. (1993) The politics of disability: post-school experience, *British Journal of Sociology of Education*, 4(4): 445–55.

Theophilides, P. (1995) Lecture given in course EPA311, Introduction to Special Education, 16 October.

Tomlinson, S. (1982) *A Sociology of Special Education*. London: Routledge.

Vlachou, A. D. (1997) *Struggles for Inclusive Education*. Buckingham: Open University Press.

Wolfensberger, W. (1989) Human service policies: the rhetoric versus the reality, in L. Barton (ed.) *Disability and Dependency*. Lewes: Falmer Press.

 **13**

Disability, human rights and education in Romania

Michele Moore and Karen Dunn

This chapter is deeply informed by the voice of Oana Benga, Catedra de Psihologie, University of Cluj-Napoca, Romania.

Overview

This chapter is based on recent visits to look at the situations of disabled and vulnerable children living in two institutions in Romania. The complexity of education and human rights issues is enormous. Some children receive 'home-school' provision and others 'home-hospital'. The latter have no entitlement to education. The majority are excluded not only from the wider community, but also from family life, and not always for reasons of choice. The voice of the Romanian contributor affirms that in a climate where the voices of all major stakeholders have previously been omitted or silenced in the policies and practices that shape their entitlements, those who work with disabled children and their families would welcome change. An interesting question for the post-communist era is whether the voices of disabled people, their families and representative agencies will be influential in bringing about a more inclusive system of rights-based education.

Introduction

This chapter is based on reflections on disability, human rights and education made in two institutions in Romania. The first institution is for approximately 600 children, most of whom are without family connections in Lugoj, a medium-size town 63 kilometres from Timişoara and close to the border with Serbia. Children here are classified into categories, which determine degree of entitlement to education. Children placed in the category of 'home-hospital' do not receive education. The school director told us, 'You have to know that you are in one of the best institutions in Romania.' The deputy director corrected, 'Not *one* of the best, *the* best'. The chapter also draws observations from an institution in Cluj, the capital of Transylvania and a large university and industrial city. This is the only school in Romania to take hearing impaired children belonging to families who are members of the Hungarian cultural and linguistic minority. Consequently, children can be separated from their families by many thousands of kilometres. Unique social, cultural, political and psychological debates surround deaf children and their human rights and education, and these provide the focus of a separate discussion (Moore *et al.* forthcoming). Here, we intend to discuss questions that are relevant to all children with whom we have had contact, irrespective of the nature of impairment.

Some information about the Romanian educational system and the position of disabled children within it will help to set the scene. With few exceptions, education for disabled children is organized around the following domains:

1 Kindergartens for children three to six years old.
2 Special schools, with eight years of study for children aged six and above described as with mild deficiencies, considered 'recuperable'.
3 Professional schools, with three years of study 'for adolescents considered recuperable'.
4 Home-schools for children described as 'only partly recuperable'.
5 Home-hostels for adolescents considered 'partly recuperable'.
6 Home-hospitals for children and adolescents 'considered somehow irrecuperable'. This provision can be 'closed' or 'half-closed'. (We have only seen that which is termed 'half-closed'.)

Many professionals feel the extent of educational provision for disabled children is seriously inadequate. 'Home-hospital' provision, in particular, is grossly oversubscribed and usually situated in old buildings, in far flung parts of the country.

Aims and problems

The aim of the chapter is to offer an analysis of the ways in which disability, human rights and education are constructed within the focal institutions. We also want to look at connections between these constructions, and the response in terms of theoretical understandings and research practice, which the two of us who are British academics have made through working in Romania and being informed by a key Romanian contributor. This chapter is the first attempt by the three of us to write collaboratively. The process has thrown up many concerns about cross-cultural research production, which is one of the overarching themes of the book.

Originally, when we were briefly together in Britain discussing the writing plan, we envisaged including all of our voices as equal partners. We realize now that we had a vested interest in using co-authorship as a means to make visible our mutual respect for each other. Because our working relationship was new, and this compelled us to talk obliquely about some of the more troublesome issues which were eventually to become the focus of the text, we imagined joint authorship could provide a gloss of shared ownership on complex issues. Problems with this unspoken agenda were quickly exposed through dependency on e-mail communications, which obliterate subtlety around sensitive issues. It became evident that while the opinions of our colleague in Romania could be sought, her presence as an author was heavily constrained. There were dangers because the emerging, supposedly 'co-authored' text threatened to render her accountable for an analysis which was only superficially informed by her voice. We have had to move away from the pretence that affinity is a product of joint naming. Establishing mutual regard in cross-cultural research practice requires a much greater leap of faith than can be contained within joint authorship. We have taken risks with our relationship in the content and structure of this appraisal of disability, education and human rights in Romania, but all three of us feel that owning up to this much has taken us a stage further towards building a platform we can share for the purposes of coalition and resistance.

Background

Our starting point for becoming involved with institutions in Romania was an invitation in 1996 from representatives of two charitable organizations, Mencap and Child Action International. These agencies have taken pride in the response they made to the emergency uncovered in Romania by the revolution in 1990. They raised a great deal of money and transported huge amounts of aid. They built an entirely new school pavilion to begin the process of relieving the chronic overcrowding which had necessitated the employment of two full-time grave diggers in the school at Lugoj in 1990. But celebrating the role of charity in children's lives places emphasis on dependency and conflicts dramatically with our academic commitments to rights and to equality of opportunity (Oliver 1996; Oliver and Barnes 1998). We were apprehensive about perpetuating personal tragedy and charity-based involvement in disabled people's lives. We became involved as much to test our own understandings of entitlement in the pursuit of social justice for disabled children as for any other reason. Our experience has prompted much debate and critical examination of our perspectives on disability, human rights and education. Our reflections are now full of contradictions.

At one time we thought that we recognized and understood the inherent contradictions in the relationships forged to establish our involvement with the two schools. We had soon to admit that lofty assumptions that these were between ourselves as 'academics committed to sophisticated understandings of disabled people's rights' and charity workers we deemed 'committed to practical notions of Christian benevolence' were wholly disingenuous. On the night of our first departure for Romania we found ourselves completely unable to resist packing clothes our children had outgrown. Despite all our supposed academic certainties, we were coming up against the multiple confusions that infuse cross-cultural understandings of disability, human rights and education matters. We had to begin owning up to the jumbled contradictions in which this writing, and our understanding of disability, human rights and education in Romania, are steeped.

Beyond this, it will also become obvious that despite our concern to offer reflective and grounded critique, we are aware that we cannot separate the fundamental emotionality of children's lives from disability and human rights issues. We have wondered whether we should resist the encroachment of emotionality in our academic writing and attempt a rather more sophisticated level of engagement with disability, education and rights issues, but find we cannot eliminate these threads from our thinking. We have opted, therefore, not to shy away from breaking out of the usual impersonal tone but to show how our concern with disability, education and human rights in Romania is bound up with real difficulties in real lives.

The project brief

The brief for our first visit was to explore possibilities for providing specialist back-up via a programme of professional exchanges. The abolition of training for specialist teachers, psychologists, social workers and other non-medical specialists in Romania since 1979 has taken a heavy toll on levels of professional knowledge and expertise and, as other writers have acknowledged (Oliver and Barnes 1998), the first (post-revolutionary) cohorts of psychologists and special school teachers are beginning their careers in near catastrophic circumstances. Our idealistic vision prior to the trip was to work with professionals, parents and disabled adults to look at ways of supporting disabled children in their rights to an ordinary education. But, of the 2000 children we would meet in just one week, only a tiny handful have any knowledge of or contact with relatives. We saw no disabled adults – other than beggars – in any social setting. No one we met could put us in touch with an organization of disabled adults that might support the work of the institutions we were visiting.

Contradictions and hypocrisy

We realize that we will inevitably make a host of problematic assumptions in this chapter. We identify these as part and parcel of the worldwide discussions on children's rights which provide an important backdrop to this book (Archard 1993; Franklin 1995; Moore *et al.* 1996). The issue of defining 'rights' is immensely problematic:

> The discourse of rights is entwined with discourses on responsibility, needs and degrees of dependency. Rights do not exist in the abstract as

the liberal humanists position would claim. What comes to be defined as a right emerges out of specific power relations and forms of knowledge.

(Marks 1996: 115)

Many of the assumptions that we make are regularly attributed to the liberal humanist position, such as that all children are entitled to a full and decent life. We would go further and argue that children have a right to dignity, to respect and tolerance and to participation in the life of their own community, as envisaged in Rachel Hurst's submission for Disabled Peoples International to the UN Committee on the Rights of the Child (Hurst 1998). Before we go on to discuss these rights in the particular context of Romania, which is internationally regarded as failing to preserve many fundamental entitlements of vulnerable children, it is essential to express the view of our Romanian contributor that the pressures made by many European countries and the USA regarding human rights and especially regarding the rights of minority groups have often been felt as 'pure proof of hypocrisy'. There is a tendency to assume that there is what could be described as 'a human rights system' operating in Britain, but we know this to be mythical.

In the UK we remain embroiled in a domestic struggle to achieve basic rights for children. Only recently the European Union has had to intervene to prevent the elevation of parental wishes over children's rights in matters of physical abuse. It is vital to remind ourselves, before launching into the body of this chapter, that while the mission to protect and defend the rights of disabled children in Romania currently has a very high international profile, all societies have a duty continually to look to the preservation of children's best interests. Many people in Romania resent the hypocrisy of the outside world's procrastination on their human rights record, and are very uncomfortable being treated as if they do not know how to deal with their own situation. For our Romanian contributor, 'probably this has something to do with human rights . . . it has happened to me only few times with foreigners, that [I am] treated as someone equal.' And our colleague is not a vulnerable child. She is one of the leading psychologists to emerge since the Romanian Ministry of Education began a national programme to promote the educational and social integration of children with special educational needs in 1993.

It is important to recognize that there are many stakeholders in any discussions of the complex relationship of disability, human rights and education. Having said all this, we cannot, and do not wish to, get away from the fact that within hours of arriving at the two schools, as observers completely new to a setting, we felt an overwhelming compulsion to contact a human rights agency. We have no sense of the validity or objectivity of our responses to what we saw, but we experienced a compelling and devastating sense of abuses and violations of children's rights. We suddenly found ourselves unable to articulate any coherent academic viewpoint on disability, or education, or developmental psychology, as was expected of us. We were totally swamped by the feeling that in these two schools, human rights and civil liberties were being contravened.

The brief of supporting disabled children in their rights to an ordinary education fast became a nightmare of inconceivable naiveté. We began to glimpse the uselessness of denouncing conditions in the institutions or of outrage at the circumstances that separate parents and children on such a colossal and irretrievable scale. When one of the directors told us 'solutions have seemed impossible in our eyes', the futility of our own position was brought into sharp focus. A deputy director said that he and his colleagues held out little hope of meaningful assistance from well intentioned professional people like us, making visits from privileged countries. He meant no offence, this was just the fact of the matter. The notion of human rights as culturally produced and as interpreted in different ways in specific contexts by each set of observer eyes struck forcibly home.

Shadows around disability, human rights and education

While horrifying images of, for example, disabled children dying from AIDS contracted through the necessity of reusing needles for purposes of mass sedation have been important in story-making narratives about disability, human rights and education in Romania, they have created many barriers to the dismantling of human rights abuses. It seems possible that such images have led to other ways of storying the circumstances of disabled children in a kind of policing process of a national shame. These alternative narratives emerged during our school visits through the presentation of expert knowledge and through the mapping out of our journey around the schools. So, while some children were identified as evidence of the school's achievements in advancing disabled children's human rights and education, others were rendered invisible. A whole category of children labelled 'home-hospital pupils' lack entitlement to education and so could not only be removed from debates about education, but also 'forgotten' when the gaze of outsiders falls on human rights.

Control of our access, particularly around one school, illustrates the current reality of this problem. We were taken on guided tours of all the most impressive features of provision. We saw a pleasant multipurpose pavilion built by British aid workers and newly adapted workshops. Care attendants, sitting smoking in the sunshine when we were at a distance, hurried children into the semblance of a game as we approached. We were escorted to carefully conducted lessons, given access to show-piece individual sessions with children and sat for several hours in front of a prized video showing aspects of best practice in great detail. The story of disability, human rights and education that was being played out confirmed recognition of the rights of significant numbers of children to the best possible provision. But a lack of rights possessed by others was reinforced through the production of a fiction in which they simply did not occupy a role. Clearly, this way of storying the institution's achievements was felt to be necessary in order for the professionals seeking our affiliation to come across as responsible and not as guilty of serious neglect or profound abuses of children's basic human rights. We realized that allowing our visits under any circumstances demanded a great deal of official courage.

Most if not all of the children we saw, even under the official gaze, were profoundly scarred by a battering of psychological abuse which has abject poverty, malnutrition and social exclusion at its roots. Many children experienced physical as well as emotional suffering. The absence of the sounds and noise familiar to us from the schools in which we have worked in England suggested that the use of drugs for sedation purposes cannot possibly be dismissed as past. Crowds of children were conspicuous in their loneliness, completely alone though constantly surrounded by each other. Most were desperate to be held or even touched. Many held back, risking only to touch our clothing as we walked by. Toddlers we saw were so traumatized they no longer cried but sat quietly, hoping for nothing. Eight-year-olds looked four. Each child appeared to be a boy, because they mostly have shorn heads and gender is discounted when clothes are few and far between. The story we were being given produced and specified a particular response to disability, human rights and education. It acknowledged the position of children as victims, but it was obviously incomplete.

After several unsuccessful attempts to evade close regulation of our movements, we managed eventually to be left alone. Our freedom remained relative and was marked by periodic sightings of the director, so that we knew that our whereabouts were always known. Even so, we did enter buildings which we had been determinedly steered away from. In one we were confronted by padded doors. A commotion ensued and we were firmly ushered out. We were repeatedly told that the director of this building was away and we could not be permitted to see around. We are therefore unable to comment on issues of human rights and education for the disabled children who are within that building, and have been unable to gain further information about what goes on in there and in an adjacent similarly restricted block. Our eviction filled us with anxiety. We made ourselves enter two further 'off-limits' buildings and both began to be overtaken by uncontrollable shaking. We had come face to face with the sight and sound and smell of the most appalling violations of disabled children's human rights. We need to give details, in order to avoid colluding with keeping the experiences of these children hidden from view. We are aware that our account should try to limit the possibility of speculative inferences and emotions but it is impossible to convey adequately the situation we encountered.

There were no staff on the ground floor of the first building we entered. Outcast children paced aimlessly around empty rooms and corridors engaged in stereotypic, often self-injurious, behaviours. Others sat rocking on the floor or unresponsive on broken chairs. Some were sobbing, some silent, some shrieking; all bewildered, all utterly bewildering. Upstairs one care worker and an unpaid helper were attempting to spoon feed 20 or so non-ambulant children. Several teenagers were confined to cots and clearly in acute physical and emotional distress. At least four children were evidently dying. All the children were bony, filthy, bare-footed, clothed only partly at most, in rags. Many were covered in sores and faeces. The buildings they occupy brought to mind those Martha Gellhorn must have seen when she described orphanages in Italy in the 1940s: 'asylums where children must live [which] are sickening echoes out of Dickens and the darkest, heartless past' (Gellhorn 1989).

At the moment of leaving these buildings we realized that there were hugely negative implications in having seen what we had seen in terms of our continuing relationship with the school. Expressing devastation and anger at what we had observed would have entailed rejecting their way of storying what goes on in their institution. To reject the identity staff were seeking to establish and maintain would render our attempts at partnership a failure. The alternative, which we went along with, involved collusion in maintaining silence around what we have seen. This is the position we chose and, as unintelligible as this response *feels*, we have since argued that the seeds of some resistance may lie within it. We chose to collude because we felt certain that exposure of what we are interpreting as a sense of national shame would have jeopardized our access to the school once and for all. There is hypocrisy in our response. There are many contradictions in our thinking, but we feel that without access to the complex worlds of disability and education in key institutions in Romania there is no practical way of engaging with human rights issues.

Once the nightmare scenario of our witnessing the shameful suppressed realities of hundreds of children's circumstances, and then opting for self-imposed silence, had been lived through, a different kind of discourse emerged. It became possible to start talking about the oppressive consequences of exclusion of any child from education and to move away from preoccupation with diagnostics and syndromes which had formerly absorbed our hosts. We were no longer confined to empty talk about things the school were already doing well. Now, although we could rarely talk explicitly, we could advance opinions about violations of disabled children's rights and put forward a view on the social origins of disability. We could begin what for us was a much more productive dialogue about the impact of oppressive attitudes and political restrictions in children's lives.

We realized that we had been allowed through what are, for some professionals in Romania, the most difficult – actually unspeakable – faces of disability, human rights and education issues. We opted to preserve the professional story about disability, human rights and education in Romania and are arguing for the subversion of a culture of blame. We feel that herein lies the possibility of change. We feel our belief that resistance to human rights violations can begin to take root even in situations where the structures maintaining those violations cannot easily be challenged has been corroborated by the response of the school director:

> You take us as equal partners and not that we are something very small and that you have to grow us up. And most important, you saw the institution. You saw what is going on and we have trust in your observer eyes. It is very hard to explain what's going on and what we are trying to

do. To keep on developing ourselves we need to have assessment through other eyes. We are so used to seeing the same reality. From time to time we need someone from outside to look differently, to see how the children feel.

Our Romanian colleagues frequently express sensitivity about the enormous gulf between our respective human rights systems, breaking in to say 'I hope you are not depressed by this' or 'I hope you won't find any of these [ideas] offending.' Human rights and education issues for significant numbers of disabled children are confined to shadowy areas of discussion, but they do occasionally occupy a space which might one day constitute an arena within which to begin bringing about change.

To keep on developing ourselves . . .

However we see the possibilities inherent in the responses of professionals in the focal school, we remain unconditionally critical of violations of human rights which emerge when disabled children are excluded from education. Prospects for change in the focal institutions are currently limited by a discourse that concentrates solely on reinforcing categories of entitlement through the construction of misplaced (and insufficiently analysed) categories of disability. The categories of disability that are used have become part of the storying around children which explains their exclusion and to which violations of their human rights can be attributed. Changes in the education of professionals and policy makers will need to play a huge part in bringing about change in Romania. The evidence we have suggests that training of educators and related professionals has not fundamentally addressed the human rights of disabled people, and subsequently thousands of disabled children are excluded from entitlements to education and inclusion which they, and their families, could expect in other parts of Europe. This is the main change with which we wish to be associated through our work in Romania.

There is, of course, some emphasis on matters of human rights for disabled children. For children who have learning difficulties described as 'mild' we heard extensive discussion of their right to have lessons in a different building from that in which they sleep and eat. Children in this category are positioned as having elaborate rights to do with issues of physical environments and space and exhaustive efforts are being made to complete an impressive new classroom suite to facilitate this differentiation of domestic and school life. In contrast we found children and young people with little or no mobility, and categorized as 'home-hospital', locked in a small upstairs room. They rarely get out of the room because time is short when one person has 80 or so children in his or her charge. They have hardly ever been outside because there is no one to carry them downstairs and then back. We have no comparative experience from which to draw sensible understandings of the widespread disablement and human rights abuses of these underfed, little cared for, unwashed children who have only flies with which to play. The 'home-hospital' category is not the only province of human rights abuses: all of the children in the institutions we saw were living with devalued identities in a society where there is a tradition of belief 'that disabled people, especially those with more severe disabilities, should be isolated in institutions, that they should in some cases be regarded as "incurables", and they should remain invisible to the community' (Diaconescu *et al.* 1995: 69). But children who in Britain would be formally assessed as meriting *most* entitlement have least in Romania. We realized we were locked into a very difficult way of seeing. A hierarchy of rights operates which is very dubiously constructed.

Observations like this call everything we do into question. We feel ourselves to be operating in the absence of a current worldwide action plan concerning disability, human rights and education, and that this means we need to interrogate every aspect of our practices. Convinced of the importance of children's rights to a decent and happy life, even those of us who have a degree of awareness and informed understanding need only to glimpse children suffering to find ourselves shifting the boundaries which keep at bay the charity discourses, oppressive attitudes and condescending practices that are part of the national and broader context in which human rights are ignored. In relation to the particular context of Romania which we are describing, a critical discussion of human rights in relation to disabled children and their education *is* where we would want to begin. But, in the face of such acute social conditions and such widespread deprivation, imposing silence on the voices of those who find rights issues tricky to negotiate and boundaries around charity inevitably blurred must run the risk of making the problematic discourse more powerful. We do not wish to naturalize the role of charity in disabled children's education but to signal the difficulties of working in a context where the respective discourses of rights versus charity so fiercely, and so confusedly, compete.

We receive constant reminders from our allies in Romania that there are many people in positions of power who are not fully engaged with the struggle for rights-based ideologies around disability. But the response that met even passing remarks during the visits to both schools encouraged us not to underestimate the desire for knowledge and good practice skills of overworked and underpaid staff in nearly impossible situations. They command respect because it takes immense strength not to give up in the face of so little prospect of change. We set about working up a plan in collaboration with our Romania colleagues, to establish a three-year programme of ongoing staff development and evaluative research which would respond to the focal schools' immediate concerns for practical innovations and change. It was agreed that this could best be achieved by developing both local and international exchanges and transfer of good practice. Locally recognized qualifications will be important and links are being carved out with Romanian universities. In the long term our strategy is to facilitate the involvement in education planning and policy making of families and children's representative organizations, and of disabled adults such as the Disabled Peoples

International Romanian Assembly. We know it is imperative that disabled people determine their own priorities for the national disability, education and human rights agenda.

We remain convinced by collaboration with disabled people that we are right to emphasize the social model in any discussions that advance their interests with practitioners and policy makers. This is unproblematic in many senses, since the social model is born out of disabled people's experiences of oppression, *except* that in order to do this effectively we have to set up structures which accredit engagement with the model. At this point both our aspirations for development – that it should wholly reflect local priorities – and our resultant model of accreditation can be seen considerably to lack rigour.

When systems are in place for accreditation of personal and professional development, individual professionals are invested with the right to choose the way in which they want to be developed and, in relation to this, to choose the way in which they work. There is a lack of rigour in our framework because, notwithstanding the genuine commitment to improving disabled children's education that we have witnessed in Romania, disability, human rights and education matters have traditionally been, and often still are, viewed as if they were unrelated. Our assumptions about the fundamentally interconnected and interwoven nature of disability, human rights and education is not universally accepted, and many of our peers in Romania would contest what is, for us, the guiding principle of maximizing rights to equal opportunity.

It has always been difficult to choose to work with the most vulnerable children in Romania, and this is structurally reinforced by a categorization system which places some children outside the legitimate concerns of educationalists. No one wanted to show us the 'home-hospital' children, and those professionals who expressed a view admitted that they would not choose to work with them. The extent of these attitudes was reinforced when we suggested to a television director filming our visit that he included some footage of the children, but he explained that news programmes do not usually contain pictures of disabled children. We have to recognize that there are layers of change involved in interventions around disability, education and human rights, and these have to be worked in different ways. We are entering a horrendous landscape of contradictions with our desire to endorse the social model, because in order to push this model forward we have to recognize that still the rights of the most oppressed children will be suspended. Thus, we feel, it is both necessary and appropriate to reclaim the language and meaning of tragedy when thinking about disability, human rights and education in the context of Romania.

Reclaiming tragedy

We have accepted that, at least for now, many professionals working in the arena of disability, human rights and education in Romania feel they must safeguard their personal career development by increasing specialist training which focuses on the interests of particular groups of children. At some times, and in some places, it is felt that beginning a process of expanding expertise may eventually start to break down the boundaries that currently exclude large numbers of children from their right to participate in education. But this model of development, reproducing as it does an emphasis on personal problems and individual adaptation to a hostile world, is an anathema for us. The reality of our dilemma is that we want something else. We cannot leave the most vulnerable children out of our vision of an inclusive and rights-based education for all. We *are*, in effect, wanting to control the professional rights of our Romanian counterparts. We are asking them to do something that does not fit with their priorities. This is why we feel we are far from rigorous in our theory of accreditation. A major criticism of our approach concerns our wanting to do something which touches on this very real tension: we want to develop accreditation of our way of seeing disability, human rights and education. We have accepted that there is hypocrisy involved in order to set up a relationship which can work for change, but we also know there are many further layers of contradiction and confusion and we have continually to interrogate these.

Lately, part of the process of interrogating our own practice has led us to revisit our own resistance to the notion of personal tragedy in the area of disability, human rights and education. The language of personal tragedy, with its legacy of establishing and maintaining negative images of disabled people, has undoubtedly, and we would argue rightly, been shamed by the social model (Barnes 1990; Oliver 1990, 1996; Morris 1993). That this should be so has been largely accepted by writers in the field of disability studies, human rights and education (Vlachou 1998). Our acceptance of the theoretical movement away from notions of personal tragedy to look at the social and political origins of oppression has, however, been heavily shaken by what we have recently witnessed. In terms of the history of disability in Romania, we would argue, disability *is* couched heavily in, and perpetuated by, personal tragedy. There *is* tragedy in the fullest sense: tragedy which involves innocents, and abuses and inadequacies and confusions. There is wreckage in the wake of disability that needs dealing with. For us, the notion of tragedy simply has to be reopened if we are working in an international context.

Perhaps now we are making some of the most contentious statements that can currently be made around disability, human rights and education, but we are finding that opening up some possibility of reclaiming the concept of tragedy opens up the possibility of expanding much else about our understanding of the issues. Gaining international perspectives is rapidly expanding our notions of our own shortcomings and rightfully contributes to debates around where we are in terms of understanding disability, education and human rights in our own country. We have found our own models shifting and discovered that there is much to learn as we are shifting. To return to one of the opening themes of this chapter, for example, part of what we have learned has made hard and fast materialists out of us. Nowadays we are often conspirators in the distasteful business of amassing resources so that we can take out useful aid. We are much less confused about the issue of the economic base that underpins a nation's response to disability, human rights and education. Indeed, our own right *not* to participate in the charity business in transitional circumstances has been strongly challenged by both professionals in Romania and disabled activists in Britain, who are taking the view that it is simply inhuman, if one does have resources, not to share them. This is one example of how we are finding that situating our work in a more global context has helped us to think more sharply about how we adequately address debates around disability, human rights and education from the relatively cosy position of our own place on this earth.

In addressing the question of possibilities inherent in the responses to disability we have encountered in Romania, we need to respect the right of our Romanian counterparts to lead the way. This is the right of professionals, and as professionals they have the power to preserve this right. We can reopen the debate about the impact of their representations of children and the deep problems which lie within this, but the social model strategies we would wish to transport will be constrained by the rights of any professional to ask another to do things differently. Ultimately we are seeking to exploit the rights of our professional peers in Romania in order to try to get around what for us is the appalling problem of the children that no one wants to work with. And so the theme of hypocrisy rears up again, just as our Romanian contributor warned us it always does. We have to remind ourselves that we do have exactly the same problems. In Britain children with multiple difficulties who are also poor are the least well provided for. This is a fact of social provision (Burman 1994; Clough 1998; Dunn 1998). Exactly the same discourse of poverty, prejudice and oppression runs through responses to disability, human rights and education in Britain, as is suggested by the problems we have commented on in relation to Romania.

We have no easy solutions on how to promote an alternative human rights approach to disability and education in Romania, although we share the view of our Romanian colleagues, and of the British aid workers who initiated our involvement, that the need for change is critical. In many senses we have found our engagement with the world of disability, human rights and education in Romania to be numbing. We have found ourselves talking our own provision up and entering into that most oppressive rights discourse of the philanthropist. We have not found the usual solace on projects that are to do with dismantling disabling barriers, which comes from affiliation with, and the experience of, disabled people and their representative organizations.

We have in our project team a disabled person who is internationally known for pioneering advocacy of disabled people's rights and who has spent many hours thinking through her pivotal role in the emerging politics of a new social movement aimed at maximizing disabled people's rights in Romania. But we are currently embroiled in considerations that are difficult and uncomfortable for us all, as we try to work through the issues involved in disabled people taking their experience of the social model to the institutions we have connections with. There are reservations around all that we are learning about the inherent disadvantages of the social model. There are anxieties about the requirement for a disabled person to take her history of pain and struggle with her into a context in which she knows pain and struggle are guaranteed to be revived on a colossal scale. And here is hypocrisy again, because we cannot even properly include this person within key discussions at our Centre for Inclusive Education in a top-ranked British university without imposing pain and struggle and contravening her basic rights to safety and dignity.

We feel left with the element of surprise which characterizes all ethnographic journeys. We do not know how best to proceed, although we wish to hold on to personally valued principles of taking the most open and honest and collaborative approach to bringing about change that we can possibly muster. There are issues about 'letting go' of the social model and what this will mean. We know that understandings of the social model will be used for different purposes, and a dearly held view of our Romanian contributor is that, in view of the lack of a social support system, the right of the state 'to take the child from their parents and put them in a decent institution if needed' should be preserved. She points out:

> if you take the case of autism in Romania, where most of the children have no *choice* of institutional help and stay *helpless* [original emphasis] with their parents, you would see the other side of the story. It was very interesting for me in England, while I was thinking about proper services for autistic people, to hear parents voices saying that it is not the thing they wanted! But to be left with their child . . . even for the English standard of life I'm afraid that [adequate support] is not possible at the extent parents want it because there are a lot of costs. It was clear that even in England only wealthy parents, or those who had enough money, could afford to have the best services (at least at home) and even in this case they were not always happy. I am afraid that for Romania things will be much more difficult. Because you do not have the same financial opportunities and children have the right to benefit from services in institutions or home, depending on the parents' resources.

Evidently there are deep rooted differences, even at the basic level of our interpersonal collaboration, where we frequently find ourselves wanting to override the way our Romanian colleagues have of doing things or they want to challenge our input. We are constantly reminded that we have to be very critical of our own model and the assumptions that we are trying to export. We are continually gaining insights into the imperfections of our own provision from our Romanian colleagues, and our partnership constantly brings these into sharp focus.

It would be misleading to suggest that the tensions and disagreements revealed in this chapter have been easily negotiated. They have not, and the process of expanding our understanding of disability, human rights issues and education in Romania continues to be exacting and at times bewildering for all partners involved. We are trying to build new responses, and although this feels interminably problematic we are learning many enduring lessons. Notwithstanding the difficulties we have described, we see the wholly realistic words of the Romanian contributor as formative and encouraging:

> I think the first thing would be to consider strategies of developing awareness of disability for all kinds of people at all levels of education. To convince them that disabled people are not a 'threat'. And I'm pretty convinced that while the need for pity and charity for disabled people might be important at the beginning, it is more advantageous to turn it soon into a different message: a message that disabled people are human beings who have the right to live as others do.
>
> Second, no matter what would be the choices of disabled people, they must have alternatives to choose from. And here I think it is vital, to prepare, to train people to become real professionals and to help parents and children and disabled adults to fight for their rights in a legitimate way. *Nearly* the same as they are doing in England.

An exercising project is identified which links commitment to change in Romania to a necessary critique of UK practices. It is vital to remain censorious of claims which might be made for our own setting.

Conclusion

This chapter is troubled by many muddles. Part of the struggle has been to reconcile our powerful positions as researchers and authors with our powerless positions as mothers and would-be children's allies. We have argued that this struggle will invariably influence our responses to disability, education and human rights issues in Romania and to disguise it would be unnecessarily reductive. However, it is clear that since we cannot tidy emotionality out of our work, our commitment to changing the dependency-creating discourse – which we know to be at the root of abuses of disabled children's rights and denial of their entitlements to education in the contexts we are commenting on – requires constant examination. In view of the undeniable infringements of basic human rights we have witnessed in the lives and education (or lack of education) of disabled children in Romania, we have ventured in this chapter to argue that the concept of personal tragedy cannot easily be dismissed from our growing cross-cultural understandings of entitlements in education. Likewise, the social model of disability, with its emphasis on entitlements and inclusion, seems precariously situated in the context we have described. Despite what at times has seemed like incoherence in our thinking, we feel that laying confusions out for this chapter has led us, and we hope will lead the reader, to challenge assumptions about disability, education and human rights in different contexts, including our own. There is much to be gained by more effective inclusion of disabled people in the process of bringing about change in Romania, and vexing questions must be posed about how to secure their participation. We hope the chapter will widen and stimulate discussion of these debates because what we have seen (and found hidden) of disability, human rights and education in Romania indicates that there are enduring consequences of oppression yet to emerge, which will not be entirely explained by the Ceauşescu era.

Questions

1 One of the main fears we have as non-disabled academics working in Romania is that if we get too close or too friendly with the professional community we will lose our credibility with disabled people and their representative agencies and become less able to engage with the critical edges of their experience. How can insights and resources of disabled people, who are usually excluded from participation in the life of the community, be brought in to discussions and decision-making forums which shape policy and practice around education and rights in the contexts described in Romania?

2 How can the process of circumventing the real barriers to participation for disabled people be managed most effectively in contexts where there is a fragile economic base and a profoundly disabling recent history of discrimination and oppressive attitudes?

3 Where would you begin the process of promoting the educational rights and entitlements of disabled children in Romania, given that the interests of disabled people have barely surfaced to date?

References

Archard, D. (1993) *Children, Rights and Childhood*. London: Routledge.

Barnes, C. (1990) *Cabbage Syndrome: the Social Construction of Dependency*. London: Falmer Press.

Burman, E. (1994) *Deconstructing Developmental Psychology*. London: Routledge.

Clough, P. (ed.) (1998) *Managing Inclusive Education: from Policy to Experience*. London: Sage.

Diaconescu, R., Ionescu, M., Chis, V. and Daunt, P. (1995) Teacher training and the integration of children with special needs, in P. Mittler and P. Daunt (eds) *Teacher Education for Special Needs in Europe*. London: Cassell.

Dunn, K. (1998) Conceptualising childhood difficulties. Paper presented at the International Sociology of Childhood Conference, Montreal, Canada.

Franklin, B. (1995) *The Handbook of Children's Rights: Comparative Policy and Practice*. London: Routledge.

Gellhorn, M. (1989) The children pay, in M. Gellhorn, *The View from the Ground*. Cambridge: Granta Books.

Hurst, R. (1998) The world's disabled children, *Disability Awareness in Action*, Newsletter 62, June/July.

Marks, D. (1996) Constructing a narrative: moral discourse and young people's experiences of exclusion, in E. Burman *et al.* (eds) *Psychology Discourse Practice: from Regulation to Resistance*. London: Taylor and Francis.

Moore, M., Dunn, K. and Benga, O. (forthcoming) The situation and rights of deaf children who are members of cultural and linguistic minority groups in Romania. Discussion paper in development.

Moore, M., Sixsmith, J. and Knowles, K. (1996) *Children's Reflections on Family Life.* London: Falmer.

Morris, J. (1993) *Independent Lives: Community Care and Disabled People.* London: Macmillan.

Oliver, M. (1990) *The Politics of Disablement.* London: Macmillan.

Oliver, M. (1996) *Understanding Disability: from Theory to Practice.* Basingstoke: Macmillan.

Oliver, M. and Barnes, C. (1998) *Disabled People and Social Policy: from Exclusion to Inclusion.* Essex: Longman.

Vlachou, A. (1998) *Struggles for Inclusive Education: an Ethnographic Study.* Buckingham: Open University Press.

 **14**

'Is there anyone there concerned with human rights?' Cross-cultural connections, disability and the struggle for change in England

Felicity Armstrong and Len Barton

Overview

This chapter raises issues about the ways in which human rights can be conceptualized in relation to disability issues in different settings. Connections are made between education and human rights and wider social and cultural contexts. Discourses which situate human rights issues as relating to 'others' rather than 'one's own' society and practices are critically discussed. The question of exclusions in society is examined in relation to dominant discourses, which focus on notions of citizenship rather than rights. We make some necessary connections between different kinds of exclusions made through the curriculum in education and disability issues and human rights. The chapter then moves on to a critical account of the development of special education in England and its roots in systems of categorization and exclusion. We argue that the question of the rights of children has not been on the agenda. Recent moves on the part of central government suggest increased openness towards the idea of inclusive education. However, an understanding of the central importance of adopting a human rights approach which is necessary to achieve such a change is still missing.

Introduction

As we set out to work together on the second draft of our chapter, public debate and questions about the meaning and status of human rights are being

– temporarily, at least – raised more urgently in the media. On the front page of today's *Guardian* there is an account of life in Kosovo refugee camps. Families are living out in the open under plastic sheeting; nearby a school provides shelter for 150 other refugees. They have no electricity or heating and their diet consists of bread and red peppers. Children are suffering from severe bronchial problems. They all live in fear. A man shouts at the newspaper reporter: 'It would be better if they killed us because we are not living in conditions for any kind of normal life. What is Europe doing to help us? Is there anyone there concerned with human rights?' (*The Guardian* 13 October 1998:1). Yesterday there was another story about a report published by the UK Institute of Public Policy Research (described in the newspaper as a 'centre-left think-tank'), which criticizes the government for refusing to set up a human rights commission which would strengthen the effectiveness of the Human Rights Bill by 'creating a culture in which human rights are routinely observed' (Lord Woolf, quoted in *The Guardian* 12 October 1998: 8).

These 'stories' are not immediately about disability or education (although the implications of the transformation of a school into a refugee camp must not pass unnoticed), but they do highlight one of the major concerns of this book, which is to try to make some connections between different perspectives and experiences relating to human rights and formal (or official) 'human rights' discourses.

In our chapter we shall use the term human rights to mean a set of principles based on social justice, a standard by which the conditions and opportunities of human life can be evaluated. These principles are concerned with health and well-being, security, opportunity and choice, freedom of speech, respect for individuality and an acceptance of difference in all spheres of life. They are concerned with an idea of citizenship which is about the right to full and ordinary membership of society for all human beings, regardless of differences between groups or individuals. How these principles are realized through the lives and struggles of people in different cultures and communities will be very different.

Disability and social exclusion

In July 1998 the government introduced a White Paper setting out proposals to establish a Disability Rights Commission. The Commission will be concerned with the elimination of discrimination against disabled people. This will include supporting and helping disabled people to secure the rights which the new legislation will have created for them.

Although the provision of education is exempt from the Disability Discrimination Act of 1995, the European Commission on Human Rights will construe the rights of disabled people to include the right not to be denied access to education. This will have important implications for the Human Rights Bill before Parliament at the time of writing, in terms of the removal of discrimination in education. The extent to which this will make an effective impact on policy and practice is still an unknown factor. However, and rather ominously, the United Kingdom has lodged a reservation to the effect that this right is accepted 'only in so far as it is compatible with the provision of effective instruction and training and the avoidance of unreasonable public expenditure' (as quoted in *Skill Newsletter* 37, 1998: 3). This will equate to a get out clause and a means of weakening the legislation, and raises serious questions about the political will of government in relation to this fundamental issue.

How we define disability is of central importance in relation to our expectations of, and interactions with, disabled people. A socio-political approach to disability emphasizes the importance of difference, diversity and the heterogeneity of what it means to be human. Views of disability as a tragedy, a dependency-creating condition or an individualized problem are all the subject of a powerful critique in which the struggle for rights, equity and participatory citizenship is of fundamental significance. A major issue is about control, and in a discussion about getting out of the 'charity-trap' in which disabled people are encouraged to be grateful for the support they are given, Morris (1992: 11) illustrates this perspective in the following questions: 'Who has the right to say what we need? Who has the right to say how we should be presented to the public?' In seeking to gain control over the power of naming, the interest is in positive self and collective images and identities. It is about being proud of who you are.

The demands for equity and non-discrimination are derived from an informed understanding of the extent and stubbornness of the disabling barriers within society. It is these that need to be identified, challenged and removed. Nor is this merely an attitudinal problem, but one of institutionalized discrimination and oppression. This is most vividly recognized by Barnes (1991: 233), who maintains that:

> The abolition of institutional discrimination against disabled people is not a marginal activity; it strikes at the heart of social organisations within both the public and private sectors. It would not be possible to confront this problem without becoming involved in political debate and taking up positions on a wide range of issues.

A public affirmation is required that discrimination against disabled people is totally unacceptable. Supporting this stance is the struggle for anti-discrimination legislation that prioritizes human and civil rights. This is based on the conviction that the world is changeable and we need to find alternative ways of struggling to get things changed (Richardson 1991).

This must not be viewed as an easy task, particularly as the key concepts need to be understood as contestable, and their meaning and applicability across different cultural contexts as problematic and contradictory.

Historically, the 'voices' of disabled people have been largely absent from discussion and decisions affecting the quality of their lives. Powerful professional bodies and organizations *for* disabled people have protected their vested interests, while articulating a language of facilitation and individual needs. Part of this experience has, for disabled people, been that of social exclusion and restriction. But what does 'social exclusion' mean and how serious an issue is it? In a discussion of the values and priorities of successive Conservative governments over the past 18 years, Walker (1997) maintains that particular assumptions informed social policy and the welfare system during this period. It was assumed that the welfare state created slothfulness and dependency. Further, self-help from within the family or the market were viewed as superior to welfare from the state. Finally, it was assumed that the most successful people would be altruistic, and this support would 'trickle down' to the most needy. Inequality was viewed as a basis for motivation, further incentives and enterprise. Against this context, Walker (1997: 8) argues, social exclusion:

> refers to the dynamic process of being shut out, fully or partially, from any of the social, economic, political, cultural systems which determine the social integration of a person in society. Social exclusion may, therefore, be seen as the denial (or non-realisation) of civil, political and social rights of citizenship.

Exclusions experienced by particular groups from ordinary membership of society in different historical, social and cultural contexts reflect particularities in relation to the dominant social and political interests and ideologies within those contexts. At their most extreme, such exclusions have taken the form of genocide, concentration camps and extermination, and include the particular mentality underpinning the eugenics movement.

More familiarly, exclusions operate at many different levels of society, often made natural or invisible through the discourses and practices which surround them. Discourses such as those referring to *'illegal* immigrants', *'single parent* families', 'children *with SEN'* or *'EBD* kids' mask the actual oppression and marginalization of some groups in society on the basis that they transgress socially constructed ideas of 'the normal'. Paradoxically, while such discourses hide from view, they also mark out and make explicit exclusions in society. Discourses of exclusion are embedded in policy making through formal and informal policies and practices.

Dominant presentations of 'the problem' of social exclusions are couched in terms of 'citizenship' rather than 'rights'. Oliver (1996: 44) comments:

> 'Why we should rediscover citizenship at the end of the twentieth century is an interesting question in itself. It seems that when the relationship between the State and its population is in crisis, citizenship becomes the device whereby such a crisis is talked about and mediated.
>
> . . . While politicians, policy makers and professionals have rediscovered the notion of citizenship, disabled people have begun to redefine disability not as human tragedy requiring therapy but as collective oppression requiring political action. Thus for the former group, the history of citizenship can be seen as the achievement of certain political, social and civil rights for everyone. For the latter, *disability is nothing less than the denial of basic human rights to certain groups in society.*

(Emphasis added)

In the present period debates about 'citizenship' and 'rights' and the importance of overcoming social exclusion have been accompanied by countering discourses from the same sources, such as 'zero tolerance' and 'family values'.

Neither is there a predictable one-to-one relationship between the ways 'rights' are publicly articulated by particular groups or bodies and the ways they are interpreted by them. The state is both the provider of 'care' and the protector of particular power relations in society, which underpin market forces that create poverty, unemployment, discrimination and exclusions in the first place. It is 'the state', through central government legislation, that imposes educational structures, practices and discourses based on competition and exclusions and within which there must be 'winners' and 'losers', while at the same time making claims to be trying to achieve 'excellence for all'. Not only has the 'welfare' state failed to ensure the rights of all its citizens, but it has frequently passed legislation that actually curtails people's freedom and rights (Oliver 1996).

Inclusion necessitates the removal of the material, ideological, political and economic barriers that legitimate and reproduce inequality and discrimination in the lives of disabled people.

Human rights

The term 'human rights' rolls effortlessly off the tongue, predigested, like terms such as 'natural selection' or 'SEN'. We know that the term 'human rights' means something special and outside the ordinary because it often has capital letters (like 'The Queen'). It is used as a collective noun as if 'human rights' was a given, uncontested principle or part of the established order of things, standing above and apart from ordinary life but always present. Such discourses are oppressive because they close down questions, arguments and critical examination, rather than opening them up. That is why the question asked by the Kosovo refugee in our newspapers is shocking. Suddenly something is required of us and we are unprepared.

The term 'human rights' has a universal ring to it, suggesting that human rights are enshrined in the protective guardianship invested in bodies such as the United Nations or governments. The UN Convention on the Rights of the Child (1989), for example, is seen as 'a good thing' and something that will protect children and make the world a better place. Similarly, legislation in the UK that is presented as protecting the rights of particular groups, while not usually being high on political or media agendas, is probably also considered to be 'a good thing'. But world declarations and the passing of legislation do not, in themselves, guarantee that human rights are respected.

The terminology of 'human rights' can itself be used in ways that distract attention away from oppression in 'our own' societies, and direct attention to oppressions elsewhere. Public references to 'human rights' in England are nearly always made in relation to groups of people perceived as being oppressed in some other place through war, famine, poverty, imprisonment and other forms of social exclusion. These public 'human rights' discourses are embedded in social and cultural practices in England. Indignation and pity directed at foreign others is ritualized through political discourses and images – often rooted in English colonial history and fashioned by a colonial gaze – projected into our homes by the media. We can turn these images on or off, at will.

Pity and concern are also directed towards some groups 'at home' in England, but only rarely are issues relating to social exclusion and discrimination presented as ones concerned with human rights. Instead, a 'needs' discourse is adopted, suggesting that difficulties, which are seen as belonging to people rather than being created by the social, economic and political relations in society, can be overcome by technical solutions. In education, the entrenchment and persistence of the idea of 'having special educational needs' is a prime example of a 'needs' discourse.

A 'human rights' position is fundamentally different from a 'needs' position because it challenges power relations, structures and practices in society which are held together and sustained by the state. A 'needs' position, on the other hand, looks to the state as possible mediator and problem-solver in situations in which a particular group – or people ascribed to a particular group – are constructed as vulnerable and dependent. It suggests that law making is rational and that policies relating to people's needs are made by rational governance, evenly and fairly implemented by paid officials and elected officers at different levels in society. Thus, a 'needs' discourse is disempowering because it focuses attention away from the possibility of individuals, groups and communities taking responsibility for undertaking action themselves to bring about change.

Human rights, integration and inclusion

A human rights approach challenges the state because it evokes rights that are opposed to the principles that underpin 'rights' accorded by the state. An example of this can be found in the opposing values that underpin the idea of 'integration' and the principle of inclusive education. Integration is based on a particular kind of 'rationality', referring to the 'right' of disabled children to attend their local schools provided the 'rights' of others are not threatened (1981 Education Act). It is contingent, provisional, dependent upon the 'efficient use of resources'. Inclusive education is concerned with the human right for all children to attend their local school. Such a principle is in fundamental conflict with principles of integration and with the state, because:

> Inclusive education is not an end in itself, it is a means to an end, that of establishing an inclusive society. Thus, the notion of inclusivity is a radical one, in that, it places the welfare of all citizens at the centre of consideration. It seeks to engage with the question of belonging and solidarity, and simultaneously, recognises the importance of the politics of difference.
>
> (Barton 1998b: 84)

Human rights have never been the concern of formal educational policy makers in England, or part of ordinary educational discourses. In the following sections of this chapter we shall discuss the exclusion of disabled children as part of a larger pattern of inequalities and discriminations experienced by groups and individuals in different contexts.

Education and exclusion

When we think about exclusionary policies and practices within schools there are three aspects of the problem that need to be engaged with. First, there are those disabled pupils who have been placed in ordinary schools, but in settings that are essentially segregated and supported by limited resources and little meaningful change organizationally. Second, there are those disabled pupils who have never participated in an ordinary school and have spent all their school careers in segregated forms of provision. Finally, there are those young people within ordinary schools who are excluded from full participation. These decisions take a temporary and permanent form. The reasons are varied and in too many cases trivial. However, there are some groups of pupils who represent a disproportionate risk of exclusion (Blyth and Milner 1996). These include boys, Afro-Caribbean pupils, children from lower socio-economic backgrounds, children in care; and, as Pearce and Hillman (1998: 17) maintain:

> The incidence of exclusion amongst those with special educational needs or emotional and behavioural difficulties is around six times higher than for others . . . In many cases the act of exclusion triggers the statementing process (indeed, the exclusion process may be pursued deliberately by a school in order to secure faster access to additional resources for a young person). However, the exclusion of a young person on the grounds of special needs or emotional or behavioural difficulties may represent a response to disciplinary problems or the perceived cost of educating a pupil within a mainstream environment.

The pattern of exclusions across schools is very varied, with some schools more willing to exclude than others (Donovan 1998). The age at which pupils are being excluded is becoming lower. Finally, those young people who experience a permanent exclusion order rarely re-enter the mainstream system. When they do continue their school experience, it is often in special units or on a part-time basis within the home.

These arguments relate to literal exclusions, in which children and young people are denied access to, or removed from, ordinary schools as places. Exclusions are also experienced on a massive and unmeasurable scale in terms of the ways schools and colleges are organized, the content of the curriculum and ways in which teaching and learning are understood. Tomlinson (1982: 135) argues that the curriculum is itself a vehicle for creating and sustaining inequalities:

It is the distribution of different kinds of knowledge and skill through the curriculum to different groups of children or the withholding of certain kinds of knowledge that largely determine their future status, social and occupational, in society. Those who are involved in curriculum decisions thus have great power.

By selecting particular kinds of knowledge rather than others, by fostering particular value systems and privileging certain conceptualizations of teaching and learning over others, education systems deny the rights of full representation and inclusion in the curriculum for vast numbers of children and young people. For us, these are also violations of human rights. In England, the introduction of the National Curriculum following the Education Reform Act 1988 was accompanied by central government discourses of 'rights to a common curriculum' which all pupils have access to, and notions of 'entitlement' and 'empowerment'. But, argues Harris (1994: 58), drawing on existing commentators' insights,

> such claims for equality of access are at odds with much of ERA [Education Reform Act], which used the rhetoric of empowering parents and consumers but which primarily was an attack on local democracy and an attempt to win back control of public services from the 'mismanagement' of local authorities. And while proclaiming the importance of parental rights the government has increased central control with an unprecedented growth in the powers of the Secretary of State for Education.

In addition, the National Curriculum in England and Wales has promoted a particular 'heritage culture', imposing 'knowledge' and values belonging to an imagined common 'British' culture. As David Trend (1994: 225) reminds us, 'Nationality is a fiction. It is a story people tell themselves about who they are, where they live, and how they got there. As such, it is a complicated and highly contested text.' The 'story' told to students by the English National Curriculum about 'who they are' excludes the lives, values, cultures and knowledge bases of a large proportion of children and young people. As such, it denies their rights for recognition and inclusion (Armstrong 1998). For us, this is also a violation of their human rights. Positioned as part of a wider set of complex processes of exclusion and marginalization within a highly differentiated and rarefied education system, the exclusion and oppression of disabled children and young people become part of a common struggle. Through this discussion, we are seeking to establish connections between the violations of human rights routinely experienced by students in ordinary settings in England, and those experienced by disabled students.

Inequality, education and historical context

An awareness and examination of historical context allows us to make important connections between the different processes, varieties and levels of productive and reproductive social practice, policy making and enactment. We can, for example, make connections between social inequalities perpetuated during a particular historical period and those experienced in other settings and at other times. We can search for voices from these historical periods which have been muffled or regarded merely as interesting examples supporting dominant narratives constructed about the past, rather than evidence that helps us to understand the present.

In a historical analysis of working-class secondary education, McCulloch (1998) maintains that the English system of provision has a deep-seated tendency in favour of social differentiation in secondary education. In a specific examination of the experiment of the secondary modern schools, their developments, achievements and ultimate failure, he forcefully demonstrates the two-nation mentality underpinning policy and provision, which he contends catered for, on the one hand, a minority of academically able pupils, and, on the other, a majority of 'ordinary', 'average', 'less able' children. Through a careful critical scrutiny of research findings and ideas, official documentation and claims, he contends that 'division, hierarchy and social inequality' have been 'continuities in educational provision' (p. 157). One of the benefits of this historical approach is to remind us of the ways in which, in the past, practice all too often contradicted theory. As McCulloch (1998: 157) argues:

> Hence a key factor in the failure of educational reform over the past century has been the difference between *theory* and *practice*, as the well meaning and benevolent experiments directed at working-class children and the ordinary child served overall to limit their capacity to overcome their social disadvantages. It seems especially important for educational reforms of the present and future to draw on their historical experience and especially to note this persistent tendency for the practice to refute the theory.

This is a timely reminder when one considers the more recent government discourse as articulated, for example, in *Excellence in Schools* (DFEE 1997a), in which the emphasis on modernizing comprehensive education is expressed through such language as promoting diversity for all children and providing a broad, flexible and motivating education as part of a commitment to deliver excellence for all pupils. Yet, and here is the contradictory nature of policy and practice, this is to be achieved in a system of provision in which competition, choice and selection are simultaneously and aggressively being promoted. Far from eradicating the deep-seated tendency that McCulloch alludes to, it would seem that the New Labour government is contributing to its exacerbation (Chitty 1998).

Disability and education

Education in England is historically grounded in systems, structures, processes and curricula based upon the division, assessment and categorization of learners. These divisions have taken place according to formal and informal measures relating to place, class, gender, race, academic performance and assumptions about learners based on all of these. Education also has roots in charitable and philanthropic projects which developed separately from state-controlled educational provision. To make matters more complicated still, churches and religious groups, firms and industries, trade unions and workers' organizations have also made important contributions to the complexity and character of what is referred to as 'the education system' in England.

Within this messy framework, it would be difficult to trace a linear history of special education and the positioning and movement of disabled children and young people within it. Schools in England have never been 'for all'.

Mass elementary state education was introduced in England through a succession of Education Acts in 1870, 1876 and 1880. (There had already existed a number of privately run 'public' schools, mainly for the sons of the aristocracy and wealthy middle classes, for hundreds of years.) The eighteenth and nineteenth centuries were periods of scientific, philosophical and aesthetic experimentation and questioning, and there are many accounts of experimental attempts to train or teach children perceived as having learning difficulties or those who were deaf or blind in schools, 'idiot asylums' and institutions designated for the categories of the day. At the end of the nineteenth century, a rapid but staggered introduction of state provision for disabled children took place, beginning with the opening of a special class for deaf children by the London School Board in 1874 and followed by the 1893 Elementary Education (Blind and Deaf Children) Act. And so began a period of massive expansion of the special education industry, with the proliferation of categories of handicap, specialists of all kinds and a rapid growth in schools and institutions to accommodate them.

Tomlinson (1982) argues that dominant accounts of the rise of special education in England as being the result of 'altruism and disinterested humanitarianism' fail to take account of the influence and constraints of 'prevailing cultural values and social interests':

> the history of special education must be viewed in terms of the benefits it brought for a developing industrial society, the benefits for the normal mass education system of a 'special' sub-system of education, and the benefits that medical, psychological, educational and other personnel derived from encouraging new areas of professional expertise.
>
> (Tomlinson 1982: 29)

The development of special education in the late nineteenth and early twentieth centuries was linked to a number of complex factors, not least of which was the emergent and sometimes competing professionalism of teachers, doctors and psychologists, and a growth of official interest in the health of school children. What is certain is that educational provision was not based upon a recognition of the 'rights' of children.

In general, 'education' was not the first concern of special schools and institutions. On the contrary, historical accounts of the dehumanizing experience of life in special schools and institutions in the first half of the twentieth century and beyond emphasize the restrictive, harsh and unstimulating regime in special schools, in which remediation, care and control provided an organizing framework for the daily lives of those within (Humphries and Gordon 1992).

Like the massive growth in asylums during the nineteenth century, in which the insane 'found themselves incarcerated in a specialised, bureaucratically organised state-supported asylum system which isolated them both physically and symbolically from the larger society' (Scull 1979: 14), the number and size of special schools grew dramatically between the end of the nineteenth century and the 1960s. The early part of the twentieth century, under the influence of the eugenics movement and the burgeoning medical professions, was characterized by a particular concern with 'care' and 'control', especially in relation to 'feeble-minded' and 'defective' children and the development of 'mental testing' (Tomlinson 1982). In this climate, there was an important increase in segregated residential institutions and schools of all sorts. Children sent to residential special schools were separated from their families and communities, and those who attended day schools were denied the ordinary experiences and opportunities of going to their local school with their peers.

The development of special education is a social process and – as such – has not followed an orderly pathway, or one based on rational principles. Pritchard (1963) offers a particular example of the unpredictable patterning of social and educational structures and processes in his account of some of the unplanned and unexpected effects of the Second World War on educational provision for disabled children. We have included this rather long quotation because it powerfully suggests the complex, multiple levels, the unplanned departures, the irrationality and opportunism of policy making:

By the summer of 1940 children who had been evacuated nine months earlier were streaming home. The air-raids of the following autumn and winter reversed the flow, and the second period of educational disorganisation commenced. The first, at the outbreak of the war, had affected special as much as ordinary schools. Indeed, in many ways special schools were more severely affected. The handicapped children attending them could not easily be billeted as ordinary evacuees. Hence day special schools in the threatened areas were re-established as residential schools in the reception areas. But some of the children previously attending them remained behind, since their parents were unwilling that they should be evacuated. They could, therefore, attend only ordinary schools which had remained open. Equally, as the threatened air attacks failed to materialise, children who had gone to the residential schools drifted back to the cities to attend the ordinary schools.

. . . Because of the reduction of boarding places available, there existed for the first time in many years a shortage of accommodation for handicapped children and consequently the number of children attending special schools fell sharply. In addition, the demand for labour induced some authorities to allow children to leave special schools at fourteen. At the same time fewer children were being ascertained as in need of special education, partly because of the shortage of accommodation, partly because of the general disorganisation of the education services, and partly because medical officers were pre-occupied with extra duties connected with evacuation and Civil Defence. It is therefore understandable that in 1941 the number of London, mentally and physically handicapped children attending special schools had decreased by fifty per cent. Other cities reported a similar decline.

(Pritchard 1963: 207–8)

Here there are no references to children's rights – or even 'needs'. Pritchard's account is a reminder of the unpredictability of the relationship between historical events and social structures and the fluidity of change in human society. It also demonstrates that 'planning' and 'policy making' should be seen as being constantly fragmented, reinterpreted and reworked at different levels in response to changing contexts. In the midst of all this, children's rights have not been on the agenda.

After the Second World War, there were changes in attitudes towards special schools and recommendations were made that they should be brought into 'the general education framework'. The 1944 Education Act, as well as introducing a system of mass primary and secondary education, made local education authorities (LEAs) responsible for the education of children 'in accordance with their ages, aptitudes and abilities'. Children who were labelled 'ineducable' were excluded from this legislation and remained outside the education system until the passing of the 1970 Education (Handicapped Children) Act. Ministry of Education regulations following the 1944 Education Act replaced the existing four categories of handicap with 11 – preparing the way for a further proliferation in bureaucratic procedures relating to identification and categorization and the burgeoning of new professional identities and careers. The new categorizations represented new refinements in the decanting of children:

Partially sighted and partially hearing children were separated from blind and deaf, delicate, diabetic, epileptic and physically handicapped formed four separate categories, educable defective children became educationally subnormal, and two new categories, speech defect and maladjusted, were created.

(Tomlinson 1982: 50)

The numbers of children labelled and placed in special schools increased despite processes linked to greater 'democratization' in other spheres of the education system:

The expansion of categories is not surprising, considering that for the first time England and Wales were about to develop a co-ordinated system of compulsory, mass primary and secondary education. Central and local education authorities, having experienced the problems particular groups of children had posed after the introduction of mass primary education allowed no chance for secondary education to be similarly upset. To develop a workable system it was essential to exclude as many children as possible who might obstruct or inconvenience the smooth running of the normal schools, hence the need for careful categorisation. In addition, the 1944 Act allowed for the tripartite system of secondary schooling by 'age, aptitude and ability'. Selection by 'ability' sanctioned selected by 'disability'.

(Tomlinson 1982: 50)

If we regard the separation off of groups of children from their peers in segregated institutions as a violation of their rights, then what is, during a particular historical period, regarded as modern, progressive and humanitarian can also be understood as reactionary, as institutionalizing and perpetuating discrimination. As Corbett (1998: 12) argues, 'It is a naive assumption to equate the passage of time with inevitable progress. In many respects, regression and destruction are more often experienced as innovative ideas are superseded by oppressive legislation.'

Important connections can be made between Tomlinson's analysis above and an analysis of contemporary exclusions of 'children who might obstruct'. Between 1982 and 1996 the overall percentage of children aged 5–15 years in segregated schools dipped from 1.72 to 1.4 per cent (Norwich 1997), but the numbers of children and young people excluded as presenting behavioural problems has risen steadily. Many of these are placed in 'off-site' pupil referral units or passed on to other schools (Ofsted 1996). This has been accompanied by an increasing 'medicalization' of disturbing behaviour through the introduction of new categories such as 'attention deficit disorder', placing the 'problem' within the student. Where a medical label cannot be found, disturbing behaviour is explained as arising from inadequate families. Such approaches deny possible discussion of the relationship between behaviour and school organization, ethos and curriculum, and how these could be changed.

Human rights and 'special needs'

Over the past 20 years 'special education' has, in important ways, been relocated within 'ordinary education'.

The Warnock Report of 1978 appeared to shift the focus of the special education project from educating 'handicapped' children and young people to a concern with 'meeting special educational need'. It was argued that impairment did not necessarily imply a 'special educational need', and the subsequent 1981 Education Act sought to 'abolish' categories of handicap as not helpful in the context of education, replacing them with the mega category 'special educational needs'. At the same time, categories which had been in use and were regarded as negative were replaced by other categories and sub-categories, such as 'children with learning difficulties', 'children with moderate learning difficulties' and 'children with severe learning difficulties'.

The Warnock Report extended the population of children 'having special educational needs' to around 20 per cent, which meant 'that the majority of children with special needs will have to be not only identified but also helped within the ordinary school.' New groups of children now came into the 'special needs' category, leading to a massive extension in assessment and formal and informal monitoring and record keeping, involving an array of different professionals and education officers.

Statementing procedures, set up as an essential mechanism to secure resources and specific educational provision, became the focus of intense activity involving major deployments of human and economic resources. Statements, based on multi-professional assessments involving educational, psychological and medical professionals, as well as LEA officers, are vital ingredients in triggering the release of resources if they establish that a child has a particular disability, learning or behavioural difficulty, requiring specialist provision. The agenda here is both bureaucratic and political. The processes involved entail struggles for dominance between different professional groups and interests. In the clamour of competing professional voices, those of parents and the children concerned are frequently absent.

Medical diagnoses of children, which often form an important part of the assessment procedures, serve to sustain medically based categories and impairment-led attitudes to children. What is, in effect, the attachment of resources to particular named impairments obscures the socially constructed nature of disability and the social and educational interests of children and young people. As such, their human rights are denied. Far from categories being 'abolished', they have multiplied – some taking on qualities of stardom – forming a hierarchy ranging from the 'exotic' ('AD-D', 'Aspergers Syndrome', alias 'Cocktail Party Syndrome') to the pedestrian ('moderate learning difficulties').

The 1981 Education Act was vague and muddled in many respects. It did not arise out of a period of gradual change involving a decrease in the number of segregated special schools. On the contrary, in his study of the complexities and contradictions surrounding policy making, policy interpretation and integration during the period preceding Warnock and the subsequent government white paper, Tony Booth (1981) charted the strengthening and expansion of segregated provision between 1950 and 1977. The discussion in his paper highlights the wide variations that occur in the reading and interpretation of policy documents, leading to the creation of myths and discontinuities in understanding and implementation and the creation of popular mythologies.

Such muddles in interpretation have been compounded by the particular mechanisms through which formal policies are made in England, with major Acts of Parliament being followed up by government circulars which present the details of how the Act may be implemented, but which 'only have the force of recommendations' (Norwich 1990). This explains – at least in part – the enormous variations in ethos, structures and practices in different local authorities in England. Local councillors, LEA officers, governing bodies of schools and headteachers have the power to interpret government policies in deciding who schools are for, what they are like and the kinds of educational experiences and opportunities students have in them. Other factors, such as the particular ideologies and practices underpinning important services, such as the Schools Psychological Service, in different LEAs also play a role, especially in relation to assessment practices and philosophies. Formal and informal traditions and practices established in different arenas concerning working practices of and between agencies, the levels of honesty at work in terms of the nature of 'consultation' with parents and the degree to which children are listened to, as well as the cultures of local communities, councils and levels of accountability – all play a part in creating local education systems. Added to this is the important question of resources, frequently evoked as reasons for particular policies being adopted, eschewed or abandoned. These factors explain the wide, visible differences in policy making relating to 'special education' and inclusive schools across LEAs in England and even within cities. Thus, in 1996 children were eight times more likely to find themselves in a segregated special school in the London Borough of Wandsworth (2.67 per cent of school population) than they were in the London Borough of Newham (0.32 per cent of the school population). The average percentage of children in special schools in 1996 was 1.40 per cent (Norwich 1997).

These variations in levels of acceptance of difference between schools and across LEAs raise some important questions concerning the human rights of children and young people. They underline the ways in which disabilities, differences and exclusions are socially constructed. These 'constructions' have important consequences in terms of the rights of individuals and groups, and connections need to be made between them and the social contexts and value systems within which they take place.

There are no immediate 'socio-economic' or other explanations that some might use to account for the differences in numbers of segregated placements across LEAs. The trend towards a steady reduction in segregated provision in England since the early 1980s has been accompanied more recently by an increase in the number of statemented children in ordinary schools, and by 1994 more than half (51.70 per cent) of all statemented children were placed in ordinary schools. By 1996 the population of special schools had dropped to 88,849 (1.40 per cent of the total school population aged 5–15 years), the 'lowest percentage ever' (Norwich 1997). While these figures are interesting and encouraging, we do need to know more about how the figures have been collected in other surveys, as well as what they mean in practice. For instance, many ordinary schools have un-ordinary characteristics, such as separate units designated for children identified as 'having' particular named difficulties or impairments, or special classes for withdrawal lessons.

The reasons for the increase in the numbers of statemented pupils in ordinary schools are complex. While it may represent a move towards a greater acceptance of differences and principles of inclusion, there are other forces at work. With the increased marketization of education, the introduction of SATs (Standard Assessment Tests) and the publication of league tables following the 1993 Education Act, and the insistence by government that schools 'raise standards' under the threat of public naming, shaming and possible closure, schools have become increasingly concerned with tapping in to available resources to support children who are experiencing difficulties. They may well be concerned, too, with providing formal 'evidence' of the presence of children identified as 'having special educational needs' in their classrooms. In addition, as the workings of the *Code of Practice on the Identification and Assessment of Special Educational Needs* (DFEE 1994), which introduced clear structures and assessment procedures, make their way into the thinking, planning and practices of schools, the identification and response to children who experience difficulties have a higher profile. Teachers, parents and governors are better informed about statementing procedures. The increase in accountability and surveillance of schools by central government, through inspection procedures, for example, has further encouraged schools to demonstrate that they give value for money and are 'effective' in all areas of their work. This again has had an impact on strengthening a 'special needs' ideology in ordinary schools.

The publication of the government Green Paper *Excellence for All Children: Meeting Special Educational Needs* (DFEE 1997b) resuscitated formal, public debate about disability and inclusion, which – as a focus for discussion of contentious issues – had lain almost dormant for some time, with attention being directed towards technical and practice-based issues concerning the interpretation and implementation of government policy initiatives (such as the *Code of Practice*).

Of course, the debate was continuing during this 'dormant' period, but in other arenas. In addition to the many struggles for inclusion taking place by young people, their families, members of the disability movement and their allies in local authorities across the country, organizations such as the Council for Disabled Children have been active in developing policies in favour of human rights.

The Council's Principles, taken from its Policy Statement from The Integration Working Party (April 1994), read:

1 The Council for Disabled Children believes that no child should be denied inclusion in mainstream education provision.
2 Mainstream provision should offer the full range of support and specialist services necessary to give all children their full entitlement to a broad and balanced education.
3 The Council for Disabled Children believes that parents of children with special educational needs should be able to choose a mainstream school for their child on the same basis as parents of children without such needs, and that the present element of compulsion in places is inequitable and against the best interests of disabled people and their families.

4 The Council for Disabled Children endorses the UN Convention on the Rights of the Child, which recognises the rights of all children to education, to be achieved progressively and on the basis of equal opportunity, and to facilitate the child's active participation in the community.

(Council for Disabled People 1994: 1)

In contrast to the principles presented above, those which underpin the Green Paper are not concerned, first and foremost, with human rights. References to rights occur only twice in the entire document, once as 'civil rights', a concept which is limited to conceptualizations of 'rights' as understood within the framework of particular state legislation and policy making. Later on, the Green Paper reads: 'All our measures will be designed to protect, or to enhance, the rights of vulnerable children and their parents' (p. 26), thus perpetuating the construction of disabled people as 'vulnerable' and needing protection.

While we cautiously welcomed the Green Paper as an opportunity for opening up issues of education and human rights for critical discussion, there are a number of major shortcomings that need to be considered. First, the reference to 'rights' is no more than a token gesture. This is made clear by the fact that the reference to rights in the Foreword to the full version of the Green Paper is absent from the summary version, which was circulated to schools and sent round to all parents. Second, the document makes it clear that its commitment to inclusive education is only partial, conditional and provisional, maintaining the continuation of special schools and units (Barton 1998a). As Dessent (1987: 97) reminds us:

Special schools do not have a right to exist. *They exist because of the limitations of ordinary schools in providing for the full range of abilities and disabilities amongst children.* It is not primarily a question of the quality or adequacy of what is offered in a special school. Even a superbly well organised special school offering the highest quality curriculum and educational input to its children has no right to exist if that same education can be provided in a mainstream school.

(Emphasis added)

A further shortcoming of the Green Paper was that it did not address important issues involved in curriculum, teaching and learning, but focused more on issues relating to 'target setting', 'assessment' and the implementation of the *Code of Practice*. Curriculum and pedagogy are of major interest and concern to all teachers, especially those concerned with inclusive education and the rights of all children (Armstrong 1998). To acknowledge this is to recognize that the transition from segregated special schools to inclusive ordinary schools will involve not just careful planning, sensitivity and consultation, but a massive leap of the imagination on the part of the whole community.

Underlying the Green Paper lies a romantic idea of schools opening their doors to all children (apart from some pupils in the special schools, which, it is clearly envisaged, will remain), and *a failure of political will* to bring about fundamental change. The Green Paper fudged issues concerning resources, stating baldly that 'The pace of change will be linked to the availability of resources.' Finally, the proposals in the Green Paper, couched in an 'SEN' discourse firmly located in an individual deficit model of disability, are put forward in isolation from all the other social and education policies contained in other legislation and policy documents.

The New Labour government has left intact – and built upon – policies, values and practices that are far removed from considerations of human rights, based on the marketization of education, put in place by their predecessors. Only by *making connections* between exclusions in society through poverty, unemployment, access to benefits and representations in official discourses and the media will the vision of building a system of education based on human rights become realizable. As such, policy making and practice in England have been – and remain – far from exemplary, although there are some local authorities that are struggling against all the odds to recognize the human rights of all children in their schools. These pockets of experience, in which barriers have been broken down and new ways of thinking flourish, are 'advance guards' that we can learn from.

Conclusion

We have approached this chapter through a discussion of disability issues and human rights. This has involved placing our questions and arguments within the framework of wider social issues and attempting to make connections between ideas, perceptions and experiences in different contexts. It has involved a recognition of the simultaneous nature of policies that are contradictory. This has led us to a consideration and discussion of the history and complexity of special education in England and today's struggles for an end to exclusion and discrimination in education. We have found that a consideration of human rights is almost entirely absent from the history of education in England. Only very recently have official discourses begun – timorously, tentatively and provisionally – to make links between policy making and children's rights. For us, issues relating to human rights are at the heart of questions concerning education for all.

The necessity of struggle for an inclusive society arises from the inequalities and discriminatory nature of the social relations and conditions within society. To engage with these is to engage in a 'form of cultural politics' (Slee 1999). Making connections between different kinds of social relations and inequalities, and building an understanding of their entrenchment and pervasiveness and complexity in a multitude of settings in society, are necessary parts of the struggle for human rights. The connections and understandings should start with ourselves, our own assumptions, experiences, work contexts and communities, leading outwards. Only when we begin to wrestle with the barriers to inclusion lodged in our own attitudes, thinking and practices can we begin to engage with the struggles 'out there'. These must never be underestimated. The struggle for inclusion comes out of that.

Questions

1 How far is an interest in human rights realistic in contemporary contexts?
2 What role has education to play in the struggle for an inclusive society?
3 To what extent can connections be made concerning how difference is defined and used both in this chapter and in others in the book?

References

Armstrong, F. (1998) The curriculum as alchemy: school and the struggle for cultural space, *Curriculum Studies*, 6(2): 145–60.

Armstrong, F. (1998) Curricula, 'management' and special and inclusive education, in P. Clough (ed.) *Managing Inclusive Education: from Policy to Experience*. London: Paul Chapman Publishing.

Barnes, C. (1991) *Disabled People in Britain and Discrimination: a Case for Anti-discrimination Legislation*. London: Hurst and Company.

Barton, L. (1998a) Inclusive education and human rights, *Socialist Teacher*, 65: 27–30.

Barton, L. (1998b) Markets, managerialism and inclusive education, in P. Clough (ed.) *Managing Inclusive Education*. London: Paul Chapman Publishing.

Blyth, E. and Milner, J. (1996) *Exclusion from School: Inter-professional Issues for Policy and Practice*. London: Routledge.

Booth, T. (1981) Demystifying integration, in W. Swann (ed.) *The Practice of Special Education*. Oxford: Blackwell.

Chitty, C. (1998) Selection fever, *Guardian Education*, 13 October: 4–5.

Corbett, J. (1998) *Special Educational Needs in the Twentieth Century: a Cultural Analysis*. London: Cassell.

Council for Disabled Children (1994) *Policy Statement from the Integration Working Party, April 1994*. London: National Children's Bureau.

Department of Education and Science (1978) *Special Educational Needs (Warnock Report)*, Cmnd 7212. London: HMSO.

DFEE (1994) *Code of Practice on the Identification and Assessment of Special Educational Needs*. London: HMSO.

DFEE (1997a) *Excellence in Schools*. London: HMSO.

DFEE (1997b) *Excellence for All Children: Meeting Special Educational Needs*. London: HMSO.

Dessent, T. (1987) *Making the Ordinary School Special*. Lewes: Falmer Press.

Donovan, N. (ed.) (1998) *Second Chances: Exclusions from School and Equality of Opportunity*. London: New Policy Institute.

Harris, S. (1994) Entitled to what? Control and autonomy in school: a student perspective, *International Studies in Sociology of Education*, 4(1): 57–76.

Humphries, S. and Gordon, P. (1992) *Out of Sight: the Experience of Disability 1900–1950*. Plymouth: Northcote House.

McCulloch, G. (1998) *Failing the Ordinary Child? The Theory and Practice of Working-class Secondary Education*. Buckingham: Open University Press.

Morris, J. (1992) *Disabled Lives: Many Voices, One Message.* London: BBC.

Norwich, B. (1990) *Special Needs in Ordinary School: Re-appraising Special Needs Education.* London: Cassell.

Norwich, B. (1997) *A Trend towards Inclusion: Statistics on Special School Placements and Pupils with Statements in Ordinary Schools 1992–96.* Bristol: CSIE.

Ofsted (1996) *Exclusions from Secondary Schools 1995–96.* London: Ofsted.

Oliver, M. (1996) *Understanding Disability: from Theory to Practice.* London: Macmillan.

Pearce, N. and Hillman, J. (1998) *Wasted Youth: Raising Achievement and Tackling Social Exclusions.* London: Institute for Public Policy Research.

Pritchard, D. G. (1963) *Education and the Handicapped 1760–1960.* London: Routledge and Kegan Paul.

Richardson, R. (1991) Introduction. A visitor yet a part of everybody: the task and goals of human rights education, in H. Starkey (ed.) *The Challenge of Human Rights Education.* London: Cassell.

Scull, A. T. (1979) *Museums of Madness.* London: Allen Lane.

Simon, B. and Chitty, C. (1993) *SOS: Save Our Schools.* London: Lawrence and Wishart.

Slee, R. (1999) Identity, difference and curriculum: a case study in cultural politics, in L. Barton and F. Armstrong (eds) *Difference and Difficulty: Insights, Issues and Dilemmas.* Sheffield: Department of Educational Studies, Sheffield University.

Tomlinson, S. (1982) *A Sociology of Special Education.* London: Routledge and Kegan Paul.

Trend, D. (1994) Nationalities, pedagogies, and media, in H. A. Giroux and P. McLaren (eds) *Between Borders: Pedagogy and the Politics of Cultural Studies.* New York: Routledge.

Walker, A. (1997) Introduction: the strategy of inequality, in A. Walker and C. Walker (eds) *Britain Divided: the Growth of Social Exclusion in the 1980s and 1990s.* London: CPAG.

Whitty, G. (1990) The New Right and the National Curriculum: state control or market forces?, in M. Hammer and M. Flude (eds) *The Education Reform Act.* Lewes: Falmer Press.

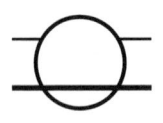

Index

RESEARCHING DISABILITY ISSUES

Michele Moore, Sarah Beazley and June Maelzer

This book is designed to meet a growing need for clear illustrations of how to carry out research which seeks to explore disability issues. It aims to demonstrate the value of a critical attention to social, rather than medical starting points for researching disability, through reviewing a variety of studies which look at different aspects of disabled people's lives. Different quantitative and qualitative methodological frameworks are considered ranging from analysis of observation data concerning disabled children in schools to rich conversation-based data which focuses on family life. A central theme concerns the pivotal role of disabled people in research. The book provides substantive examples of the dilemmas which face researchers and connects these to ideas for individual personal action. Disabled and non-disabled researchers, professionals and students from a wide range of disciplines will find the presentation of both research findings and debates informative and of interest.

All authors have considerable expertise in relevant areas, including many years of teaching research design and methodology on undergraduate, postgraduate and in-service courses. The book has emerged from years of applied disability research experience and their successful development of a unique course in Psychology, Research and Empowerment. June Maelzer is herself a disabled person, and has won national acclaim for her personal contribution to the pioneering advocacy of disability issues.

Contents
Questions and commitments in disability research – Conventional commitment: traditional research and the creation of disablement – Divided commitment: researching with service users and providers – Making commitment: siding with disabled people – Uncertain commitment: the interests of children – Developing new pathways for disability researchers – References – Index.

112pp   0 335 19803 1 (Paperback)   0 335 19804 X (Hardback)

STRUGGLES FOR INCLUSIVE EDUCATION

Anastasia D. Vlachou

This is a lucid, authoritative and original study of teachers' views and attitudes towards the integration into mainstream schooling of a particular group of children defined as having special educational needs. It offers one of the clearest and most comprehensive analyses of the socio-political mechanisms by which the 'special' are socially constructed and excluded from the normal education system that has so far been produced.

Sally Tomlinson,
Professor of Educational Policy at Goldsmiths College,
University of London

In its detailed analysis of primary school teachers' and pupils' attitudes towards integration, this book locates the question of inclusive education within the wider educational context. The wealth of original interview material sheds new light on the reality of everyday life in an educational setting, and shows us the nature and intensity of the struggles experienced by both teachers and pupils in their efforts to promote more inclusive school practices. The author's sensitive investigation of the relationship between teachers' contradictory views of the 'special' and their integration, and the wider social structures in which teachers work, adds to our understanding of the inevitable difficulties in promoting inclusive educational practices within a system which functions via exclusive mechanisms.

The book will be of interest to students of education, sociology and disability as well as teachers and policy-makers involved in inclusive education. The original methodologies adopted when working with the children will also appeal to students of attitudinal, disability and educational research.

Contents

Introduction – Part 1: Setting the theoretical scene – Disability, normality and special needs: political concepts and controversies – Towards a better understanding of attitudes – Part 2: Teachers' perspectives – Teachers and the changing culture of teaching – Teachers' attitudes towards integration (with reference to pupils with Down's Syndrome) – Part 3: Children's perspectives – Integration: the children's point of view – Disabled children and children's culture – Conclusion – Appendices – References – Index.

208pp   0 335 19763 9 (Paperback)   0 335 19764 7 (Hardback)

DISABILITY DISCOURSE

Mairian Corker and Sally French

- Why has 'the discursive turn' been sidelined in the development of a social theory of disability, and what has been the result of this?
- How might a social theory of disability which fully incorporates the multidimensional and multifunctional role of language be described?
- What would such a theory contribute to a more inclusive understanding of 'discourse' and 'culture'?

The idea that disability is socially created has, in recent years, been increasingly legitimated within social, cultural and policy frameworks and structures which view disability as a form of social oppression. However, the materialist emphasis of these frameworks and structures has sidelined the growing recognition of the central role of language in social phenomena which has accompanied the 'linguistic turn' in social theory. As a result, little attention has been paid within Disability Studies to analysing the role of language in struggle and transformation in power relations and the engineering of social and cultural change. Drawing upon personal narratives, rhetoric, material discourse, discourse analysis, cultural representation, ethnography and contextual studies, international contributors seek to emphasize the multidimensional and multifunctional nature of disability language in an attempt to further inform our understanding of disability and to locate disability more firmly within contemporary mainstream social and cultural theory.

Contents

240pp   0 335 20222 5 (Paperback)   0 335 20223 3 (Hardback)